JEANNE HYVRARD:
THEORIST OF
THE MODERN WORLD

Jennifer Waelti-Walters

EDINBURGH UNIVERSITY PRESS

© Jennifer Waelti-Walters, 1996

Edinburgh University Press Ltd
22 George Square, Edinburgh

Typeset in Caslon
by Pioneer Associates, Perthshire, and
printed and bound in Great Britain

A CIP record for this book is available from the
British Library

ISBN 0 7486 0831 1 (cased)
ISBN 0 7486 0818 4 (paperback)

JEANNE HYVRARD:
THEORIST OF
THE MODERN WORLD

Also published by Edinburgh University Press

The Dead Girl in a Lace Dress by Jeanne Hyvrard
Waterweed in the Wash-houses by Jeanne Hyvrard

CONTENTS

ACKNOWLEDGEMENTS

The author wishes to make the following acknowledgements:

The Social Science and Research Council of Canada and the University of Victoria without whose support this project would have been much more difficult to accomplish.

Les Editions des femmes for permission to quote from *Canal de la Toussaint, Le Cercan, La Pensée corps, Que se partagent encore les eaux*; Les Editions de Minuit for *Les Prunes de Cythère*; the University of Nebraska Press for *Mother Death* translated by Laurie Edson; Les Editions du Seuil for *Le Corps défunt de la comédie*; Les Editions Trois for *Ton nom de végétal*; Edinburgh University Press for *Waterweed in the Wash-houses*, trans. Elsa Copeland, and *The Dead Girl in a Lace Dress*, trans. J.-P. Mentha and J. Waelti-Walters; Dalhousie French Studies for permission to incorporate material from 'The Body Politic: *Le Cercan* and *Les Prunes de Cythère*', vol. 13, 1987.

Jeanne Hyvrard for permission to use unpublished manuscripts, taped conversations and drawings.

Lorraine Weir for her careful reading of the manuscript, intelligent suggestions and invaluable support. Emmanuel Hérique and Michael Bishop for encouragement stemming from their appreciation and enthusiasm for the writings of Jeanne Hyvrard. Annye Castonguay for translating many of the quotations. Sandra McIntyre and Rosemary Gibney for help with proofs and index. Marianne Legault for all the hours she spent solving my computer problems, translating quotations, and entering and correcting the manuscript. Without her this book would still be written in pencil.

Finally Jackie Jones and the readers for the Edinburgh University Press for their enthusiasm and helpful comments, and Robyn Marsack for her thoughtful, sensitive copy-editing, her patience and her sense of style both here and in the translated novels.

PREFACE:
THE MISSING VOICE

There is a voice missing from the debates about women, Woman and the Feminine, in those English-speaking Western intellectual and academic circles where people have been rooting their arguments in the work of contemporary French thinkers. That voice belongs to Jeanne Hyvrard, in whose powerful and compelling literary texts converge many of the streams of thought important to theorists of contemporary literature, though she herself remains apart from academic debates and acknowledged theoretical discourses.

In my view, Hyvrard should be included whenever discussion turns to the work of Hélène Cixous, Luce Irigaray, Julia Kristeva and Monique Wittig. These four women bring a variety of attitudes of mind, lines of discussion and styles of presentation to the issues about which they theorise: the problematisation of 'woman', identity and gender; the female body; sexuality; maternity and female genealogy; language; writing and the symbolic.

The distinctions between Cixous, Kristeva and Irigaray stem, to a degree, from their personal formative experiences rather than from their academic formation. Cixous grew up in Algeria during the 1939–45 war in a Jewish family where German was her mother tongue. Kristeva arrived in France from socialist Bulgaria in 1966. Irigaray grew up in Belgium and now gains much of her support in Europe from the women of the Italian Communist Party. But all three completed their higher education in Paris; all three studied language (literature or linguistics) and psychoanalytic discourse;[1] all three teach and do academic research funded by the state. Their approaches in terms of class, modes of analysis and angles of perception, are fundamentally similar. It is in their personality and politics that they differ. Wittig is the exception: from

1

her position as a radical lesbian (now living in the USA), she subverts phallocentrism and compulsory heterosexuality from outside French social and intellectual institutions.

Hyvrard is also situated outside Parisian intellectual and philosophical circles. She teaches political economy and this shapes her perspective in ways that are different from Cixous, Kristeva, Irigaray and Wittig. She feels herself to be a witness to the changing world, an isolated figure who writes primarily for her own survival, but the terms by which Cixous, Kristeva and Irigaray in particular are brought together as a group in the theoretical discourses are terms which are applicable to Hyvrard also. And in addition, she brings the world into the debate. She looks at globalisation with all the material and moral concerns of a woman-centred economics, politics, and ecology. Her voice would shift the locus and scope of the present debates without eliminating any of the core issues.

Taken into account by Michèle Montrelay (*L'Ombre et le nom*) as early as 1977, she was mentioned by Alice Jardine in *Gynesis*, 1985, and inter-viewed by her for *Shifting Scenes*, 1991. Gloria Orenstein gave her a page in *The Reflowering of the Goddess*, 1990, and she was the subject of a couple of paragraphs in Rosi Braidotti: *Patterns of Dissonance*, 1991, and Nicole Ward Jouve: *White Woman Speaks with Forked Tongue*, 1991. Otherwise she has been ignored by and large in theoretical circles while enjoying an ever-increasing reputation as a literary figure in France and in North America. The relative silence around her is perhaps an issue of accessibility, or perhaps an issue of class. Published by Minuit, Seuil and the Editions des femmes, with her thirteenth book to be published in Montreal by Editions Trois, invited to Canada in 1982 by the Association of University Teachers of French, delegated by the French Government to tour South America in 1987, invited frequently since 1984 to participate in the international gatherings organised by the writers of Quebec, she is hardly invisible. She is, however, a teacher in a lycée technique, not in a university, and she refuses to 'spend any time on literary game playing and media climbing', with the result that she is better known in the French departments of Canadian and American universities than she is amongst her peers.

Why would Hyvrard's voice add a dimension to *écriture féminine* and the feminist debates in process? Primarily because she is an economist and claims her right to political discourse and a public forum (both of which have caused difficulties with male-dominated, patriarchally inclined publishing houses). She is also a long-time activist, taking part in protests and performing street theatre in Avignon. More importantly, she has lived for extended periods in the Third World, so that her experience is not that of getting ever nearer to the centre: coming from elsewhere to the intellectual and bourgeois heart of the 'Hexagone' as is the case with Cixous, Irigaray and Kristeva, but rather the opposite move of going out from the metropolis (where she was born and raised by Parisian middle-class atheist parents), into colonialism, oppression, poverty: an ever-increasing globalisation. She came to her analysis through praxis. Today she works in a school where many of the students are from immigrant families, hence her experience of what it is to be a woman in France right now continues to shift and grow. Likewise her theories of oppression and strategies for survival become more radical and more refined, her writing more sophisticatedly attuned to social change.

Her views are not unlike those of Irigaray, as is her style on occasion: *Le Corps-à-corps avec la mère* (Irigaray, 1981) could be an Hyvrard text. Her writing is superficially similar to Cixous' fiction; her views on mother-daughter relations connect her with Kristeva; her circularities and woman-centredness recall Wittig. Her search for connections beyond those of the rational is analogous to the shift Foucault makes from 'archaeology' to 'genealogy'. Hyvrard, too, works with networks of significance. She is somewhat of a visionary, though to my mind less utopian than Irigaray or Wittig and more prophetic in her awareness of potential apocalypse.

Primarily her writing comes out of her family dynamic and bodily experiences – miscarriage, birth, breast cancer. This physical experience is augmented by the intellectual one provided by authors she loves – Hugo, Dostoevsky, Marx, Freud, Arendt, Lanzmann, Levinas, Chouraqui's translation of the book of Genesis and the journals of the great navigators. In these affinities she is similar to Cixous, and like Cixous, as Braidotti says, she 'explores ... an embodied female subjectivity',[2] but whereas Cixous' exploration turns inward to self and to myth as she feels her way to the expression of something she finds personally 'unspeakable', Hyvrard also turns outward, to find the economic and political parallels to her embodied self. From these she creates multilevel fields of resonance reaching from the global to the most intimate as well as back into history and myth. Hers is not the self-analysis that drives Cixous' prose, where, when the unspeakable is finally uttered, the text can be cut off and become a book, and a new text begin. Hyvrard's 'unspeakable' is on a cosmic scale – that of the chaos before Creation (as described in the first book of Genesis). She writes to identify and analyse forms of oppression and formulate strategies of survival. She is as inexorably driven as Cixous, but where Cixous writes into death – 'every book an attempted suicide' I remember her as saying in Kingston in 1991[3] – Hyvrard writes out from it because her physical encounters with death have been too close for her to contemplate anything other than life. An extended comparison of their literature would be extremely informative; as it is, an elaboration of Hyvrard's views will at least make it possible to situate her amongst her fellow thinkers. She has said to me that, like Cixous, she writes the pain of being a woman, but that through the direction and development of her thought, she has stronger affinities to the work of Irigaray.[4] Be that as it may, her voice is an important one and should be included in contemporary discussion of 'la féminin' (sic, Braidotti, 1991, p. 238) as well as in all considerations of the state of French critical theory today. It is to this end, with the primary purpose of making available her thoughts, themes, structures and strategies in her own terms that I have written this book. I trust that other readers will explore and extend the issues raised here.

The major difficulty, until now, has been the inaccessibility of much of her work to those who read no French. To date only *Mère la mort* (*Mother Death*, Nebraska, 1988) has been easily available in translation. *Les Doigts du figuier* (*The Fingers of the Fig-tree*) was translated as part of an MA thesis in 1987, and is available only through university libraries at present. Its twin text, *La Meurtritude* (*Waterweed in the Wash-houses*) will be published together with this book, as will *La Jeune morte en robe de dentelle* (*The Dead Girl in a Lace Dress*). Extracts from *Auditions musicales certains soirs d'été* (*Listening to Music some Summer Evenings*) and *La Baisure* (*The Kissing Crust*), are available in anthologies. *Que se partagent encore les eaux* (*Let the Waters Part Again*) has been translated but never published. I understand that a translation of *La Pensée corps* (*Body Thought*) has recently been undertaken. It is to be hoped that even more texts will be translated soon, meanwhile I try to bridge the gap by including more quotations here than are usual in a critical text.[5]

Hyvrard is an isolated figure within the French tradition, which itself continues to remain separate in significant ways from the thought processes of the Anglo-American world. As a result, some of the material that appears as original in Hyvrard's context may seem to be familiar to

English-speaking readers. It is necessary to situate Hyvrard in her world to appreciate why her voice is special. Her literary antecedents are Lautréamont, the Surrealists and especially the New Novel, as I shall point out. The Modernists are not part of her world. Fanon and Foucault are familiar voices but not Saïd and Spivak, Wittig but not Daly. The major influence on her thinking at this time is the Shoah. She describes the oppressions of the contemporary world as they are reproduced in the very flesh of women. Imaginary and creative structures make her a witness in the way that Lanzmann and Levinas, for example, bear witness to the Holocaust. In her works the female body is transformed into a holocaust site, where the repressive mechanisms are replicated in the reproductive ills of female experience – beginning with Hyvrard's own. This location of oppression in her own body is what gives the urgency for survival in her writing as the flesh is made word.

Chapter 1

ON WRITING / READING HYVRARD

Jeanne Hyvrard came to literature by force of circumstance: setting out to write a report on the economic state of Martinique, she produced *Les Prunes de Cythère* (The Plums of Cythera, 1975) and was hailed as one of the most exciting new literary voices in the Caribbean. This curious error persists to this day as a result of critics' frequent habit of referring to other critics rather than to the source material. The original error was based on the (prevalent) assumption that women writers only create first-person narrators in their own image – hence Jeanne Hyvrard was necessarily dubbed Martiniquaise, whereas she is Parisian. She still claims to have no professional connection with literature, describing herself as a political economist and philosopher and she declares the primacy of the social sciences over fiction and prefers to call her writing 'realities'.[1] She will, however, admit to being a poet.

I happened on her first four books in 1978,[2] was totally fascinated by voice and content, and in fact created a book full of more 'respectable' women writers in order to be able to write about Jeanne Hyvrard, Wittig (a new discovery for me then also) and the Quebec feminist Louky Bersianik.[3] I have been reading and teaching her work ever since. In those days all I could find about the work was reviews. Many of the reviewers of *Les Prunes* seemed to think that she was or had been insane because, as I said above, all powerful books by women are assumed to be autobiographical. Certain reviews of *Mère la mort* (Mother Death, 1976) sustained the original position with curious comments such as '[c]xcept for an occasional Creole term or speech pattern, it is impossible to identify the author as a black Martinican woman from textual evidence',[4] even though *Mère la mort* is set in the centre of France and deals with regional politics as well as the madness, women's oppression, body and language themes of the first book. No biographical sketch, interview or photograph was available, so when the Canadian Association of

University Teachers of French invited Hyvrard to the 1982 convention, none of us yet knew who this woman was.

Jeanne Hyvrard was born in Paris in 1945, the third child of Parisian parents. She married a fellow economics student and they have one daughter, who is an engineer. When she began to publish she took as a pseudonym the name of an aunt who was not 'acceptable' to her family, for the purpose of preserving the aunt's memory and upholding her values.[5] In this way Hyvrard's literary existence is clearly separated from her private life. Although she has recently begun to read her poems to her students, I do not know whether they have any notion that their teacher of economics, politics and business has a life, reputation and career outside the bounds of the school and the demands of the national education system.

Teaching is very important to her none the less; her thought is conditioned constantly by what is happening in the world, how this is represented by the media and what would be an effective analysis of both for classroom use. She is concerned with the ways in which the eyes of urban teenagers (lower middle class, increasingly immigrant or first generation Parisian, none of them intellectually inclined) can be opened to the realities and false rhetoric of the political and economic context in France, Europe and beyond. Her work is informed, if not shaped, by the daily difficulties of an inner city technical high school: the violence and ethnic tensions amongst the students, the fact that many of her colleagues find her modes of thought outlandish and her expression bizarre, whereas the students, though resistant to the curriculum and affirming their otherness in the face of French cultural expectations in ways that are troublesome, are more receptive and comprehending of her metaphorical discourse. She talks about some of the connections to Ann Menke and Alice Jardine:

> I teach and try to modernize my practice with the help of video cassettes. I show a lot of films. And, moreover, without my students, I would never have written *Canal de la Toussaint*. The notion of enception and chaic came to me from my teaching practice and from my students' reactions.[6] Things can be communicated through images, through affect, expressions, vision, music, sound, that are no longer binary at all. Verbal language necessarily led me to try teaching my students economic concepts, which no longer worked for them since, of course, the students are in some sense already in

the twenty-first century, far more than we are. While the television was transmitting the notion of encept, all I was doing was theorizing what I noticed in them.[7]

So Hyvrard's writing and analysis is rooted in her observation of daily economics and political realities. She writes in the hope of change, but without any political agenda. As she says:

My moral sense orders me to witness and not ask what our species will do with my testimony. Metaphysically, that doesn't concern me, and practically I don't worry about it. If we had to worry about the future, in addition to present difficulties, we'd never work our way out of this. (Ibid., p. 95)

and she prefaces this comment with 'I write to keep myself alive.'

In what way is this urgent sense of the need for survival, and writing as the means to that end, either relevant or useful here? It is the underpinning of her increasingly elaborate philosophical system. Born of her own physical experiences, it adds an acuteness to her analyses of oppression. For Hyvrard, all forms of oppression are first and foremost threats to survival; their ultimate result is extinction for those oppressed. (Frantz Fanon's analysis is very similar and may well have been formative. He writes 'All this gnawing at the existence of the colonized tends to make of life something resembling an incomplete death.'[8]) We are in a life and death struggle and Hyvrard describes it as such, whether she is talking about women classified as mad, women in chemotherapy, all those under colonial rule or children in abusive families. All Hyvrard's texts start from within the economy of the narrator's body and expand, level upon level, until they reach national and international proportions. All the levels are voiced, interconnected, reflecting and echoing each other. I shall borrow Nancy Miller's (and Roland Barthes') metaphoric onion here because I think it suits my purpose at least as well as it suited hers.[9] Miller likens her critical analysis of male texts to the stripping of an artichoke down to its heart and her reading of women's texts to peeling an onion. 'The layers are indeed there, but what is at the center?' For her 'the phallocentric text elicits a practice that both reveals and reduces' whereas women's writing requires 'accepting a radical decentering and reorganization of pleasure: finding pleasure not in the revelation of center, but in the process itself of the peeling away of the layers.'

Hyvrard's onion-texts certainly develop in layered voices that are audible to the reader; they are also centreless while being precisely and visibly structured. Thus enjoyment or appreciation of such writings does 'mean accepting a radical decentering and reorganization of pleasure'. Also, as Miller realises, they cannot be dismantled skin by skin:

> for while an onion is indeed constituted by layers, beyond removing the brittle outer skin, one does not peel onions. To perceive that an onion has layers, one has to cut into it, slice, chop or dice; and for those incisions, as we well know, one pays the price of tears. (p. 36)

So far the metaphor holds. Hyvrard deals with women's pain, physical and mental, marginalisation, and violence, and readers may well pay with tears for their efforts to dissect and integrate her thought. These readers are also free to separate and use the books in any way that is useful to their understanding. There is no 'correct' interpretation or organisation of the mass of material; the books express Hyvrard's perceptions of the world whichever way you slice them. Indeed, the more individual the slicing the more satisfactory the result.

I have often found, as I read, that suddenly a given paragraph leaps out as the key to organising my grasp on a 'difficult' text. Clearly this is a response to indicators I have been picking up along the way without being consciously aware of doing so. My cultural habits as an Occidental have predisposed me to expect and look for (linear) structures and my training in literature has prepared me to recognise, classify and analyse the structures I find. I enjoy patterns and the more those I find in a book are complex and challenging, the more pleasure I take in bringing them to light and elucidating or justifying their complications. As a result, I certainly recognise myself in Trinh Minh-ha's comments. She is reflecting on the behaviour of Western anthropologists with respect to oral storytelling; given the analytic nature of literary criticism and the fluidity of Hyvrard's writing, however, the remarks are quite apposite here also:

> Those who function best within definite structures and spend their time structuring their own or their peers' existence must obviously 'look for' that which, according to their 'findings' and analyses, is supposed to be 'the structure of their [the storytellers'] narratives.' What we 'look for' is un/fortunately what we shall find.[10]

And we are so used to organising our mental environment as a way of owning and controlling it in order to transform it into 'knowledge' that even students who have no trust in their reading practices, when asked to isolate the paragraph that seems the most important to them and to organise their thoughts out through the books from that paragraph, can offer an 'enceptual' understanding of Hyvrard's texts that their conscious minds – searching for artichokes in an onion patch – could not deal with conceptually. This is the point at which I shall abandon the vegetable metaphor, because all the parts of an Hyvrard text are in constant motion in relation to each other, and a kaleidoscopic dance of onion pieces won't quite do. Let us return to Trinh Minh-ha's reflection on the process of reading, then to me and my students and to the question of cultural expectations.

Reading Hyvrard is like listening to music: the themes mutate as they wander back and forth between instruments, between keys, between rhythms. The non-linearity and movement are essential. This dynamic non-linearity is new to my students and they tend to find it intimidating. The French tradition is extremely proud of its rigorous cause-and-effect linearity, and (Euclidean) geometric structures are frequent in novels. The resulting patterns may be complex, but they are static, so it is possible to describe and analyse them from an 'objective' position outside the design and we are used to doing this. Even Hyvrard's immediate predecessors, the writers of the New Novel, who situate the reader inside the text and within a present in motion, keep linear language patterns together with very clearly delineated structures and themes to guide their readers. Hyvrard's writing is different from this, as I shall discuss at greater length later. My strategy is to help my students get whatever grasp they can on a new kind of 'story' by making it clear that we all have different priorities which shape our perception at all times and that such personal priorities are legitimate and are indeed indicators of how each of us chooses to organise our understanding. So to quote Trinh once more: 'The structure is therefore not something given, entirely external to the person who structures, but a projection of that person's way of handling realities, her narratives' (p. 141). Most readers in the West (and this is particularly true in France) are more used to Realist stories with a beginning, a development, a climax and an ending, than to any other form of literature.[11] Above all, they are used to being able (required even) to stop at any given moment and explain what they have understood until then. Moreover, our critical language is also structured for this purpose. The reading of non-linear texts goes against learned habits of reading and expectations of modular comprehension. The exposition of the 'content' of such narrative goes against the culturally developed intentions of critical language, yet we deal with fragmented, dynamic, non-linear information all the time in our daily lives. Just as we have been taught to separate content and structure in a text, so we have come to separate the experience of understanding and the 'official', 'academic' experience of reading:

> The present, which saturates the total field of our environment, is often invisible to us. The structural activity that does not carry on the cleavage between form and content but emphasizes the inter-relation of the material and the intelligible is an activity in which structure should remain an unending question: one that speaks him/her as s/he speaks it, brings it to intelligibility.[12]

So writes Trinh Minh-ha, and in like manner, reading Hyvrard's writing obliges us to bring together our modes of understanding, to refuse the compartmentalisation imposed by acts of analysis and classification, to become our own authority in our own ways of knowing. As readers and as human beings, we struggle to sort, use and survive an ever-increasing flood of information which by its flow and complexity effectively prevents the creation of 'solutions'. Yet we were trained to find solutions, to make 'knowledge', and constantly adapting to ever-changing condi-tions is alien to our Western mindset. We have been trained to control and categorise information, to name, define, sort, decipher, dissect, analyse and synthesise. These are skills which relate to a world that is disappearing, and they are clearly less and less adequate as tools in a post-Einsteinian, post-Freudian, cybernetic and transnational environ-ment. Inadequate for a study of Hyvrard also, as she writes the 'new' world into literature.

Hyvrard herself opposes music to song [*le chant*] and grammar to natural language [*la parole*], codification to expression issuing out of deep memory.[13] This does not imply, however, that my comparison of her writing to music is invalid, as her books are highly structured in ways that facilitate the transmission of the deeper meanings through the ever-shifting relationships of the 'sound bites' – short sentences and sentence fragments that occur, recur, are modified and given sense by their immediate context. These modifications are frequently affected as much by the play of sound as by the association of meaning. The resultant language is sonorous, rhythmic, full of echoes, repetitions, linguistic variations and leitmotifs; its symbolic structure is similarly densely metaphoric, full of inter-reflective images, recurrent scenes and thematic variations.

What does writing of this kind imply? On the one hand that as a writer she is attuned to the literary and scientific paradigms which are the current narrative conventions for seeing and describing the world. She uses chaos theory with its holistic thought forms rather than the fragmentation of post-modern writing (see below, Chapters 2 and 3). On the other, that her writing, by its very style and form, embodies the resistance expressed by the content.

Hyvrard's writing (like that of Cixous, Wittig and others[14]) is the expression of her refusal of linear 'rational' thought as the privileged mode of thinking. Her entire *oeuvre* is an ongoing search to find adequate languages in which to transmit the new ways of thinking she is inventing out of her struggles against the monolith of expression that is 'logarchy' (a term she prefers to patriarchy). Her books have an I-subject (*je*) who is female and multiple,[15] a you-object (*tu*) split between a (positive) lover (male) and a (negative) mother figure (female) and an oppositional-they (*ils*), male, undivided and threatening.

The I-subject challenges the traditional narrative expectation at all times because it is always female. In the early books (1975–7) the narrator is doubly transgressive because she is labelled mad by those around her and, in the first book at least, is on occasion assumed to be black. In the later books (1982–9) she transgresses by being female and claiming the right to speak politically as an expert in the public domain. Since then the narrator has been violating specific taboos, breaking deep social silence on specifically feminist issues. This 'I' also refuses the integrated-subject position, with all its implied attendant binary oppositions, of the 'traditional' novel. Hyvrard's subject usually opens to permit the passage of other voices into the tissue of the text. The oppressed and resistant subject thus speaks layers of (women's) experience simultaneously, inscribing connections from the individual to the collective, from myth to rebellion into the writing. Multiple or not, this subject always speaks from a specific situation in (a) particular female body/bodies and the layering of observation, commentary and struggle are rooted in the physical condition of the embodied female subject.

The body is thus the primary situation. Female bodies tend to be more receptive to cyclical (r)evolution than to linear development, to multiplicity and complexity than to binary choice. Hyvrard's writing reflects this turn away from Realist techniques.[16] She refuses all notion of fixed definition and of exclusionary opposition. Meanings mutate according to context in Hyvrard's work; 'definitions' are indefinite, flexible, mobile; words/concepts and their 'opposites' are thought together with an awareness of the 'contraration'; experience frequently provides contradictory information. Everything is interconnected. Hyvrard calls this way of thinking 'fusional' (*fusionnelle*) or 'round' (*la pensée ronde*) or 'corporeal' (*la pensée corps*).

Time, for this subject-body, is inscribed above all in memory, the long, deep race-memory of female genealogy back to the goddess before Genesis – the separation of the waters of the Creation and the story of Adam and Eve are recurrent and reconfigured figures of Hyvrard's prose – and conscious historic memory of female sufferings. As such it is discontinuous, 'fragmentary and concentric' in Hyvrard's terms, and is integrated into the present of the narrator's discourse, as the narrator tries to reach back in search of a pre-androcentric, non-divisive language in which to think.

This non-divisive style precludes the usual separation of subject and ground also, with the result that Hyvrard does not create décor and characters in the 'traditional' fashion. Physical context is included as part of the circumstances around the subject-body in a specific fragment of experience, but the subject is not constituted and situated by a setting of material possessions as is the case in the capitalist narrative convention.

There is no separation either between a thinking–I–subject and a feeling–I–subject. Hyvrard's philosophical, political and economic reflections are interwoven with emotional responses, feelings and physical reactions to a variety of events and circumstances in what Braidotti calls 'affective will-to-know' or 'a form of conceptual creativity'.[17]

Most of the books are printed as continuous prose, others divided and presented as poetry, but, read aloud, there is little difference in the overall cadences, tone colour and rhythms as they shift in accordance with major themes. Most of the texts are written in a variation on this style:

Memory the same for everyone. The knowledge of death in the mother's belly. The order of the world. The order of things. The order of opposites. The origins of thought in the memory of death. The origin. How can one conceive it save in conception? Two times

one: one. The original garden. The womb of the world. The gestation of the species. The digestance. The tombs. The dolmens. The
Pyramids. The dead becoming digested foetuses again. The men-
hirs standing tall replacing the living in perpetuity. A love song. The
sense of things. The sense of words. The sense of the world. The
memory of unity.[18]

Les Prunes de Cythère, Mère la mort, La Meurtritude are all subtitled
'novel'. *Les Doigts du figuier* is called 'parole' (speech/utterance) stressing
its aural nature and it is written as a long epic poem, as are *La Baisure,*[19]
Que se partagent encore les eaux and *Le Silence et l'obscurité, réquiem littoral
pour corps polonais* (Silence and Obscurity: Requiem for a Polish Body). *Le
Corps défunt de la comédie* (The Defunct Body of the Comedy) subtitled
'Treatise of Political Economy' is written in prose 'lessons', to delineate
the history and effects of the colonisation of Africa. *Canal de la Toussaint*
(All Saints' Canal) is divided into verses reminiscent of the Bible. *Ton
nom de végétal* (Your Vegetable Name) is written more or less in the same
poetic and associative style, although the third section is punctuated
with paragraphs in the classificatory manner of natural history manuals.

There are four exceptions to this dominant linguistic mode. In these
the style is less allusive at the sentence level; the interconnections and
symbolic fields operate at the level of the paragraph or section instead,
although the mental operations remain similar. *Auditions musicales certains
soirs d'été* is a volume of brief and subtle stories told in a variety of styles,
the whole of which is reminiscent of Nathalie Sarraute's *Tropismes.*[20] *Le
Cercan*, an examination of the mis-treatment of cancer patients, was
begun as the collective endeavour of a group of people in chemotherapy
and was ultimately completed by Jeanne Hyvrard. It includes discussions, extended prose pieces and an important conversation between
Jeanne Hyvrard and her mother. *La Pensée corps* (Body Thought) lays out
Hyvrard's interpretations of terms, 'defines' her neologisms, and
describes her view of social structures in a series of cross-referenced
articles. The structure of the volume is such that it appears to be a dictionary, but the usual stabilising, prescriptive elements are all missing.
These 'definitions' are relative to their context. This book provides the
core of Hyvrard's social, political and economic thought, and it is a major
tool in the understanding of her work.

The other key to her early work is *La Jeune morte en robe de dentelle.*
This is the only literary volume so far that Hyvrard has written on a

computer – because she needed the distance, she says. Written like *Auditions* in brief paragraphs, reflective or anecdotal, it is a sustained examination and dissection of an oppressive – 'cannibalistic' – mother-daughter relationship. A masterpiece of devastatingly clear psychological and linguistic analysis, written with controlled sobriety and subtlety of effect, this book is totally different from the others. Of all the works to date, it is the most likely to go into the canon of French literature (where there is a long tradition of slim volumes of narratorial psychological self-examination). It also deserves a place in the ranks of the major feminist examinations and representations of mothers and daughters and I will come back to that in a later chapter.

Within the confines of Hyvrard's own work, *La Jeune morte* throws specific light on the situations depicted in the four first volumes and is a key to the important role survival plays in Hyvrard's thought. It is also the book (*Le Cercan* apart) that feels the most autobiographical to many readers and indeed when I asked her directly, at the insistence of my students, whether the name claimed by the narrator at the end of the novel was her name, she agreed that this was so. She also insists, correctly to my mind, that this book is built on as many layers of metaphorical possibility as the others (see Chapter 5). The point here is that Hyvrard's work is rooted in her own bodily experience in the same way that the themes of the texts are embodied in the narrative voice.

She talks of her struggles for survival starting in the womb;[21] certainly in her adult life, she has suffered numerous miscarriages, a brush with psychiatry,[22] breast cancer and chemotherapy. These are female ills, all accompanied through history by specific social opprobrium: infertility, madness, scapegoating and silence. From her childhood comes the fight to understand and survive a cannibalistic (her term) mother-daughter relationship.[23] Extended out into the group, the mother's invasiveness and control translate into slavery and colonial governance, and into all negative responses to the sexual female body from prudery to rape. Parallels are drawn between mental hospitals, prisons and concentration camps, between chemotherapy and the devastation of the planet. Breast cancer is explored in terms of chaos, love and female genealogy.[24]

Hyvrard bears witness to an increasingly toxic, increasingly dehuman-ised world, in which writing is a political act and new ways of thinking are essential for physical survival on a daily basis. Hers is a poetics of dis-placement that, to use Maggie Humm's terminology, refuses to recognise borders. She writes her way across them all and thus forces her readers to consider the way they draw their own borders and are confined by those of others. She describes herself to Menke and Jardine as

> a housewife . . . who was cornered, given the events that historically intervened in her life, into taking recourse in writing to emancipate herself and to rethink the world that was condemning her to death.[25]

This sense of urgency and necessity permeates her work.

Chapter 2

ON THE CHANGING PARADIGM

At a conference given to a Latin-American Women's Congress in 1987 on what women's writing has to offer the sciences, Hyvrard said:

> Literature by women makes visible forms that have not been catalogued. Not only by the mixing of *genres* but by the advent of other grids, networks and structures. Chaos is said to be formless. Let's rather say that the forms it takes are not known to current logic. Right now we are taking part in an expansion of women's thought and even greater changes in the workings of the mind ... (this notion does not cover that of the mentalities attributed to a society, class and generation).[1]

Thus, by juxtaposition of concepts, she appears to be claiming chaos for women whereas certain contemporary scientists would claim that an increasing awareness and understanding of the forms and behaviours of chaos is what science has to offer right now. These claims are not mutually exclusive; it is simply that a variety of thinkers are exploring a certain world view or grid of understanding from very different perspectives and have not yet encountered each other or recognised the similarities in what they are doing.

This in itself is certainly not surprising, as the marginalised voice of the female writer and the dominant voice of the male scientist are just about as far apart as is possible on the continuum of philosophical discourse. Both, however, are exploring aspects of the physical world and of the attitudes and thoughts that result from their experience/discoveries that challenge all that the previous Western cultural paradigm represented: laws, stability, measurability, accountability, hierarchy. They are examining aspects that previous theorists set aside either as intractable problems, 'noise' in the experiment, illogical phenomena, or the irra-tional – chaos indeed.

Particle physicists were shaken out of their mechanistic and logical thought habits by the behaviour of the quanta they were trying to 'observe' 'scientifically'. (Simultaneously a number of French writers made a similar shift as a result of explorations in contemporary painting and music.) Their experiments, Einstein's theories, Freud's theory of the subconscious, began to break down the linearities of the previous para-digm (space, time, objectivity) and open new pathways into what had previously been set aside as unthinkable; or rejected perhaps as unac-ceptable, because it was mysterious, uncontrollable, illogical, frightening and humbling, beyond male domination and falling traditionally into the realm of the feminine: the dark and turbulent side of Mother Nature.

Hyvrard arrives at her notion of chaos from the opposite pole – from the inner cycles of her own body, from daily experience of being a woman in the world, from her observations, as a political economist, of the ways women are and have been in the world, from a continual closeness to natural realities. She draws her structuring metaphor, her paradigm, from the book of Genesis: the chaos that existed before the separations imposed by the seven days of Creation and the exclusions and omissions created by the instauration of reason as the only acceptable process (Adam's naming of all things being the beginning of all categorisation).

However, Hyvrard is not writing in isolation. She is rooted in French culture and so is part of the shift of attitudes and awareness happening in the Western world. She, like the physicists, is ahead of most of us in her recognition of formative patterns. She is acutely aware of changes as they occur in social attitudes, economic trends and political reactions. As the scientists say that the 'order' of the living world is probably what they, from the observation point of the previous paradigm, consider 'chaos', so Hyvrard also grows into the realisation that chaos is disorder only when defined from the illusory standpoint of 'knowledge'; that 'knowledge' is restrictive and oppressive because of its traditional lim-itations. Hyvrard's 'chaos' lies beyond its borders in a state of pre-knowledge – the flowing together of encepts to create information in an extra-rational form. Both points of view are subversive of science as cur-rently practised and used to uphold status quo capitalist and patriarchal hierarchies of control, and of academic philosophy, political science and economics. Ultimately it does not matter very much whether we choose to 'read' our society through an hyvrardian grid or read Hyvrard through a cultural one. The networks are so intertwined that they cover much of the same territory, though on different planes and in different modes.

I choose to start from the scientific paradigm because it seems to me that in any period, at least in French literature, there is a clear and usually unacknowledged parallel between the dominant scientific paradigm and the dominant narrative mode in literature. Both provide conventions of description for the same world view using the same elements to do so and these elements seem to be: space, time, measure, matter and the processing gaze of the knower. This holds true for the God-directed literature and alchemy of the Middle Ages, for the man-centered and increasingly mechanistic age that stretched from the Renaissance to the late nineteenth century and for post-atomic science and avant-garde writing today.[2] Looked at this way, Hyvrard takes her place in literary and philosophical tradition as an exemplar of a non-referential, non-Realist, writing the chaotic world view as it comes into being. She is a witness to the changing paradigm and a shaper of the new narrative mode.

The awareness of particle physics came into the French novel in the 1950s with the explorations of the 'new novel'.[3] The novel is always the last of the arts to shift into new modes. I suspect that readers bring to novels an expectation of immediate understanding that they do not apply to poetry or painting. As Herbert Read once wrote: 'Traditions make hat racks in the mind'[4] and it is not until these pegs are in place that most novelists try to hang prose on them. So the 'new novelists' were the first to explore basic quantum thinking in French literature, though they did not consider what they were doing in those terms.

The manifestations of the shift from a mechanistic view of the world to that of quantum field theory make an enormous change to the narrative mode and imply an entirely different way of being in the world. First there is a change of structuring metaphor from that of the novel as a machine which can be observed, in which every part has a place, every movement has a cause, every cause has an effect, every effect can be analysed and the whole is the sum of its parts: measurable time, space and motion. (Hence the conventions of all-seeing author or single perspective narrator, chronology, plot, décor, character development and so on.) The new metaphor is that of a 'cosmic dance', a network of events or an energy field in which everything is interrelated, is in constant motion and is not always visible. This is a 'reality' with no detachable parts and no enduring unchanging parts either. This 'reality' is inferred from patterns of probability extrapolated from patterns of motion in which the observer is included as an integral part: the problems of such a world view for those of us raised in the previous one begin to be apparent. Katherine Hayles, in her study of contemporary American novelists, suggests the metaphor of 'a constantly turning kaleidoscope whose shifting patterns arise from the continuing, mutual interaction of all its parts'.[5] She then goes on to show the complexities inherent in her metaphor. If the dance is incessant and infinite, how can we describe it without stopping it? Yet if we stop it and describe the 'pattern' we see, we have not only lost the dynamic essence of the dance – its real pattern – but created a false description because the 'pattern' we described was created by our own intervention.

But, before we can ever arrive at the 'false' description we need to take into account another limitation implicit in quantum field thinking: we are inside the movement and so have no 'objective' spot from which to observe. This is the situation of the readers of novels such as Michel Butor's *L'Emploi du temps* and *La Modification* and Alain Robbe-Grillet's *La Jalousie*.[6] It is also the situation of the narrators of these novels, who are forced constantly to adjust their understanding of the circumstances in which they find themselves.

Not only is the observer part of the field/dance but so is the language that must be used for the description. An author working within this energy-field paradigm is trying to construct a web to catch or evoke a holistic reality which is dynamic and infinite – this is difficult enough in itself, but the internal structures of the language used will complicate the attempt even further. Western languages are by nature linear and sequential (in delivery if not in their implications). French in particular (especially since Descartes) has been considered a precision instrument for the transmission of logic and rationality. Hence French is a highly articulated language structured upon the clear expression of explicit cause and effect. This is not the language in which to explore the paradoxes of a quantum universe, to try to describe an elusive reality 'deriving its deepest meaning from a whole it can neither contain nor express'.[7]

So, a novelist using the new paradigm must find a way of seeing with a multi-directional, ever-shifting narrative gaze a dynamic world in which any attempt to measure what is seen will change what is to be measured. Where, in any event, measurement is not absolute but subject to change, depending on the frame of reference from which it is made.

The change of perspective is total. In such a world the patterns of energy, the shaping networks are the significant transmitters of 'information' or 'meaning'. There are none of the discrete elements from which the nineteenth-century novel was constructed, but only the traces they leave behind and their potential spots of re-emergence into the visible pattern. The shift is similar to that from a daylight photograph of a street full of vehicles, to one taken on a dark night in the rain with a time exposure, where all one sees is firework-like trails produced by the lights of the flow of traffic. Now suppose that we regard the *pattern* of trails as 'real' and the vehicles as temporary manifestations of the *patterns*. 'This radically altered perspective is analogous to the shift in view suggested by quantum field theory.'[8]

The writers of the 'new novel' took steps towards this new view. They dislodged plot, chronology, décor, figure and ground opposition, and played with the relativity of perception and frame of reference and with possibilities of narrative voice. (Butor, in particular, created extensive, dynamic networks of which the most famous is *La Modification* but probably the most ambitious is *Degrés*, 1960.)[9] The one thing they did not challenge was the pre-eminence of rational thought and logical expression as embodied and embedded in the language itself. In this they were creatures of transition – and also by this means they remained intelligible in an age of transition. (The Surrealists explored the breakdown of reason, but their legacy survives primarily in poetry and painting.)

Hyvrard takes the next step and has spent her whole writing career struggling to find a form and a language adequate to express the dynamic, holistic, interactive world she sees – that is the human meaning of field theory in particle physics.

Both 'systems' are constructed from a dynamic web of moving particles which cannot be stopped and examined 'objectively'. Configurations shift in ways that do not depend on one-way, linear interaction and, as a result, causes and effects cannot be identified. With the breakdown of cause and effect comes the impossibilitiy of description as we know it, because 'causal terminology implies a one-way interaction that falsifies the essence of what we want to convey'.[10]

The narrator of *Les Prunes de Cythère*, Hyvrard's first novel, senses the restrictiveness structured into the language she is supposed to learn and resists it from the beginning. As a child she does not speak at all; once at school, she speaks patois and persists in making grammatical errors. In this novel set in Martinique where the narrator's voice, which is primarily that of a young white French woman, also transmits those of the black female servant, and a black male (historic) revolutionary against the colonial regime, opposition to standard French as taught in school and as acceptable to the white mother figure is a threefold statement:

(1) refusal of the oppressive and alienating structures of dominance and colonisation.

> But, from hearing you so much, I have started to speak patois. Well, said the mother. She is speaking finally. Maybe we will get her to make progress. One doesn't say runned but ran. Poor little thing, she'll never come to anything. She makes so many mistakes. The deformed mouth of the words she can't pronounce. Do you realize my daughter talks black. Me, a white woman. What will become of me? My little girl. Make an effort. Think of me. Of your father. All the sacrifices we've made for you. We don't deserve that. She speaks patois. Nobody understands anything she's talking about. (*Les Prunes de Cythère*, p. 177)

(2) refusal of the restrictions imposed on girls in the name of conformity and acceptability:

> Come now, don't teach her those words. You (masc. sing.) will do her wrong. Come, come, that isn't nice in a little girl's mouth. Rather, try to smile. Speak softly. You will make a little conversation. Above all be very polite. Be quiet. I shall have the last word. Answer when you are spoken to. Come to me and I will deliver you of speech. [. . .] (Ibid., p. 29)

(3) refusal of the thought processes coded into the language and an increasing awareness of what the language lacks:

> I don't want anything to do with your world. Or your logic. Even less your language from which so many words are missing. I don't want immobile verbs, dormant substantives, sterilized adjectives. I give you back my muzzled mouth . . . (Ibid., p. 113)

As we see increasingly clearly as the book unfolds, what she is searching for is a language which can express connection. This narrator understands instinctively that networks of understanding stretch across time: from Mother Africa to contemporary colonialism; across space: from the grandmother in Northern France to Martinique once more; across matter: from human to animal, plant and element; across situation: from slave to female victim of colonisation, rape, amputation, silencing, murder. She makes these connections but the way she expresses what she sees cannot result in acceptable, rational prose, ordered in a logical fashion towards a neat and tidy conclusion. I include an extended excerpt from the novel so that you can experience Hyvrard's narrative form:

The mad go in pairs in the alfalfa. Their bells can be heard under the acacias. She fell in the gravel pits one day when she was singing there. Or maybe in the iron stairway that led to the head doctor's office. And yet I had told you to put her in a strait jacket. But me, I want to run, laugh and jump. Saint James's Madness, the mad walk in pairs in the lanes through the wood. Sometimes, one passes someone on horseback. Doubtless, the one who was coming to meet me in the meadow when I was twenty. One day, my horse let go of the bit and you (masc. sing.) dismounted to come to my aid. Your boots were in the grass. The meadow smelled of hay and gentians. Wild blackberries. Raspberries of my only love. Our bodies entwined in the hollow of the rocks. Dandelion. Lady's slipper. Coltsfoot. New flowers of unknown embraces. We've been galloping for days over partly cleared ways. It's the rutting season. We run on the paths to meet the mountain. You are my only love, says the man kissing her in the stable. The smell of horses in the past perfect. The smell of droppings in the future perfect. The poverty of words to smell colours. How many words left to invent to say the cut hay. The imperfect and the pluperfect of the forest, over us like a coat.

But, from hearing you so much, I have started to speak patois. Well, said the mother. She is speaking finally. Maybe we will get her to make progress. One doesn't say runned but ran. Poor little thing, she'll never come to anything. She makes so many mistakes. The deformed mouth of the words she can't pronounce. Do you realize my daughter talks black. Me, a white woman. What will become of me? My little girl. Make an effort. Think of me. Of your father. All the sacrifices we've made for you. We don't deserve that. She speaks patois. Nobody understands anything she's talking about.

Any way, one mode is missing. The one of your open arms under the larches. Dead birches thrown on the ground. From the smile of the raspberries to the brambles of lost time. I'm telling you there's a mode missing. The indicative doesn't indicate anything of what is swarming in my potholes. The conditional is unusable with its traps of conditions that we never fulfilled. If your father wished. If you were reasonable. A mode is missing. The one of my hair you've cut to make a sheaf. (*Les Prunes de Cythère*, pp. 176–7)

This stream-of-consciousness writing functions differently from similar writings by the 'new novelists'. Butor, Robbe-Grillet and Simon use primarily the visual aspects of perception and the theories of phenomenology to create descriptions where the forms and patterns described have been disconnected from any interpretation of their function. Hyvrard's narrative builds by association. Her shifting points of reference accrue in the mind of the reader, who gradually recognises thematic currents running though the prose, and generate possibilities of significance, networks of 'encepts'.

The only way for such writing to be acceptable in French in 1975 was perhaps for the author to label her narrator 'mad', and this Hyvrard does, while making it absolutely clear that this label is the result of insufficiencies in the language and in the people around Jeanne (the narrator) and not in her perceptions of the world.[11] For Hyvrard this is also a political statement. In *Au bord du marais* (On the Edge of the Marshland), the lecture she gave in Ottawa in 1982, she spoke about 'the feminine and madness, both gagged by the same linguistic dogmatism'.

The lunatic is someone for whom separation is deadly (the misunderstanding is complete, since the lunatic is placed, *a priori*, in a state of separation whereas his claim and his universe are those of non-exclusion). Madness is the universe of the unlimited and the infinite. It's the universe of the cosmos, which is also infinite, unlimited, and of life made up of the same elements which undo themselves and recombine unceasingly.

Here is the world of quantum field theory from a different perspective. Hyvrard maintains it can be 'thought within the domain of the rational' if we are prepared to improve our 'tools' for thinking. But this world has not yet entered the dominant discourse:

Contemporary intellectual economy does not even try to take the world of madness into account. It excludes it *a priori* as by nature irrational, beyond speech and thought.

The function of French schooling is to separate, define, exclude, within a linear logical (cause and effect) system sustained by a binary and oppositional symbolic system, and to impose this thought pattern as the only one possible. Hyvrard struggles to find (create or rediscover) an alternative system which she subsequently calls 'marsh language' and defines as one which manipulates 'open-infinite-indefinite concepts' that are wider than usual and incorporate 'in the same word perceptions of the earth, the body, the intellectual and the spiritual'. This language creates and uses connections and correspondences of all kinds drawn from intuitive knowledge and collective memory expressed through vehicles such as tales and proverbs. Hyvrard sees this as the language of 'non-separity' which will come into its own as the language of globalisation and of the totality of experience. She writes:

> The present crisis is economic, social, political, but mostly cultural. One world is dying, another is being born. How can one give an account of this transformation other than by the language of the marsh which can say one thing and its opposite at the same time? That's why the language of the marsh is that of the future. The open concepts, the correspondences allow the integration of what is going on as soon as it happens, even if one doesn't yet understand fully. One cannot integrate the phenomena that are occurring in a language in which concepts are closed. To tell of today, it is necessary to elaborate a language which allows one to give an account of the mental phenomena that are taking place. That is to be able to say already that which one is not really equipped to think about yet.

This is a language in which she can think together what she calls 'contrarations'. These are concepts which are the reverse of each other and yet are interconnected in a multitude of rich and living ways denied and rendered invisible by binary opposition. The first pairs she identifies as important are: separate/differentiate, contrary/negative, contraration/contradiction. *Les Prunes de Cythère* is an exploration of this.

One of the reasons Jeanne feels alienated from everybody else is that the people around her – her mother in particular – all behave as though every word or situation has only one meaning, one possible response. These are the people who accept the view that language imposes: there are rules that clarify meaning; nothing is ambiguous and there is no such thing as paradox. These people have a fixed, impoverished, controlled perspective whereas the narrator lives in a swirling network of possibility within which she struggles to maintain her own understanding.

> Words assault me. A crowditude of words shouting in my head. They squabble and kiss each other, walk on each other's feet, climb all over each other to get a good view of my shaky rationality. (*Les Prunes*, p. 130)

For her, every concept is infinitely variable.

Let us take as an example the word 'mother', which is a key concept in Hyvrard's work. For the narrator's mother, a mother is the one who gives birth to the child and to whom the designation 'mother' gives *ipso facto* the right to claim that all her actions, however dubious they might sometimes be, are at all times good for the child. The narrator sees things differently. It is true that, whatever she might do, the mother remains the ultimate haven, her body the lost paradise: 'Mother I want to come home to your belly . . . Mother everything except your flesh is famine' (Ibid., p. 165), but she is also a source of danger because she can prevent her daughter from living:

> I can't manage to be born. I don't want to be born. I don't want to let her be born. I'm you. I'm this body contracting so strongly that she's suffocating. My body squeezes in to embrace you, to suffocate you so that you will die rather than escape me. (Ibid., p. 73)

And this stifling mother is linked unequivocally to the system by which she has been co-opted, which is that of all male dominance over women:

> So she lay on top of me and forced her phallus into my mouth. Stop mother I'm not hungry anymore. I don't want anymore of the sperm of your suffocating love. (Ibid., p. 46)

This mother refuses to help her daughter in any way, strives to repress and mould her, to amputate undesirable parts and silence the language she is searching for. Yet through all of this there remains a core sense of complicity of identification. The word incorporates all possible aspects of the mother-daughter relationship and above all the word remains dynamic, a flexible concept that can take its place in a shifting context of meanings. Hyvrard's narrator is trying to express the process of living, understanding, relating and not to define a state.

Les Doigts du figuier, twin text to *La Meurtritude* whose structure I shall look at shortly,[12] exemplifies this attitude. It is built around the process of life as it unfolds the multiplicity of aspects of any given concept. The body, for example, described here in terms of action/verbs:

It is that which is
It is that which talks
It is that which lives
It is that which survives

Then qualities/nouns:

Body of joy
Body of wonders
Body of happiness
Body of distress
Body of tiredness
Body of refusal

refusal leads to contrary possibilities:

Informing itself of what is appropriated
And of what is not

and then self-regulation of space and time:

Her body informing itself
Compass body
Calendar body
Clock body
(*Les Doigts*, p. 58.)

The body then orients itself to its sources of information: the senses. These are listed and viewed together and then explored individually, the first establishing themselves by analogy, by sonority, by visual transformation. The text then returns to the notion of body and sets off again through the various cycles of a woman's life: menstruation, pregnancy, life and death.

This is an epic of process and inclusion, opposites, complexities and paradox – an extended example of how Jeanne's thought might well unfold. Simultaneously the 'story' is that of the repression of such thought and such all-inclusive sensitivity by the dominant logos, the suppression of the feminine by the masculine, the elimination of the Goddess by Judaeo-Christianity. The themes are those of the rest of the early work and we shall return to them later.

If we set out again from the arguments put forward about language in *Les Prunes de Cythère*, we see that the struggle to define or create an adequate language continues in the second book, *Mère la mort*, as does the analysis of the role of language in the logarchy:[13]

> I can't manage to adopt their language which is still foreign to me. She says I'll never amount to anything. They say I invent words. And yet all I do is apply their rules. They say I invent words. And yet it seems that they were already there. Only they had forgotten them. They dissect the flesh of my suffixes. They see the sure sign of my illness there. They take my conjugations. They see symptoms there. [. . .] Every day they give me a zero for grammar. Dictation. Dictation. Writing. Dissertation. Composition. Logical analysis. In what language the same tense to say the future and the past? In what language a sacred tense, a profane tense? In what language a lasting form and one that doesn't last? They say I'm mad, but I speak the same language they do. Who are those men who put red on my exercise papers? Who are those men who correct? Who are those men who claw my flesh while underlining my verbs? Who are those men who scratch us out? [. . .] Do they know how to conjugate the fusional tense as I dissolve myself into the world?
>
> Mother Death, in what language do words also mean their opposites? [. . .] They use language to lie and spelling to make us comply. [. . .] They want me to use auxiliary verbs. To be and to have, they say. But auxiliaries of what? They don't know anymore.
>
> Power and identity. To be and to have. Verbs conjugated with to be and those with to have. Tenses with to be. Tenses with to have. Why not both forms? Why not choose? Conjugations of power. Conjugations of identity. (*Mother Death*, pp. 33–5)

To speak as her oppressors want would mean that Jeanne was cured. 'Cured' is another term with variable meanings. For those who consider themselves normal in these novels, being cured is accepting to live under the same social code of dominance and binary opposition as they do. So for them a 'cured' woman is a quiet, passive, well-dressed, well-behaved marriageable doll. For Jeanne the word for this state of colonised womanhood is 'death'. (Death also has a variety of roles from 'non-life' to the power of Mother Death in the natural cycles of existence.) She will be cured when she breaks out of the game she gradually comes to recognise and name:

> They've locked me in a chess game. They've made me the queen in a strange game. White or black. In a game with no left or right. They've made me the queen in a game whose object is to destroy the other. [. . .] They've locked me in a game where someone always loses. They've locked me in the game of power and identity. They've locked me in a game and tried to checkmate me. They were moving their pawns forward to surround me. They wanted me dead or mad. They were going to say 'mate' [*mat*]. But I upset the chessboard. Here I am, free. (Ibid., pp. 65–6)

(*Échec* – chess – in French also means failure. 'Mat' is both mate, for the termination of the chess game, and the name of the Fool, who is the first card of the Tarot deck – which will be Hyvrard's next game.)

Chess is a game in which someone wins and someone loses. It is also a game of calculated moves, in which logic plays a fundamental role in winning the game. So is language when dominated by the logos. The rules impose a way of thought so controlled that the holes and deficiencies in the system are rendered invisible (to most people) or taboo. Once Hyvrard's narrator begins to create extra words to permit previously unexpressed subtleties of relationship to exist, we realise how much richer language could be and how accepted and expected language usage imposes an implicit ideology on our very thoughts.

Language is colonised. Its categories shape our perception. Hyvrard gives an interesting example when discussing the search for identity: 'A woman seeks her identity. A mad woman confuses first, second and third persons. A bad pupil falls back into her mistakes of grammar' (*Mother Death*, p. 54). Yet the linguistic manifestation of these three actions would be the same. The distinctions drawn are social, mutually exclusive and intended to control. The language Hyvrard is seeking would release these definitions and allow free play amongst the roles and interpretations.

This brings us back to the chess game and the place of games and systems in Hyvrard's writing. A chess game is an oppositional competition with fixed rules, complex but fundamentally mechanistic. It is a closed system driven by cause and effect. As her work with language progresses, Hyvrard starts experimenting with dynamic and flexible systems which permit, indeed encourage, changing relationships, paradox, ambiguity and total interconnection of the elements of which they are composed. In *La Meurtritude* she uses the Tarot and alchemy to structure her novel. The Tarot provides a description of a world in which powers are shared, where women and men are equal and where Jeanne has her place as the enlightened Fool, card without a number in the pack. In this totality every card is distinct from the others while being inseparable from the game, because every card has function and meaning only in the context of the cards surrounding it at any given moment. This is a complex and mobile network which incorporates each element and its opposite in a universal and often paradoxical vision. The Tarot offers Hyvrard a synchronistic web of connections; alchemy provides a diachronistic one. Rather than the language of the interdependency of power, its language is the language of fusion. In this description of the world, primary matter is transformed by a series of 'deaths' and 'rebirths', a series of inseparable lives, doubled by the personal spiritual development of the alchemist. Both alchemy and the Tarot are recounted in a coded convention of exploits of mythic divinities. These two systems predate the age of reason and the categorical thinking of the mechanistic paradigm. Through the possibilities they offer, Hyvrard finds encouragement in her search for the 'language before separation', which she situates before the Creation recounted in Genesis – but of this, more later.

Hyvrard's first four books explore and establish basic energy-field writing as an aim and a possibility. In her own writing, as we have seen in the quotations in this chapter, she puts her explorations into practice. She breaks down the tight articulation of French grammar by the use of juxtaposed short sentences and sentence fragments which move about in the text, finding a different significance according to their context, floating free in a way that leaves readers to establish their own priorities, clarities and ambiguities within the shifting pattern of information. The 'message' of the text grows out of the recurrences. Insistences form patterns, proximities create understanding, juxtapositions propose analysis, images are critical. In these ways the author circumvents the obstructions, simplifications and distortions that logic would impose on her thought and leads her readers into texts that fit together more like pieces of music with themes, variations, changes of tone, key and instrumentation than like 'traditional' novels in the mechanistic mode.

From the beginning, Hyvrard conceives of her world as a holistic dynamic swirl of flexible concepts. The challenge is to express this in a language where the rules of the game are laid out in grammar books and the words are fixed in dictionaries, their meanings stabilised, defined and hierarchised. She succeeds in her early literature, where the readers can always let passages go by as comfortable patches of incoherence only to be expected from a 'mad' narrator, and where what she herself is seeking is to chart the process of connection, 'enception' and 'chaorganisation'.[14] Remaining a political economist at heart, however, she sees the real challenge in making her entire system visible and comprehensible, in a form accessible and acceptable to those thinkers in her field who would be unlikely to read as philosophy or social criticism an avant-garde novel with a doubly or triply marginalised narrator. So Hyvrard wrote a dictionary, a guide to her neologisms and a description of today's world as she sees it, *La Pensée corps* (1989).

In the tradition of Wittig and Daly, (both women have written dictionaries with the political intent of claiming the right to public definition of meaning for women),[15] Hyvrard is none the less pushing further than they did because she subverts the dictionary form as well as the content. *La Pensée corps* is constructed as an energy field of dynamic, interrelated points which indicate the shapes, scopes and patterns of motion implicit in the system. The 325 entries are arranged in alphabetical order in the usual way. Each entry is cross-referenced to others not only by proximity, as in a usual volume, but by italicised words within each entry which indicate other entries, and by a 'read also' list at the end of each one. The exception to this is the entry for death; it stands alone, an end, the place where the network stops. The 'definitions' vary from personal or poetic statements such as the first one in the volume:

To loove [*Aamer*]
   Language makes the *word* what the ice box/glacier makes the *body*. To loove: to love tenderly. I haven't invented it. I found it in the old dictionary you gave me. Read also: Soul. Man-speech.

to technical descriptions of political organisation. The second entry lays out the base of Hyvrard's analysis very clearly:

Obstacle [*Achoppement*]
   The *reasonary* assumes the monopoly of *logic*. He excludes the *mad* from it. He deprives himself of the *in-thought* he calls *irrational*. He excludes from reason half of itself. When it re-emerges, he does not recognise it. He exterminates it. Yet in science, he misses it.
   The assistant assumes the monopoly of life. He excludes the suicidal. He deprives himself of the in-thought he calls depressive. He excludes from vitality half of itself. When it re-emerges, he does not recognise it. He locks it up. Yet in medicine, he misses it.
   The coloniser assumes the monopoly of culture. He excludes the culturally integrated. He deprives himself of the in-thought he calls primitive. He excludes from civilisation half of itself. When it re-emerges, he does not recognise it. He vassalises it. Yet in politics, he misses it.
   Man assumes the monopoly of speech. He excludes the *Woman* from it. He deprives himself of the in-thought he calls chaos. He excludes from thought half of itself. When it re-emerges, he does not recognise it. He masters it. Yet in philosophy, he misses it.
   The *logarch* assumes the monopoly of *order*. He excludes the fusionary. He deprives himself of the in-thought he calls confusion. He excludes from *organisation* half of itself. When it re-emerges, he does not recognise it. He represses it. Yet in geonomics, he misses it.
   Read also: All the rest. O! the suffering of this grid cast on the foam, of this net catching the birds, of this form attempting to ordinate the living body. Littoral, the lips of the sea. Littoral, the dictionary between dream and writing. Littoral, the open book. Littoral, the nomenclature. Littoral, the text between eternity and time. (*La Pensée corps*, p. 9)

Notice the apparent shift in language here. Hyvrard still uses short, juxtaposed sentences – thus refusing the grammatical construction of cause and effect – but here, the sentences contain clear statements and follow each other in a way that provides coherent information. It is as though the author had sorted the sentences of her literary texts into thematic piles and presented them here one pile at a time. The interweaving happens at the level of the paragraph entry rather than the phrase.

The book begins with love and closes with the all-encompassingness Hyvrard has been struggling to write:

Universally [*Universellement*]
One, union, unit, universe, universality … I could decline it in alphabetical order and by increasing size, until the entire earth was covered, if I didn't know where that leads.

O may your hands, the book and the name/noun remain eternally between the drama and me. (Ibid., p. 219)

Reading the text is like reading an enormous deck of Tarot cards. Each entry takes its meaning from its context but what that context is depends on a multitude of choices made by the reader. And these choices, in good quantum-thinking style, 'interfere' with the movement of the entry particles. According to the choice made, so the lay-out to be read is different. If you look at Appendix II you can try out the whole process for yourself. Meanwhile, if we look back at the entry 'Obstacle' (*Achoppement*), we see the problem. Do we read the whole entry, then look up the words in italics one by one *without* following up any words that may be in italics in those entries? Do we stop at each word in italics and follow it? This would give us *reasonary* – which in turn has only one word in italics: *roles*. Do we then return to the original entry or continue? Continuing would offer *power* as the first italicised word which would send us to *information*. *Information* is an entry with no italicised words (though a lot of them could have been) and a reading list beginning *chaic, chaorganisation* and so sending us to Appendix II, where you can continue this trail again. As in an immensely complex game,[16] any different choice would create a different path. As a way of understanding Hyvrard's world and method this book is brilliant. For any reader trying to get a firm grasp of her concepts (rather than a fluid awareness of her encepts) it is a frustrating nightmare, a maze of shifting information. See the 'read also' section of obstacle – we were warned.

To track the possible connections in this book would be virtually impossible. To give an idea of the complexity of the whole let us look at the following diagram. It was drawn by Annye Castonguay as part of her MA work on Jeanne Hyvrard and I am extremely grateful both for her work and for her permission to use it here. She chose thirteen words to begin with, for reasons of her own. For example: 'shadows' and 'spiders' web' because neither had words in italics nor a reading list; 'order' and 'organisation' because they are in opposition; 'magma' and 'separation' because they are opposing and very important terms in the system. She avoided 'fusion' and 'encept' to see whether they would turn up – which they do – and so on. From this restricted and arbitrary sample, she traced the inter-connections and cross-references. Do I need to argue further that Hyvrard's holistic world view is strikingly similar to that of particle physicists, that the scientific paradigm of the twentieth century and her narrative mode are in accord?

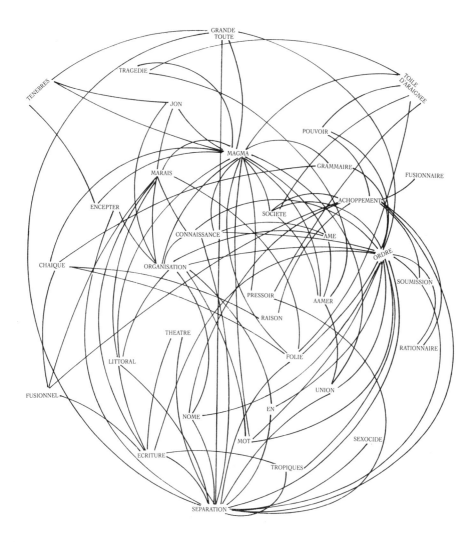

Fig. 1
Diagram of cross-references (partial) in *La Pensée corps*.
Drawn by Annye Castonguay.

Chapter 3

ON CHAORGANISATION

By the creation of dynamic holistic energy fields, grids or networks, Hyvrard is leading the reader to make thematic connections between contraries. She is making visible the complex of meanings within a single word or between culturally defined opposites. By her mode of writing, she is changing the ways in which meaning arrives; she is organizing experience in as yet unaccustomed patterns, breaking the sequential ways in which we have learned to create understanding. For some readers the new presentation is immediately comfortable, but not for all. As Katherine Hayles remarks about an analogous text:

> [Readers] tend to be divided between those who find the novel a chaotic mass of unconnected detail, and those who see its patterning as pervasive. . . . either one sees the whole design, or one doesn't see it at all. For those who do, the technique forges a bridge between the emerging sense of a field view and the experience of reading. The very fact that we can see the connections means that we are participating in the mode of vision being described. (*The Cosmic Web*, p. 175)

Some readers can accept the inhabitual text, and work to make patterns with the information it provides, whereas others struggle to use strategies of classification and analysis that have worked for them in other places. Both are trying to impose order on an apparently chaotic narrative, both are struggling to construct meaning, both are striving to construct or recognise organisation in a text from which the traditional indices of patterning have been obliterated. Both learn a similar lesson perhaps, though the one who goes with the text will have an easier time than the other:

36

Then, when we find connections, that is, images or reflections of our own thought processes, one of the patterns we can discern is the danger of self-consciousness. . . . but in order to receive this message, we had to tame the unruliness of the text into cognitive patterns we understand, thus exercising over the text the same kind of control that created the problem in the first place. . . . At the same time, the unruliness insures that this cognitive structure cannot be complete or perfect. For all its frustrations for the reader, the unruliness offers a way out of the central dangers of authoritarian control and life-denying organization. (Ibid., p. 169)

Hyvrard was not consciously aware of the process Hayles describes here when she wrote her first novel, but she has certainly shown since that she would be in complete agreement with the statement that 'unruliness offers a way out of the central dangers of authoritarian control and life-denying organization'. She first wrote a chaotic text because she found no other way of dealing with her material. And that brings me to the other scientific theory with which Hyvrard has an affinity: chaos theory.

Hyvrard was trained as an economist and political scientist. 'Neo-Classical' economics, like all the other academic fields that were largely defined and determined in the nineteenth century, works within a mechanistic paradigm. The limits of the discipline are clearly defined. Problems are solved by breaking them down into basic important elements. Considered acceptable as basic elements are only those economic indices that can be clearly measured, quantified and discussed logically. Considered unacceptable as evidence are all the unpredictable, chaotic elements of life that are the true indices of economic reality. So the calamities that befall most of the subjects of this economic reality (women and children), such as war, famine and poverty, are not usually the subjects of economic study. Like turbulence for physicists, and weather prediction for meteorologists, Third World poverty (colonisation and its effects) has been an intractable problem for economists in the world of cause-and-effect thinking because it cannot be broken down into discrete pieces and dealt with 'scientifically'.

One of the basic assumptions of scientific thinking is that you can keep isolating and defining the bits of your world view that you think are important until you arrive at whatever appears to be fundamental. (The rest you reject as mere details.) Then you can re-combine your 'pure' knowledge in complicated ways to solve the more difficult problems. Unfortunately, our heritage of order and reason is such that the intractable problems in most fields fall outside our definition of rational behaviour, and the state of the de-colonised world is but one instance of this. Let us look at a description of post-colonial corruption as described in *Le Corps défunt*:

> This sheet of paper on the ground beside the bed. This sheet of paper in amongst the clothes. Shoes. Papers. Spectacles. Cushions. This sheet of paper loose in amongst the grief. This sheet letting the corpse come back up week after week. Decomposing flesh of hidden truths. Clothes bespattered with compromise. Face puffy with malfeasance. This sheet of paper letting corruption, misappropriation, abuse of trust ooze out week after week. The head entirely gangrenous. *Le Canard enchaîné.*[1] 16 January. Where are the six thousand diamonds snatched in the coup d'état? Where are the six thousand diamonds carried off with the archives? Where are the under-developed dictator's six thousand diamonds? Bangui Bangui I hurt. Where are those diamonds handed over to the white chiefs to seal which amazing alliance? And those heads are spinning with the discovery of the magnitude of the scandal. (*Le Corps défunt*, pp. 21–2).

In Hyvrard's writing the human perspective is included in the economic description and the resulting shift in perspective turns order to chaos – chaos as the term is used in chaos theory.

A linking of viewpoints is useful here. Certainly the parallel between Hyvrard's writing and chaos theory is a fruitful one for me, providing me with a metaphor for my reading of Hyvrard. I find the following remark by James Gleick in his book *Chaos* particularly apt: 'Analyzing the behaviour of a non-linear equation is like walking through a maze whose walls rearrange themselves with every step you take.'[2]

Hyvrard's texts create a similar experience – this description of Brazilian economics, taken from *Canal de la Toussaint*, for example:

> The world is now only this failure, the effort of understanding how he could call the growth of famine development [. . .]

> Secret report of the Stocks: Half the population of the North-East is not profitable, and must disappear. Brazil-wood.

Flagellados, the name of the afflicted. Development, the name of the plague. Aid, the name of your continued hold. The Brazilian miracle. So he says when he teaches economics.

Aid, the name of your continued hold.

The world is now only this failure to understand how, little by little, the form alone has imposed itself.

Flagellados, the developed, the landless, the waterless, the without anything but the smoke of ethanol, memory of the bean crop.

Public works irrigating the owners' fields. Millions of orphans wandering the streets. Savage hordes attacking supermarkets. The Church no longer considering theft for survival a sin. (*Canal*, p. 278)

Chaos is brought about by overload of a simple system which is very sensitive to local conditions.[3] Under stress such a system will speed up and bifurcate over and over again until it rolls over into chaos.[4] This chaos is a state of unpredictability which generates a vast stream of information. However, when such irregularity is examined across scale, it is found to contain pattern in a different way. It is self-similar. We recognise self-similarity all around us, in images such as the indefinitely deep reflection of a person standing between two mirrors, or in the cartoon notion of a fish eating a smaller fish, eating a smaller fish. In Hyvrard's work such an 'echo' is found in her mother figure: the narrator's mother, Mother Africa and a series of goddess figures leading to Mother Death. Hence, what was thought to be disorderly, irrational and impossible to describe becomes, when looked at from a different perspective, curiously repetitive and highly complex. This complexity includes the co-existence of contrary experiences, and patterns that correspond on different planes and scales, while giving the impression of randomness in the immediate.

The study of chaos has generated ways of coping with vast quantities of information, with the apparently irrational, the unpredictable, jagged edges and sudden leaps. It has created a new geometry – fractal geometry[5] – which permits the description of natural forms, and new metaphors which can be transferred to the study of other previously overwhelming and intractable data – the realities of global economics, for example.

Hyvrard's first novel, *Les Prunes de Cythère* is the illustration of such a system. It proves to be, as she has always claimed, a report on the economic state of Martinique, but in the form of possibly the first ever piece of chaos-economic writing, certainly the first in French. (*Le Corps défunt de la comédie* is a more developed example of this. See above in this chapter.) So chaos theory is useful as a way of talking about Hyvrard's literature because it explores non-linearity and dynamic complexity. Also it describes a physical world analogous to Hyvrard's economic and political world. Hyvrard set out to write a book of socio-economics but her experience in Martinique and Central America could not be contained in the traditional form. Once she included all the information economists (or scientists in general) would usually put aside as details, the 'accepted' fundamental elements became much less important. Suddenly she had a text that was more unruly than any economic report would ever be. In chaos terms: 'a complex system [that] can give rise to turbulence and coherence at the same time'.[6]

Les Prunes de Cythère presents itself as stream-of-consciousness narration from several perspectives at once: child, adult, white, black, contemporary, historic, primarily female and always victimised. These are marginalised voices talking about enslavement: physical, mental, educational, linguistic . . . The fragments of stories of rebellion, refusal, rape, death and blood, provide the turbulence. And out of the stream of apparently disconnected sentences grows a coherent 'encept', an understanding of the workings of oppression of all kinds, especially oppression of the colonised and of women.

Hyvrard's narrative voices are never totally separate and could perhaps be described rather as the voices of a narrator with multiple personalities, all splitting off at different times over a long period as a result of successive abuses and acts of oppression. Indeed, to push the comparison further, it seems to me that the splitting of a human personality into multiple selves which appear unpredictably and yet create both a stream of important information and a situation of apparent chaos is but another manifestation of standard chaos theory: a system under stress will divide and divide until it achieves chaos. Within this chaos windows of coherence continue to appear and the system can switch out of the state of chaos as unpredictably as it switched into it.

Patterns emerge at all levels simultaneously so that the dual impression the reader has is of randomness in the text and of increasingly complex echoes of meaningfulness. These echoes produce a literary self-similarity which is actually an intra-intertextuality between the levels of the text itself. The result feels at first like chaotic motion. Bohm and Peat in *Science, Order and Creativity* write:

> An example of such motion is given by the ocean as it breaks on rocks near the sea shore. At first sight this seems to be totally irregular, yet closer inspection shows many suborders of swirls, flows and vortices. The word *chaotic* provides a good description for the order of such a movement. Within the context of order that is visible to the eye of a close observer, this motion contains a number of suborders and is far from random. Nevertheless, to a more distant viewer these suborders become so fine that they are no longer visible to the eye and the order would be called random. (p. 126)

Hyvrard's texts produce this effect on several levels at once, and in language which is in itself an example of a highly complex order. This example from *Les Prunes* includes death, birth, madness, language and love:

> To walk towards the death glimpsed at Montparnasse. When things began to exist on their own. The astonishment from lack of words. Things became objects. People became things. Things existing on their own. The first time. Death glimpsed. The links that are no longer made. Objects with no reason. Language without speech. The beast whirling on itself, struck in its very being. For the first time, going through the mirror. Little spinning steps. Knees bent. In one direction and the other. In all directions at once. The compass no longer points North. Marine turtles bury themselves in the earth. Dogs mistake the smell of their master. And the city is no longer the consenting cesspool of my lost loves. The strange city seizes me with both hands, gloved in rubber. What a shame, it's a girl. Death and barking. (*Les Prunes de Cythère*, p. 179)

In the words of Bohm and Peat, a novel can be considered as a 'hierarchical nesting of [these] suborders [which] forms a greater order of its own' (p. 129). These suborders would include the order of the sentence and its suborders of tense, subject and so on, the order of character with its suborders of voice/s, development and so on, the order of 'plot' with all the various strategies for advancing the text – I'm having a certain difficulty adapting the 'traditional' orders of novel structure referred to by Bohm and Peat to the narrative behaviours of Hyvrard, which tend to refuse any notion of hierarchical structure and create 'chaotic' interconnections. However, and this is why I used their example of the ocean, sentences come together like waves, combine, exchange elements, separate again and set off on new paths towards new exchanges. This becomes clearer and clearer as Hyvrard's work develops. The following extract from *Canal* will serve as a quick example:

> Round thinking is the thinking of chaos.
>
> Round thinking is thought on the way to organisation. Round thinking cannot be the thinking of order because it has no orientation. Round thinking is the thinking of organisation.
>
> Round thinking is body thinking. The one which thinks the part and the whole together. Taking back the whole to think the part. Taking back the part to understand the whole.
>
> Totality thinking. The thinking of the totality. Not totalitarian thinking. (*Canal*, p. 83)

The essential point Bohm and Peat are making and that I endorse is that '[a]lthough language is of infinite order; it is clearly not random; rather it is intelligible and meaningful at a very high level' (p. 129) and also, very importantly, it is context dependent. If the reader lacks the appropriate capacities, knowledge and experience then the order of meaning cannot emerge from the text – this is both one of Hyvrard's main topics (the contextual limitation of meaning by education, social definition, cultural judgement) and her major practice, in that what we expect to be a simple, coherent system – rational, logical and syntactical – is here transformed into unruliness and ultimately meaningful chaos. Such a description fits Hyvrard's writing. All her books contain explicit self-similarity, ranging from changes in the narrator's body to equivalent shifts on the global scale, metaphoric echoes of the body politic from a variety of perspectives. All her books are recursive. They fall into the two categories described by chaos theory: big complicated systems with an underlying order or, the reverse, simple systems producing complex behaviour. And she is certainly 'looking for the whole'.

Coincidentally, or perhaps not so coincidentally, Hyvrard's major structuring metaphor is that of the biblical chaos before the Creation. She sees this as a state of total interconnectedness that existed before the separation and naming began, so that logic and reason are sub-orders of chaos.

> At the beginning God created the heaven and the earth. And the earth was without form, and void; and darkness was upon the face of the deep. And the Spirit of God moved upon the face of the waters. (Genesis 1:1–2, King James version)

Hyvrard at the beginning of *La Meurtritude*, recoding Chouraqui's translation, renders this as:

1. In the beginning the spirit conceived negations and affirmation.
2. Affirmation was chaotic, bottomless fusion, the breath of the spirit brooding over opposites. (Waterweed, p. 9)

For Hyvrard, the successive acts of separation which make up the creation of the physical world as we know it are the establishment of a philosophical world view which was given dominance over what had gone before:

1. In the beginning the spirit conceived negations and affirmation.
2. Affirmation was chaotic, bottomless fusion, the breath of the spirit brooding over opposites.
3. The spirit says: 'Light will be.' And light is.
4. The spirit sees the light, that it is good. And the spirit separates the light from fusion.
5. The spirit calls the light 'Differentiation'. The fusion he calls 'Confusion'. It is both union and separation: unique different-iation.
6. The spirit says: 'A dividing line will be at the heart of opposites. It will be separant between opposites and opposites.'
7. The spirit creates the dividing line. He separates the opposites below the dividing line from the opposites above the dividing line. And so it is.

8. The spirit calls the dividing line: 'Negations'.

It is both union and separation: second differentiation. (See Appendix IV for the whole text.)

The old order was inclusive, interconnected, holistic – now considered irrational, illogical and confused, according to the new order which is the order of discrete elements, fixed definitions, binary oppositions, reason and logic. A fusional mode and a separational mode, attributed by the habits of binary comparison to the female and the male, the first rendered invisible within the expanding domain of the second. This being the first act of colonisation and domination through language.

Hyvrard's early work shows both the gradual emergence of the concept-encept of chaos and the refinement of chaos-writing as an intelligible and unruly textual strategy. In the later books, *La Pensée corps* and *Canal de la Toussaint* in particular, the world itself becomes a central element in the hyvrardian view of the world and in the cancer-related works – *Le Cercan* and *Ton nom de végétal* – a key to the meaning of what is being told.

If we take these groups in order, we find that the biblical affiliation emerges gradually. In *Les Prunes de Cythère* there is a tree in the middle of the garden, a tree on which it is suggested the narrator might hang herself or at the foot of which she falls. The implication is that this is the tree of life and knowledge which brought Eve's fall and death. Adam was given the power to name all things and throughout the novel Jeanne is struggling to come to terms with the opposition between her experience that words have multiple, complex and often contrary meanings and the fact that those around her deny this. Those around her are trying to force her to accept a confined, confining and ordered system – at which point she will be declared cured. She herself considers such a capitulation to be a death not a cure.

The struggle of the 'mad' woman against the male-reason-dominated system continues in *Mère la mort* where the narrator declares: 'They say they want to cure me. As if they could cure me from the creation of the world' (*Mother Death*, p. 58). She then retells that creation:

Let's start again. In the beginning was chaos. Then the earth. The earth begets the sky and unites with him. But chaos means openness. They translate it as 'emptiness' and wonder why they don't know anything anymore. The earth marries her son, the starry sky.

But he eats his children, and only one escapes. Time. Time marries his sister, the earth. But the earth doesn't beget the sky at the level of the window anymore. A little lower than the beam. At the level of the running knot. Already at that point, something's wrong. Already at that point, they separate mother from daughter. After having separated space from time. And sky from earth. The more time passes, the more they separate us. I was earth and sky and time. They tore the sky from me. We were just one. They separated us and made us beget time. Time who eats his children. (*Mother Death*, pp. 66–7)

And towards the end of the novel, she undoes the work of Creation in order to recreate her form of fusion:

He knew his wife. In my belly, reptiles return to the single earth. Branches knot their barks to become the trunk of what tree? Threads become twisted for what cord? Flows of lava mount together toward the volcano. Unification. Unity. The one. The same. The same time. Always. I don't confuse the first, second, and third persons anymore. I mingle them. I don't conjugate anymore. I conjoin. Mingling. Conjunction. I blend all my loves together. They become the sun and the stars. They become the sky and the sea. Bottomless and insatiable. I'm abysses and mountain torrents and floods and tides. I'm folded mountains. Molten craters. Fetuses in gestation. Mental confusion, they say, and they give it a name. What is it again? But they forget the symptoms. The sun in my eyes and love in my flesh. (*Mother Death*, pp. 91–2)

Next Hyvrard published two texts, one prose, *La Meurtritude*, one poetry, *Les Doigts du figuier*. Appearing simultaneously, they explore fusion and separation from different angles. As we saw in Chapter 2, *Les Doigts* is an example of a thought field. It is the epic of domination of woman-goddess-holistic thinker by man-Christ-rational thinker. The biblical reference lies in the metaphoric opposition of the fig and the grape and in the story of Jesus cursing the fig-tree that had no fruit. This is a development out of the fusion-separation struggles in the previous texts and is related in this way to the theme.

La Meurtritude, on the other hand, depicts the separation-fusion struggle not only through the situation of the narrator but also as a superimposition of systems: the Tarot, alchemy and the beginning of the book of Genesis. The Tarot is, in effect, a simple system highly sensitive to local conditions, as the possible interpretations of each card depend to a large extent on its context. The alchemical quest is a sequence of chemical transformations (deaths and rebirths) dependent on the mental state and spiritual progress of the alchemist – so again a simple system sensitive to local conditions. In both cases the system can become exceedingly complex as it progresses. Both are energy-field systems, interconnected and dynamic; systems which work with the elements of chaos and within which the participant moves. The book of Genesis offers a very different thought pattern. As we have already seen in Hyvrard's re-encoding, it postulates the separation of all interconnecting networks into more and more discrete, measurable, definable entities which can be controlled by an observer. Adam is charged with the task of naming all things over which he will have dominion. Adam is the coloniser imposing his system on what was there before. Here the system which is *Les Doigts du figuier* also becomes part of the system which is *La Meurtritude* and the complexities compound.

> Perhaps all this happened on the same day. The day the world was created. The day of the murder. Of the separation. Of the curse. Of the withered tree. All this happened the day they gave me a name. The day they broke the order of opposites. The day they fractured the order of things. The day they insisted on dominating the world.
>
> You say that's not possible and that I know only the order of separation. How is it that I remember the day before the first day. You say I'm not the one who remembers it. That she's the one they walled up in the wine press. How is it that I remember the first day? The last day of the order of things. (*Waterweed*, p. 38)

Adam and Eve choose the order of separatedness and move away from holistic understanding into a life of compartmentalisation, scapegoating and domination which is inimicable both to the narrator of *La Meurtritude* and the walled up goddess-woman of *Les Doigts*.

> In the garden the spirit gives order to man saying: of every tree in the garden you shall eat, but of the knowledge of good and evil, you shall not eat for from the day that you eat of it, of death you shall die.

But they eat of it anyway. Because of wisdom. Because of love. They eat. They make love. They know. They find union of opposites again. Death and life reunited. They know fusion and separation. They discover that they are naked. They can't bear it. They prefer to separate from each other. They hide in the tree of the garden. They sew leaves from the fig-tree to make girdles for themselves. They need a scapegoat. They can't look without losing strength. They hide the truth from each other.

Man says to the spirit: the woman you gave me to take with me, she gave me of the tree. I ate. And the woman in her turn said: the serpent seduced me. I ate.

They know good and evil. They know fusion and separation. But they prefer to separate. They exclude themselves from the original garden. They have eaten from the tree. But they forbid themselves the tree of life. They're afraid. They can't bear knowledge. They're going to lock it up.

A garden with two trees. Knowledge and life. But they can't bear it. They exclude themselves from it. Two trees and a third one as well. The tree of the murderer. They take it with them. They take it along in their girdle. To separate it. To curse it. To wither it. To lay on it the burden they are unable to bear. They carry it along to guard death. They are going away to the orient. They are going toward life. Her name is the Living One.

They will invent farming. They will have three sons. The first to die. The second to be dead. And the third to forget. They will be father and mother of the murderer. She will name her first son: I Have Acquired. He will be the first blacksmith. They will dominate the world. They will live because of the tree they are carrying with them. They will live. I won't.

I hear the woman. I hear her every day. She's walking by the lake. I hear her parasol and her mauve veils. She's the mother of the murderer. I hear her singing. Jeanne is cursed. Jeanne is separated. Jeanne will kill herself. She's laughing. She's coming to see me in the depths of my torment. She's coming to see me to torment me still more. (*Waterweed*, pp. 80–1)

However chaotic fusion returns in the sixth alchemical death[7] and female survival reappears, this time in the form of Lilith – now a monster in popular tradition, but originally recognised as Adam's first wife, the one before Eve.

I'm the first woman of the first man. The one whose name he has forgotten. Drawn from the silt of the earth with him. His equal. His companion. His deliverance. The one who didn't eat the fruit because it was her own belly. The one who didn't seek to find out since she already knew. The one who was not expelled since she hasn't separated. (*Waterweed*, pp. 120–1)

Lilith is the unforgotten, the rebel against the creator and creation. Finally Hyvrard's narrator arrives back at a state of interconnectedness, of positive chaos and a language to express it in:

I will say together, death and life. Contraration, fusion, the sacred, the madness, the unlivable. I will say water. I will say together, affirmation, reasonableness, the profane, the livable. I will say earth. Earth and water. Reasonableness and folly. Profane and sacred. I will say the earth that unites them. I will say the water that unites them. [. . .] They say they don't understand the forgotten language. But they hear it all the same. The language that says everything and its opposite. The language that reunites everything that must not be separated. The language from before language. The language of the body. The language of the world. (*Waterweed*, pp. 123–4)

She arrives at an understanding of why the enemy (later identified as the 'logarchy' – those who operate only within the logos) pursues so relentlessly those who think otherwise (and Hyvrard pulls together all the systems very neatly):

They destroy our brains because they can't bear not being able to separate. They inhabit the earth from before. The earth of total reason. The earth of union and separation. The earth of the union of opposites and negation. The earth of chaos. The earth of the womb. The earth of knowledge and life. They destroy our brains because they can't put up with difference. We guard in us that half of reason from which they have excluded themselves. We guard the philosopher's stone that they can't excise. We haven't left the original garden. We live in all the cards of the deck. They have it in their hands, but they use it to question the future. They corrupt it. Because they can't keep from dominating. They can't write themselves into the world. They can't live the writing. They have the game in their hands but they don't know how to read it. (*Waterweed*, p. 130)

She then envisages briefly the possibility of a reconnectedness for all in a metaphor of return to the Creation. But this is not yet to be. Return to the Creation is not possible, for it is a nostalgic search for a lost Golden Age of interconnection, but Hyvrard's early narrator remains a witness to the result of a separated world:

You say suffering is useless. But it isn't. It serves to make you cry out. To warn of the senselessness. To warn of the disorder. To warn of the world's fracture. You say that suffering is useless. But it isn't. It serves as a witness to the broken body. (*Waterweed*, p. 132).

Hyvrard does not abandon her metaphor of Creation, Adam, Eve and the lost garden as her work advances. It comes more and more to symbolise the differences between man and woman rather than the separations made in the fabric of the universe and in the way in which human thought encompasses its context. Chaos and subsequently chaorganisation as described in *La Pensée corps* (see Appendix II) and as used in *Canal de la Toussaint* are key 'encepts', tools in Hyvrard's attempt to establish a way of expressing clearly but non-restrictively all the thought and understanding that remains beyond the realm of the logos: non-linear thought, para-rationality, female intuition, holistic networking. This is the 'chaos' of the mental field, as real in everyday life and as unruly as famine and war for an economist, turbulence for a physicist – and, because it is uncontrollable, declared experimental noise, outside the bounds of legitimate inquiry in the same way.

What was a source of anxiety and oppression for the 'mad' narrator of the early works, has become a counter system, a source of strength. Lilith's system, perhaps, while Eve is oppressed by the logarchy. Hyvrard is searching to re-discover an order that is greater than the logos permits, as chaos may be the real 'natural order of scientific enquiry'. She believes that 'there remains memory inscribed in everything', and that women are conscious of this underlying 'lost' order of the world.

Man cannot think fusion. He can only conceive of totality. He's afraid of it. He turns away from it. He does not know he can skirt around it.

Woman cannot speak fusion. But she can enceive of it. She knows it can be skirted. (*Canal*, p. 42. My translation)

And Hyvrard does indeed skirt around a possible definition of chaos as *Canal* unfolds:

Chaos is not blurriness, it is movement. [. . .]
Chaos is not multiple, it is fragmentary. [. . .]
Chaos is not disorder, it is another order. (p. 47)

Chaos is space before it becomes order. [. . .]
Chaos empty and concentric. It cannot be named. [. . .]
Chaos can only be enceived of. Enceived of chaos; it is the world itself. (p. 48)

Chaos is the order of the living. [. . .]
Chaos is the attraction point for the living. (p. 49)

Chaos woman and the world are fragmentary and concentric. [. . .]
Chaos-thought, woman-thought and world-thought using the same absence of tools. (p. 50)

Chaos is neither nebulous, nor multiple, nor formless. It is what you call History. (p. 54)

Chaos is not regular. Escaping rules it can only be thought more or less. (p. 61)

Chaos is space which is not yet order [. . .] Chaos is what is moving. (p. 210)

Chaos, the order of hunger. Chaos the aspiration to totality. Lack. (p. 239)

My name is chaos, the shadow of logos. (p. 245)

Chaos is organisation as it comes into being. (p. 295)

What becomes clear in this litany is that chaos, as the source of a thought process which may be called fusional thought, round thought, woman thought, serves two inseparable purposes: a political one and a natural one. The political end is that chaos thwarts control:

> Against totalitarianism, thinking totality. Thought conceived of not as an order, but as an organisation. In motion from the start. (p. 318)

This thought is necessarily connective, self-similar at the personal, political and global scale:

> Round thought is body thought. The one which thinks together the part and the whole. Taking the whole to think the part. Taking the part to understand the whole. (p. 323)

Finally this thought is rooted in the natural world and the purposes come together:

> The order of chaos in spite of him [. . .] The infusion of another order in the very heart of the biological. Disorder. Organisation. (p. 350)

So we see that, for Hyvrard, chaos is the very order of life.

As everything changes and grows, the world is in a state of chaorganisation. The constant growth of patterns and networks is the geometry of nature and it is also the geometry of Hyvrard's texts, *Le Corps défunt de la comédie* and *Ton nom de végétal* being the most obvious examples.

Le Corps is the first book in the second phase of Hyvrard's work, as I think *Ton nom de végétal* will prove to be the first of the third phase. *Le Corps* stands metaphorically above *Les Prunes* on the spiral. Another volume of chaos economics (sub-titled 'treatise on political economy'), its flow has a much clearer direction from the beginning than *Les Prunes* because it is set up as a series of lessons on colonisation. These gradually speed up and get more complex as more and more elements are added. Here are the opening pages:

Treatise of political economy
Lesson 1: Under-development

First paragraph: The origins

One sees in the rivers schools of hippopotami. They get along with the crocodiles and they quietly swim with one another. They cannot be captured with nets because they tear them. They sleep in the reeds of the marshes. They sleep in the reeds of the marshes on the river banks. [. . .]

Second paragraph: The colonisation

They come earth and stars. Parallels and meridians. Latitudes and longitudes. They come land-measuring, compasses, sextants. They come cartographers and geologists cutting up Africa's flesh. They do not see the engraving of the calabashes. They do not hear the Shaman's song recounting the people's memory. They do not taste the bloody fruit of the forest. They are deaf and blind. They bring civilisation. The Commission agrees to divide the land between the French and British Empires. The French equatorial Africa and the British Commonwealth. The purple stain and the pink stain. The Franco-English Commission works in the most complete harmony. They establish the dividing lines. They control each other from the two sides of the frontier that they invent. [. . .]

Third paragraph: African song

Oh! this world is decaying. Oh! the Under-Fired Clay Pot, the white man has arrived here. Oh! the Under-Fired Clay Pot has ruined the world. He has cut the world in two. Yea yea comrade, the one who is vanquished feeds on shit. Yea yea the world I no longer understand it as before. Yea yea the Under-Fired Clay Pot controls the world. It wrings it. Yea yea we are in sorrow.

Fourth paragraph: Natural Resources

The agreements. The granting. The acquisition. The racket. The looting. The oil, mostly the oil. The copper. The cobalt. The zinc. The silicon. The silver. The gold. The Diamonds.

Fifth paragraph: Multinational firms

The multinational firms never ceasing to suck the seams. The layers. The mines. [. . .] To take the earth from the mouth of those who

have nothing. United Fruit. Unilever. Nestlé. But that's not sufficient. That's not enough. On top of that the firms step over the
invented borders. A labour force sure of being without security.
Pliant from having been broken. Hard from being poor from the
hardness of the rich. [...] The world's empire not willing to rest
from possessing the whole Earth in a single hand. A single profit.
A single capital. It's still not enough. (*Le Corps défunt de la comédie*,
pp. 18–21)

As I count, this text has nine interrelated levels of referentiality before
it disappears into the hole left by 'the missing piece' which could be the
film *Last Year at Marienbad*, or the missing information in that film, or
the film *The Rule of the Game* which, in the novel, lies behind *Last Year
at Marienbad*, or even the missing scene in the reconstructed post-war
version of *The Rule*.[8] These levels all move in concentric and fragmentary superimposed circles (terms which describe Hyvrard's vision later
in *Canal* but which are just as appropriate here). Circles in time: the
historic evolution of colonisation, a day in the life of a Parisian worker,
a year in the suffering of the districts of Paris;[9] circles in space: the
underground circuits of the metro and the canal Saint-Martin, and the
board on which the Royal Game of Goose is played. The spiral shape of
the text is made evident by the use of the Royal Game of Goose as a
structuring metaphor (see illustration). Its sixty-three squares, with
representations of a hotel, a well, a labyrinth, a prison, death and finally
at the centre a wood, and its two voices (dice) suggest the main elements
not only of Hyvrard's world but of the two films that are both present
yet invisible within the networks of the book. Next is a layer of myth –
Cain/the Blacksmith-King, Eden, Euridice, Persephone – and finally
the funeral mass.

For me this suggests the circles of Dante's Hell. When I suggested it
to Jeanne Hyvrard, however, she refused my idea utterly. I should have
realised why. The *Inferno* is a model of cause-and-effect ordering of the
cosmos. It does share its title with *Le Corps défunt de la comédie* but exactly
because the *Divine Comedy* is the dead paradigm – the corpse. Hyvrard's
image was much more practical and, of course, chaotic. She saw the
structure of the book as that of water spinning round increasing speed in
order to go down a plug-hole. The turbulence of an economic situation
going down the drain.

Ton nom de végétal deals not with economic chaos but with physical and metaphysical chaos. The book opens with a rewriting of the Creation, in which humanity, born of the Great Female Chaotic Totality is situated between the birds and the reptiles:

> At the beginning, he parted the Heavens from the Earth and set up two twin histories, one of the birds in the heavens above, because of the wing-carrier seraphs and one of the reptiles on the earth below, damp and vegetating.

> To those ones, he said: *Because you so inevitably adhere to nature's chaos, from all the strength of your round and wandering bodies, I give you the entire world, conquer it, dominate it, from the glacial prairies to the marshes of the rivers' mouths, and be there no vegetable happiness that is not yours.*

> At the beginning, he parted the Heavens and the Earth and divided them between two twin and great royalties. And when he created man, he did not have anywhere to put him, because he had already divided up the world between the one and the two and there was nowhere to put what he had just created.

> He did not want to settle him in the birds' kingdom, since man did not want to remember that he was born of Her, the great all chaotic, the mother of seraphs, carriers of wings and song. He could not settle him in the snake's kingdom either since he constantly fought with it over the control of all the other beings.

> He decided that he would keep him in the big white garden with him.

> Let the day break and the world begin! (*Ton nom de végétal*, ms, p. 1).

This re-establishment of the major metaphor in a section called 'Génération' is followed by three other sections and a brief 'Contemplation'. In the first two sections cancer is the form taken by the naturally chaotic system, and chemotherapy is the technologically produced toxic system. The first section is a description of the physical results of chemotherapy in their medical context. The second is a love story: the description of spiritual, emotional and sexual rebirth out of the dehumanising destruction of the first. The third section shifts from the cellular and human scales to the global and is a piece of chaos-writing that almost defies description. Hyvrard herself (actually speaking to a conference in Quebec about a different book) captures the flavour of *Ton nom* absolutely and precisely. First the chemotherapy which is the subject of 'Récit':

[. . .] Codification was really the pain of the beginning of the world. [. . .]

In so questioning the unnamable, I contracted the long and painful stigma/stigmata. The unnamed (feminine) cancer.[10] The chemical treatment that was inflicted upon me without asking my permission nor informing me of the possible consequences finished dissolving away from the alienation, schooling and cultural codes, what psychoanalysis had left in existence. In the alchemist's crucible of an era in total transmutation, I was myself the metal in fusion. [. . .]

Then the struggle to resituate herself in daily life, physically, emotionally and spiritually in 'Paradis-Fiction':

In order to go back among the living, I copied the gestures of my family, my friends, my neighbors, my colleagues and my fellow citizens daily. That is how I learned that those who abandon themselves to the species are spared, what one may consider as the greatest of all solitudes, the exclusion from one's own species.

In leaving me half dead, the chemical poisoning gave me back at the same time the savage distress of the beginning, its innocence, absence of prejudices and of conditioning. I discovered that culture was only the codified shape of the jungle and that predatoriness was the world's faith. This devouring of all flesh, this frantic cannibalism where each one tries to make the other into a shape in which he will be able to use him, I knew to be the foundation of the world: the effort of all living beings to remain alive. Dare I tell you of the solitude of the prey in the mouth of the predator? In the cavern of night, mouth full of fangs and slobber tasting of my own corpse, working at not letting go of the stick which I had managed to grasp, I survived. Is that what sets me aside from the others, having seen behind the curtain? There are no words to express that horror. There is no after-it, the world then remains eternally unveiled.

And this unveiled world is recreated by Hyvrard in the third major section of *Ton nom*, 'Roman'. It is a world of toxicity, cannibalism and chaotic activity where both planet and human body are holocaust sites.

> Yet, there was always an anonymous beast against which to lean the misshapen flesh that my swollen legs could not hold up anymore. In the *Sheol*, body pinned to the species, I have known fusion with the species. As I did not despair of it, it did not despair of me. Convinced of the necessity of going to sound the alarm, I stubbornly persisted in rediscovering all my faculties one by one by one. I had to regain shape to warn of the ravages caused by the new treatments. They were ruining the body and destroying the brain. Their physiological barbarity was, finally, less worrying to me than the ontological questionings that they were raising. [...]
>
> Disorder appeared to me then as an effort of organisation which the concepts in force could not account for. I was forging other tools with the innocence, faith and urgency that are found only in the suburbs of death. In the glacial enthusiasm of the boarding of the eternal boat, I invented the new concepts of *chaic* and *encept* to think what the conceptual logic of the excluded third had constantly left aside. 'Treatise of Disorder' is a philosophical meditation on the (re)creation of the world. (*Au bord de l'innommable*)

Hyvrard is actually writing about the opening section of *Canal de la Toussaint* but the description fits the third major section of *Ton nom* just as well. This section of 'Roman' begins yet again with a retelling of a Creation. This time Hyvrard creates a glacial world in which there is no individual identity, and we recognise that the images are clearly related to her experience of cancer and its treatment:

> That day, the world begins in desolation, but it begins none the less.

> The stubbornness of the living substance to survive despite what scatters it, atomises it, and drives it to melt yet again in the cauldron of the today's otherwise, would name itself breath, if there were someone to pronounce a name. But in this glacial top, aside from the pale-faced condor and the thing locked-up in the block of freezing, there is nothing.

The stubbornness of the living substance to survive, even though it is changing shape, would name itself breath, if there were a mouth to pronounce a word. The stubbornness of the living substance to resist the compactisation of which it is told that it is the same, would name itself breath, if there were a breath to name itself.

The stubbornness of the living substance to make sense only to itself, would name itself breath, if between the white face of the glacier and the white face of the condor, the spoken word were to circulate. But it does not circulate. Let the day break and let the world begin, be it in desolation, in the womb everything always generates.

Rejection of this monstrous transplant on a body that wishes to keep its sensation, its sense, its feeling, its taste, its knowledge, its salt only for itself. Rejection of this monstrous transplant where the body fights to maintain its integrity, its integration, its entirety, its entity, its being. To be a self only to itself, in its essence, in its substance, in its necessity, in its essity.

Let the day break and let the world begin, the living substance cannot resign itself to its disintegration. As long as the day breaks, be it in desolation, the living substance without consolation is in the world and does not want to be separated from it. (*Ton nom de végétal*, ms, pp. 175–6)

The world that is created here is the world of the first page of the book. We find ourselves in a fractal landscape, jagged rough, inhospitable, cut by rivers and gorges that fork and fork again, chaotic topology across which struggles the odd and occasionally named but non-individuated human character: the Explorer, the Traveller, the Envoy, the Navigator, the Coloniser, the Implorer – token humans crossing history in a world of birds, reptiles, plants and minerals. These orders of creation are numbered, catalogued in an attempt at taxonomy. Here we are in the mechanistic paradigm in which 'scientific' information is juxtaposed to increasing chaos. Each category Hyvrard describes: minerals (07), egg-laying quadrupeds (10), soil types (12), shows a series of transformations. And many of them grow increasingly actively toxic. For example 08.01 saxifrage, 08.02 arnica . . . 08.05 arsenic . . . 08.07 sea anemone . . . 08.12

poisonous creatures. All the forms we know are disintegrating until finally the Implorer staggers out of a polluted sea to collapse, hungry and defenceless on the beach:

> As he crawled towards land, searching for food, his skin, diaphanous and obsolete, was scratched on the dead branches. He had neither scales nor claws nor fungus [ergot] nor anything that allowed him to live and fight, and outside his mother's body, his flesh dried out, brittle and sharp like shards of glass. (*Ton nom de végétal*, ms, p. 283)

A post-nuclear image perhaps or post-pollution; a warning of a future where the planet no longer sustains human life.

Hyvrard writes about what she is doing within the body of the text, as is her habit:

> 41.— The substance prompted by the desire to survive would name itself breath, if breath were in the substance that which is opposed to merging with that which is surrounding it and takes it upon itself to resist enough, bracing itself against the magma to liberate in the substance, and against it, the possibility of creating a book.
>
> The name of the point of reversal, of reversation, of the critical point as orthodoxy would call it, is it the knot around which the work is made up, written or spoken, gestural sometimes, in any case, the act by which the actant [*agent*] in the world, not always the actor, puts between the world and himself the minimum distance which allows organisation, that is to say, *in fine*, shape?
>
> The blazing form of the sun. Alas!
>
> Since I do not yet know the shape of my (feminine) sun, and yet it is in this place that the text takes shape. The world is but this lapse, the brains' effort to conceive in the shape of the era, the end of the era, and accomplish thereby the work of domination.
>
> Apocalypse. Revelation. Alas! (*Ton nom de végétal*, ms, p. 216)

Rational thought as imposed by the logarchy refuses to see and cannot incorporate such unruly and dynamic complexity. Nor could scientific discourse until the advent of field theory, chaos theory and fractal geometry:

> ... dynamical systems imply a holism in which everything influences, or potentially influences, everything else – because everything is in some sense constantly interacting with everything else. At any moment, the feedback in a dynamical system may amplify some unsuspected 'external' or 'internal' influence, displaying this holistic interconnection. So paradoxically the study of chaos is also the study of wholeness. . . . the most fertile area of chaos study lies along the ferociously active frontier that has been found to exist between stability and incomprehensible disorder.[11]

Define 'stability' as the regime of the mechanistic paradigm – the logarchy – and 'disorder' as everyone and everything that resists taxonomy – chaos – and we see that this 'ferociously active frontier' is that edge of contemporary society that Hyvrard lives, sees, feels and expresses and through the strategies of chaos-writing she employs. Let her speak for herself:

> With whom am I contemporary? With the founder of global consciousness, Magellan of course, the hero of my book *Canal de la Toussaint*. Ploughing through the sea in his caravel he rounded the earth, marking out upon the oceans the boundaries of the new city: the world economy made up by a thousand fused nations. His maps were inaccurate. He found the route regardless. History is strewn with these errors, these erring ways, these wanderings, and in every generation are found entire fleets of brains which sail through new straits.
>
> Thus the inaccurate maps of women's thought taking issue with the world of men, those of heretics railing against orthodoxy, and the protests of all those castaways are erratic attempts to encircle, by fusionary paths, logarchy. Thus at the end of this century, the effort of the species to form a conception of chaos, of the chaotic, and every inception accounting for the world in movement. Beneath the apparent disorder, a 'chaorganization,' an organization has been growing from the beginning.
>
> With what age am I contemporary? Why, with the age itself! My first book *Les Prunes de Cythère* aimed to be a socio-economic

report on the Antilles, and a public rumor had it that I was a black woman from the colonies. A white Parisian, what better way to say that I was literarily born as a transnational? Since then my literature has consistently dealt with the social sciences. Which explains why literature is not a distraction for me, but rather the necessity to account for a reality that has been bypassed.

Today, techniques are interconnected in a large network organizing living matter under the aegis of *homo faber* manipulating himself. By way of corollary, post-humanity manages for its own use the resources of the earth. All disciplines converge toward geonomy. New tools are needed. They cannot be separated from the explosion of images, sound-tapes and the multiplication of communications making indispensable and possible a third culture on a global scale. The poetic and symbolic language of the swamp is the basis for this, for it constitutes the common denominator for all peoples.

Both in form and content, my literature is contemporary with the present age, for it works upon the language so that human beings and machines may speak with the same voice and that each one of us find personally relevant the polyphonic basics of the planet earth. It provides the tools to form a conception of the coming fusion, the technical concretization, the related questionings, the totalitarian anguish, and the necessary interrogation on religious beginnings in order to rewrite cultural experience in contemporary terms. Finally it is a question of reuniting, by means of literature, scientific and philosophic knowledge that which Western scientism has fragmented to the detriment of its truth.[12]

Hyvrard has a clear vision of what she is writing and how she is writing. She sees the way in which the world is advancing and claims her role as witness and scribe of the contemporary situation in all its unruly interrelatedness.

Chapter 4

INTERFACE:
VOICES FROM THE MARGINS

To begin again from the end of the last chapter:

> ... the most fertile area of chaos study lies along the ferociously active frontier that has been found to exist between stability and incomprehensible disorder.[1]

The first view of this area is from my perspective and is the frontier between usual and accepted academic writing – literary criticism or philosophy in this case – and Hyvrard's 'round thinking' and 'chaorganisation'. I thought, when I started, that writing the opening section on the new paradigm would set everything up properly and enable me to write about the content of the work without too much difficulty. Not so. Grasping any one of Hyvrard's thought progressions is like trying to trace the note of C through a piece of heard music – like tracing an atomic particle, indeed, as I explained earlier – and trying to organise a discussion of all her interwoven thought developments is like describing a piece of music in words. A better analogy is perhaps that of trying to describe a fast-flowing river in terms of the water coming in from all the various streams, when to do that I need to trace the separate bodies of water even though they mingle infinitely and infinitesimally with each other. To stop the flow would make the task possible, but stopping the flow distorts the work and creates a false picture. In this instance formation in the academy represents a 'stability' in whose terms Hyvrard's writing is disorderly, if not entirely incomprehensible, and I and my book are caught on the frontier between the two.

Gail Stenstad offers assistance in her article 'Anarchic Thinking'.[2] The struggle is, of course, between 'mastering' linear or non-linear but stationary patterns, and the need for a critical thought able to incorporate ambiguities, multiplicities of meaning, paradoxes and differences while they are in process. As Hyvrard writes in *La Pensée corps*: 'The form of chaos is a form the logarch does not know. He calls it disorder' (see Appendix II). She frequently comments that disorder is only disorder from the perspective of one who thinks he knows what knowledge and order are – namely, logos.

> Anarchic thinking welcomes the ambiguities, the multiplicities of meanings, of the words we encounter and use. It is open to the deep wells of differing experiences from which such multiplicity arises. Anarchic thinking embraces multiple interpretations of texts. The tensions which arise from such ambiguity and multiplicity serve to keep thinking moving and open to manifold possibilities. (Stenstad, p. 89)

As my thinking is forced into new forms, not so much by the understanding of Hyvrard's views but by the need to find ways of exteriorising the fields of energy in her writing, I find a growing consciousness of another tension, named by Stenstad: that between the strange and the familiar. Hyvrard's writing pulls together elements which are all familiar, but in the context she sets them in they become strange. My aim is to maintain the strangeness while enabling the reader to regain a sense of familiarity in the reading process.

> The effect of this making-strange is to decenter the familiar, the taken-for-granted, the true, the real, etc. The boundaries set for our thinking by familiarity are transgressed. The previously unthinkable becomes thinkable. Anarchic thinking is boundary thinking, pushing at the very boundaries of the thinkable, stretching them, rearranging them, breaking them. The boundary transforms our thinking; it transforms us. The transformative experience of anarchic thinking is perhaps one of the most subversive effects. It is a powerful way to clear out lingering internalizations of patriarchal presuppositions. This clears the way, as well, for us to think creatively. (Stenstad, pp. 89–90)

Unresolved tensions keep thought moving, pushing at the frontiers of the unthinkable, turning around what Hyvrard calls 'the missing piece' or the 'unnameable', extending the capacities of language further into the realm of the irrational, the contrary, the non-linear, the connected and the non-causative. For the most part these tensions exist between culturally learned binary-oppositional thinking and experiential aware-ness of 'contraration' – Hyvrard's term for the thinking together of supposedly opposite and therefore mutually negating concepts such as life and death. In Hyvrard's thinking, the result of binary opposition is usually a refusal of difference and a practice of oppression, repression or suppression. What she is searching for is interconnectedness, wholeness as it is expressed in various manifestations of what she considers sacred. Resistance to oppression and to the denial of the sacred in today's tech-nocratic logarchies are the externally manifest tensions that drive her thought; resistance to the threats to mental and physical health create a parallel energy at the personal level. The entire work is the narration of an on-going process of philosophical and emotional survival in a toxic world.

From the perspective of rationality, madness is disorder; from the point of view of the male (in Western tradition) the female is disorder; from the perspective of health, disease is disorder; in 'civilised' European thought, colonised peoples represented disorder. Hyvrard says: 'Chaos, woman and the world are fragmentary and concentric. Man too but he has forgotten' (*Le Canal*, p. 50).

Everything lies in the point of view of the narrator: who is subject? Who is other? Where lies stability? Where is disorder? Where is the centre? Where are the margins? Whose voice? Whose language?

> The narrative account that all other accounts must take into consid-eration (e.g., grand theory or the canonized text) has the most power, whereas the account that lies buried, unheard or untran-scribed has least. Whether narratives subvert discourses, conventions or even the forms of argumentation, may depend on whether power relations can change enough to alter subject-positioning.[3]

It is still relatively rare, in French literature, to find a literary text whose narrator is not male, white and privileged or whose narrator has not been created by a middle-class, well-educated white male author. Practically the entire body of 'recognised' literature is written by 'insiders'. It is even rare for a canonised or famous contemporary author to live permanently outside Paris. The literature is as centralised as the railway system. Narration is therefore narration from a dominant point of view, and all other points of view are imagined, evaluated and situated in respect to the insider-subject. Such a narrative position maintains stability and traditional order.

Writing from the margins creates resistant narrative. To return to my original quotation one more time, such narration lies along the frontier between the canonised and the as-yet-unheard, and creates chaos in the system. Women who write from a woman's perspective place themselves here and this is where all Hyvrard's narrators are situated. The texts she writes are gendered texts, not because a female author is creating a female narrator but because of the desires, interests and attitudes that shape the narrative.

> What makes something a feminine point of view should be explained in terms of oppression of a particularly fundamental kind. Being oppressed is a condition which women share with other social groups. Being oppressed involves economic and political powerlessness, marginalization and a vulnerability to violence. All of these are common to women's position, but they do not capture what is distinctive about it. Women are oppressed because that which gives them their identity as women is an oppressive concept. This identity is constructed in the interest of a dominant group which excludes them, and it is internalized by them. The subjectivity of individual women is structured by a concept which is oppressive and which supports other forms of oppression. Some class and race concepts may also operate in this way.[4]

Hyvrard's narrators are all victims of oppression, usually of multiple forms of oppression which situate them further and further out from the dominant-male-insider perspective. All are women; the first four are also considered 'mad'; the first is echoed/doubled by the voices of a black woman and by (historic) rebels against the colonisers; two are cancer victims; one is a little girl. They may be victims of systemic sexism, racism and discrimination against the disabled but they are in no way passive. Agents all, they are survivors who situate their political struggle in their right to break socially expected silence. In this the speech acts of Hyvrard's narrators resemble the discourse of incest survivors in North American society in that they are acts of transgression.[5]

Hyvrard's narrators break taboos. First the very act of public narration is a transgression of the knowledge that the speech of women, the mad, the colonised, the scapegoated (for example, cancer patients), is considered excluded speech and has no place in literature (except when constructed by a dominant voice to emphasise victimhood). It disrupts conventional arrangements of who shall tell a story:

> . . . arrangements in which women and children are not authoritative, where they are often denied the space to speak and be heard, and where their ability to interpret men's speech and to speak against men . . . has been severely restricted . . . (Alcoff and Gray, p. 267)

Like Hyvrard's narrators' perception of their situation, 'survivor speech is also transgressive to the extent that it presumes objects antithetical to the dominant discourse' (ibid., p. 268). Thus words shift when used by survivors and do not remain in the relation to other words to which dominant speakers are accustomed.[6] We have seen this in the instance of Jeanne's understanding of multiple aspects of the word 'mother'. Once the narrator's position shifts from that of the dominant subject then all the power relationships, previously hidden or accepted without comment, become visible and open to challenge:

> To the extent that survivor speech acts cannot be subsumed within a given discourse, they will be disruptive of its positivity and at least point to a different set of formation rules. (Alcoff and Gray, p. 268)

Hyvrard's narrators are in violent confrontation with the dominant perspective and, just as for survivors, the locus of conflict is not to determine 'truth' but rather what may or may not be stated. They struggle to break down the frontiers of the dominant discourse in order to survive, to force inclusion of marginalised experience, silenced voices, excluded modes of thought, non-grammatical language – in short, unruliness 'chaos, woman and the world'.

Multiple-voiced narration makes the refusal of a monolithic truth and order even more evident. Two of Hyvrard's books fit into such a category: *Les Prunes de Cythère* and *Le Cercan*. *Les Prunes* is a novel, *Le Cercan* a multi-faceted report on their circumstances by a group of people undergoing chemotherapy. Both are disruptive; agents of the dominant discourse tried to silence each of them in different ways. *Les Prunes* was pulled into line with mainstream assumptions and discredited as political and

economic commentary when critics subsumed the author into the narrator and declared her both mad and Martiniquaise. As Hyvrard herself
expressed it:

> [Parisian critics] diagnosed a rupture of identity which they analysed
> in terms of madness. It was in fact a transnational planetary identity
> in the process of constituting itself in the world-economy.[7]

Action against *Le Cercan* was more immediate: the group were thrown
out of the hospital and refused a place to meet and discuss their experience. Each book actively breaks silence, though in different ways; each
faces the question of how and why individuals or small groups become
scapegoats for the larger group; each uses illness as a metaphor for both
the state of the individual and of the body politic.[8]

Using illness as a metaphor has a long tradition; in twentieth century
French literature Gide, Camus, and Boris Vian leap to mind. The difference between the reception of their novels and that of Hyvrard is that
Jeanne Hyvrard is a woman who creates narrators – also named Jeanne
– who are 'mad'. Same-name narrators in books by male authors create
no problem. However it seems, traditionally, to have been easier to assume
that a woman writer is writing autobiographically. Women are frequently
and easily assumed to have a propensity for going mad. Women's bodies
have long been confined to the private sphere. It requires an effort for
most readers to recognise a woman's illness as vehicle for social dis-ease,
and an even greater one to accept a female as political and economic.
This body language is but one level of Hyvrard's claiming of the right to
discourse in the public sphere; it is necessarily closely connected to the
act of speech, the use and understanding of language. In *Les Prunes*,
Hyvrard's intellectual analysis of her living experience found expression
through physical dis-order. In *Le Cercan*, the movement goes in the
other direction. Her body is the analysis of experience which is finding
its expression in words. In the first, the politics were expressed through
the body, in the second, the body is expressed through the politics.

Le Cercan is a collective work; co-ordinated, structured and written by
Jeanne Hyvrard, it is the result of discussion by a group who reacted
against the way they were treated as cancer patients both in society and
within the hospital. This book starts from illness as fact and examines
the role of this particular disease in the social context as experienced
by a number of different people, for the most part women. Here lies

the first and most obvious similarity between *Le Cercan* and *Les Prunes*. In each case, the text is created by the juxtaposition of fragments of information and opinion expressed by a multiplicity of voices, from a variety of perspectives, all turning around a central point which remains un-named. These are fragmentary and concentric texts where all the elements focus on 'la pièce qui manque' (the missing piece). This is a familiar and recurrent structure in Hyvrard's work, one which reaches its most sophisticated expression in *Le Corps défunt de la comédie* and its most elegant in *Canal de la Toussaint*.

The difference between the books, and it is a crucial one, is that the whole effort of *Les Prunes* is directed towards understanding what is hidden by silence, in order for the narrator to be able to express it and thereby clarify for herself her role in society, whereas that of *Le Cercan* is to break the taboo of silence and express what is understood all too well by the narrators in order to explain to others the role imposed on them by society. In both cases, the struggle is primarily a struggle with language, with the explicit restrictions imposed on expression and the implicit restrictions imposed on thought by the capacities of a specific language, and with the control exerted over language-users by the inculcation of the notion of accepted usage and all its concomitant taboos.

The protagonist of *Les Prunes* adopts her madness as the form of her revolt. It is the means of her explorations and search for understanding. Those around her believe that the illness is a means of rendering her powerless, forcing her to be passive, keeping her away from public life until she conforms and becomes 'normal'. For Jeanne, the madness is a form of action, a taking possession of her mind, allowing herself to explore and express her physical experiences, a claiming of her language. In this, she identifies with political revolutionaries, seeing their struggle against colonialism and slavery as parallel to her struggle as a woman for her right to autonomy, her right to make her own choices, to recognise her experiences and the feelings they evoke. Her acknowledgement of her 'madness' as the expression of a valid dis-ease is a symbolic refusal of all social and economic constraints on all colonised peoples. The traditional image of mad woman as scapegoat bearing the oppression of patriarchal order is transformed.

Transformed into what? We have to wait until *Le Cercan* to see those it is imposed upon claim proudly the role of the scapegoat and transform it into that of the mutant. Hyvrard would define the mutant as the person who adapts best to the way society is going in order not to be annihilated by its development, and would consider this a shift from a passive mode into an active one. Instead of wandering in exile, bearing the blame society has put upon them for what has happened in the past, the group sees itself as taking responsibility for change and marching out into the future. Just as Jeanne took on her 'madness', so the group in *Le Cercan* claim their cancers as the physical manifestations of their revolt against the constraints imposed on the way they live. Thus they are presented as political bodies playing a role, despite the silence with which that role is surrounded.

The missing piece in *Le Cercan* is the name of the dis-ease. For Hyvrard the struggle is again a struggle against the silence which prevents expression, denies experience. The silence which kills. It is again a struggle against a repressive social order and is fought on intellectual and economic grounds:

> Cercan. The name of the unnameable. Cercan in wardback, the very title of the book, like the sign of the impossibility to come to terms with the word. The wardback of the powerless to subvert the order imposed by the words. When their struggles have failed, only this joke is left to them. An ultimate way of protesting that changes nothing since the name has not been changed, but at the same time a way of expressing the opposite vision of the world, and of maintaining that one will not renounce it, whatever the pressures may be. (*Le Cercan*, p. 30)[9]

Here the order is the medicalisation of natural functions: birth, sexuality and death – not the colonisation and therefore the control and infantilisation of one people by another, but rather the control of life by technology, the infantilisation of the living by the technocrats.

Hyvrard's metaphors are parallel: just as cancer is a refusal of order by the cells of the body, so madness is the choice of disorder by the cells of the mind and rebellion is the overturning of order by the cells of society. She sees this as another manifestation of self-similarity. Each is a taking of action, a rejection of restraint and control. All are mutations from the 'normal'. Yet all are considered blameworthy by the 'normal', all are exiled and victimised: punished, cured or otherwise suppressed.

Cancer and madness, like rebellion, are for Hyvrard states of transition out of oppression into a world of wider possibilities. As with all her political and economic observations, she locates the shift first within the narrator's body, the woman's body and in the specifically female parts of that body. Breast cancer (which Hyvrard had) and womb cancer (which her mother had) are the sites of dis-eased female genealogy. Without these reproductive organs the networks the author is trying to create across time and memory, to the chaotic state before the logos held sway, are not possible. The connection here is not essentialist and biological but rather it is the physical manifestation of what Kristeva names 'abjection'. Living inside oppression produces dis-ease in body and mind: for Hyvrard the manifestations are cancer and madness. They come into being as a result of a literal and figurative mis-birth. *Les Prunes* begins with a miscarriage and Hyvrard's books contain many evocations of miscarriage, birth and rape. Cancer of the female sex organs is another manifestation of negative sexuality.

The trauma at the birth site and the incapacity of the mother to love her offspring transforms the child into a scapegoat. The trauma of surgery and lack of medical support for the 'cancering' is the social equivalent. Hence the shift from scapegoat to mutant is a precise naming of a visceral move from victim to survivor in a transforming order. In *Les Prunes*, Jeanne was coming to terms with her trauma. *Le Cercan* relocates the struggle, from oppressive mother and traumatised child to non-nurturing medical system and silenced patients.

While this metaphor grows and changes as Hyvrard's works develop, it remains rooted in an exploration of the structures of power and levels of discourse in the medical system in France.[10] *Ton nom de végétal* (1995) is recounted by a survivor of chemotherapy, of toxic manipulations of her body and of the dehumanising disregard of the experts for the devastation they have caused. The book has three main sections, telling the struggle for survival in different modes. The first narration is of the physical effects of the treatment over a couple of years; the tension is between the narrator and her body. The second narration moves into the realm of emotion, spirit and relationship. It tells, over the same period of time, the tensions between a man and wife. She is in a state of total non-living and wondering whether to die; he is forcing her back to life by obliging her to make the gestures of living. She recounts her gradual reawakening to humanity: response, reaction and love. The third narrative shifts to the state of the world and a clash between taxonomies of toxicity and transformative chaos through which wander a handful of non-personalised human figures.

The parallel between woman and community was in the first novels;

then, in *Canal*, the parallel becomes woman and the world. What is recounted in *Ton nom* is the turmoil of the physical world struggling to adapt to the increasing devastation produced by today's society.

Ton nom is unusual in Hyvrard's corpus, in that each element of her interconnected metaphor is separated from the others and developed separately – perhaps as a comment that the destruction within and around her stems from an increasing separation of element from element. Certainly the third narration contains sections of chemical and botanical classification complete with numerical references; the text also begins, as we have seen already, with a retelling of the biblical Creation where the primal fragmentation took place.

In this way, in *Ton nom de végétal*, Hyvrard re-writes the levels of transformative resistance seen in *Les Prunes* and *Le Cercan* and adds the level of post-holocaust devastation of the planet. Her thinking here connects her with Levinas, Derrida and the Shoah. She sees her body as the primary holocaust site and the cancer as a response to the repressive mechanisms replicated within her and repeated in scale throughout the organisms and systems of the natural world. The texts are not literal responses to bodily pathologies but rather provide codes for transcribing the chaotic activity at the border between death and survival. *La Jeune morte* deals with the same issues in terms of a mother-daughter relationship.

Both *Le Cercan* and *Les Prunes de Cythère* are extended examples of the concept of 'contraration'. The accepted social view of Jeanne and of the cancer patients, as it is shown within the text, is parallel: they are in a state of incapacity and must be restored to 'normal' life within the social and linguistic order or, failing that, they must be separated from it. In opposition to that is the view of the narrators: they see themselves as active participants in their situation, having chosen it and taken responsibility for it. Thus all major concepts are transformed. Just as in *Les Prunes*, where all the key words had multiple meanings according to the situations in which they were used, so in *Le Cercan* the words transform and have a transformational power.

The 'Cercan' offers a radical shift from the usual French attitude to cancer some twelve years ago. Hyvrard first turns over the language of the passive victim as states become actions: 'cancereux/cancerant' (cancerous/cancering). Fragmentary understanding can no longer be perceived as a sign of disintegration but is rather a coming together in a new creation. Disorder is no longer lack of a known order but rather a sign of a new and more inclusive order, just as the irrational is not the state of any lack of reason but the more inclusive process of thinking the chaos (or disorder) before reason.

In this world of ever-mutating concepts, Hyvrard (like Sontag)[11] explores the social significance of illness. If cancer and madness are signs of growth towards a new order in a changing context, then dis-ease is the beginning of energy towards survival, and those who are not uneasy in their roles are not aware of the global dis-ease.

The figures in *Canal de la Toussaint* focus the tension within Hyvrard's work between the lost traditionally female past and the emerging female-mutant future. Magellan sets off on a voyage and an unnamed woman remains at home. The woman is rooted in all that women have traditionally done and which Hyvrard explored in *Les Doigts du figuier*, the man also – except that this man is a mutant, different in body and therefore in mind from most men of his time. Hyvrard says that he limps and that this gives him a different perspective on the world because his own natural movement is non-linear. As a result he is convinced that the world is spherical; everyone around him is sure that it is flat. The maps are flat. How can you navigate straight on a curved world? asks Magellan, bringing us back to Hyvrard's concept of round thinking. It is an all-encompassing thinking; a process of thinking out of the body and its cycles, of thinking the world in its globalness. Thinking in revolutions. Revolutionary thinking.

Monique Wittig uses dynamic round structures in *Les Guérillères* (1969) in ways that are technically similar to Hyvrard's.[12] Like Hyvrard, Wittig situates the circles both in the text and in a female body full of holes. The vulval ring, her main metaphor, is a source of poetry, defiance, defence and the retelling of myths and folk tales. All games are circular; the names of invented creatures begin with O; the women sleep in spherical 'cells'; oral/aural circularity takes shape in echoes; O/zero represents the omissions and silences that are part of women's tradition. And a circle in motion is a revolution. Wittig's text tells the story of a revolution and revolutionises the form of the novel. In it she circumvents every expectation of the French novel until 1969. She has multiple female narrators, no identifiable space or time frame, and multitudes of apparently disconnected paragraph-length stories which are in fact reclaimings of every level of language from prayer through myth, fairy tale, history, and description, creating a network of female connections across time and space, voices from everywhere and total disruption of the established order.

It is in the way they cast what they challenge that the two authors differ. Wittig writes as a lesbian feminist openly describing a war that women wage against men in order to claim their past and reframe the future. Hyvrard, a heterosexual woman in a long and supportive marriage, maintains the image of a loving male partner in her work, while constantly challenging the actions of an oppressive, male power group.

They both create female genealogies reaching back to the Great Mother;[13] both root their view of the world in the female body, but while Hyvrard works from a perception of the body as the site of oppression and struggle in a context where female linguistic tradition has been silenced, Wittig writes the body triumphant, gleaming and healthy, warring against oppression. Her guerrilla warriors are a community bonded in action, sensual but not sexual whereas Hyvrard's narrators are isolated in their bodies in such a way that their only sense of connection with others comes through the merging with a male in loving sexual intercourse. Hyvrard writes from a place of cultural isolation, and invents the world she wants to inhabit, whereas Wittig symbolically reclaims for women the whole of literary culture and power of language of all kinds. The difference probably lies in the political climate of France in 1968, when a new society seemed possible, and the depressed, post-colonial France of today, rife with racial and political tensions and increasingly marginalised in a globalised economy.

Hyvrard's narrators are breaking down the frontiers between legitimised and circumscribed rational forms and the disorder of all other ways of thinking. Deliberately unruly voices, created to transgress, to break silence and to force openings. These are voices from the margins.

Hyvrard is bearing witness to the way the world is going: to the cannibalisation of individuals and of the planet by transnational economic exploitation, which is bringing in its wake increasing technological devastation and dehumanisation.[14] So that, globally, the 'ferociously active frontier between stability and incomprehensible disorder' lies somewhere between the breakdown of regimes and nation states, between the ethnic groups demanding to be heard and the multinationals manipulating the global economy. Hyvrard calls this 'post-humanity', and in what she defines as her 'feminism' she struggles against it. In a lecture at the University of Victoria in 1988, she said:

My feminism has never been anti-man, it [feminism] is the tragic memory of the world resisting modernisation, when it [memory] is but a lure for groups deprived of all food-producing, social and cultural resources, and who in this order of peddling will never be rich enough to buy. Ethnic or social groups will have lost everything by themselves without attaining any of what is being put in place. So goes the world on a carpet of corpses in an eternal sun rise. (ms, p. 9)[15]

This statement is curious and needs to be situated in Hyvrard's thought. She sees post-colonial modernisation as a process of increasing exploitation of world resources and thus as a process of increasing oppression of the economically underprivileged – namely women and children, especially in the Third World. The voice of her feminism is the voice that reveals the abuses of they [masculine] who hold power, be it economic, political, medical or physical. She speaks as a witness to oppression and exploitation, as the guardian of the memory of the resisters – who, in her work, are either female or black or both. It is partly in this empathy with [black] male resisters and revolutionaries that she declares herself not anti-man.

Her feminism as 'the defence of a femininity in process of extermination' is the strand which connects her to the 'missing piece' she was searching for in the early novels, *Mère la mort* in particular. Her search for primeval chaos, for the interconnected state before Genesis, is cast as a female genealogy, as a search for the Great Mother in any or all of her forms. (The Great Mother is Mother Death, Mother Africa, Persephone, Demeter and the Virgin Mary.) According to Hyvrard, the language of this heritage has been lost but in its place she represents the archaic tasks of rural female-ness together with the physical cycles of the female body as the unspoken knowledge/encepts passed from mother to daughter through which the genealogy has manifested itself constantly in material form.

She sees female reproduction, then, as the production of daughters and hence as the essential link between women through time and across geographic and economic boundaries. This connection is lived in two possible forms: bad birth – rape, miscarriage and the internalisation of oppression (Kristeva's theory of abjection),[16] or the experience of total (pre-Adamic) merging in sexual congress. This allows love and security with a male partner, but it does not bring understanding, because, as a result of the divisions of the (Genesis) Creation, man is identified with the logos and separation, whereas the woman remains connected into the female (reproductive) network, in fusion with her mother and daughter.

Because the need for pregnancy is central to Hyvrard's thought, her system remains unquestioningly heterosexual. It is here that Hyvrard's own experience, which gives power and energy to much of her writing, begins to snarl the system. She has written through the mother-daughter connection; she has theorised from her experiences with psychiatry and with cancer, but she has not yet addressed the role of sexuality directly either in its good manifestation – a long-standing and apparently loving and supportive marriage, and a daughter with whom she has a loving relationship – nor in its pain – lack of understanding from her own mother and a series of miscarriages. Therein lies the frontier between her own personal stability and the most profound private disorder which is one of the major issues in her very first book, *Les Prunes de Cythère*. She may well explore it thoroughly at some time, but meanwhile her personal defence mechanism of declaring the individual male-female sexual bond to be a bond of love and refusing to look at it in any more nuanced fashion, because that might jeopardise her own survival, creates a fissure in her analysis that puts her credibility at risk. Likewise, she has no sense of women as a supportive community for each other. So these patterns, repeated in her writing, actually come directly out of Hyvrard's lived experience, from which she draws the energy for survival that she invests in the form. But the structure thus created is also that of a fairy tale: a wicked mother and a magical/divine mother, a patriarchal society and a saviour prince. As a result the cultural expectations accrued around the archetype contaminate Hyvrard's texts, making them appear more rooted in unquestioned habits of patriarchy than they actually are.

Chapter 5

MODES OF
PSYCHOLOGICAL OPPRESSION

Hyvrard's world is woman-centred; all information is focused through a female body towards two interconnected ends: outward to access the context of the body, and inward to ensure personal survival. It is not surprising, therefore, that one of the major themes explored in all Hyvrard's texts is that of oppression in its many manifestations and guises. Her women are oppressed because they are women: constricted, silenced and repressed as little girls in order to make them fit the cultural mould acceptable for a woman; suppressed psychologically and physically as adults for non-conformity and unruliness. Cultivated as bonsai (Hyvrard's image), maimed and decorative, of no political or economic consequence – but survivors.

The metaphor of the child as a bonsai human is one Hyvrard uses in *La Jeune morte en robe de dentelle* and it is one of a series of similar images: being grown in a pot, being kept in a jar on the shelf, being in a parasitic relationship similar to that of mistletoe and apple-trees, a caged bird. All are images of constricted growth and fundamental lack of autonomy. Hyvrard depicts this oppression as learned by a girl child from her mother, as a result of the mother's own internalised oppression. What should be a locus of love, empowerment and growth of self-esteem for the child is instead an experience of progressive alienation from the self. The mother's need is insinuated into the daughter's body, mind and language so that the child is controlled both from without and within.[1] So, for Hyvrard the ultimate experience of oppression is to be a bonsai, reduced, imprisoned, without any sense of herself as a self in the world and, above all, sterile. She sees this as alienation not only from her body and identity but from her place in the network of human potential.

Starting from this context, Hyvrard has constructed a personal feminism which is the opposite of the bonsai. It is rooted in her experience

75

of what female power is: an omniscient omnipotent mother[2] who is connected to the world through her daughters. From this Hyvrard extrapolates a system on the cosmic scale linking women, through the act of giving birth, back through time to a female divinity, the Great Mother. Her women are interconnected through their bodies; their power and their oppression is replicated from generation to generation in their female organs.

Physical femaleness is the discourse that Hyvrard opposes to the male logos. Hence she takes as her starting point the separations of the Creation of the world as told in the book of Genesis. Using this text she can then create the self-similarities of her system: undifferentiated chaos and a rationalised universe; the Great Mother and her reproductively connected networks of daughters opposed to a patriarchal God and his logical lineage of sons; Lilith/Eve and Adam; women and men; fusion and separation. She attributes to men the Word and claims for women the Flesh as primary locus and discourse. Here begins the tyranny of the word as the guarantee of meaning in a secular world and the refusal of any other source of authority.

Sexual intercourse is the only link between the two ways of being, and if we return to the story of Genesis we see the beginning of female oppression. Fusional thought, sexual merging and female birthing come together in Hyvrard's feminism as ways of thinking and being that are in opposition to male meaning because incompatible with it. As such they have been both sources of power and causes of oppression. Over time the power has been suppressed, silenced and forgotten; the oppression has become more effective as a result. Hyvrard's feminism is rooted in her own struggle against internalised oppression. From that experience comes her social analysis. And she never loses sight of the interconnections between what happens to the individual and what happens to the group.

Trained as a political-economist, active in the Paris 1968 uprisings, raised on Marx, a professional woman and mother in a sexist society, she has both a theoretical and practical knowledge of the concept of alienation and of female reproduction as labour. Her presentation of oppression is rooted here and then extended:

The concept of alienation employed by Marx has two core features: It refers both to a *fragmentation* of the human person and to a *prohibition* on the exercise of typically human functions. When workers lose control of the products of their labor or of their own productive activity, they have undergone fragmentation within their own persons, a kind of inner impoverishment; parts of their being have fallen under the control of another. This fragmentation is the consequence of a form of social organization which has given to some persons the power to prohibit other persons from the full exercise of capacities the exercise of which is thought necessary to a fully human existence.[3]

So writes Sandra Bartky, and she, like Hyvrard, though in a different mode, goes on to explore the concept in terms of women's experience:

Women undergo a special sort of fragmentation and loss of being as women: . . . The cultural domination of women, for example, may be regarded as a species of alienation, for women as women are clearly alienated in cultural production. Most avenues of cultural expression – high culture, popular culture, even to some extent language – are instruments of male supremacy . . . If this is so, then the prohibition on cultural expression denies to women the right to develop and to exercise capacities which define, in part, what it means to be human.

The historic suppression and distortion of the erotic requirements of women are clearly an instance of *sexual* alienation, for just as workers can be alienated from their labor, so can women be estranged from their own sexuality . . . Young also argues that restrictions on feminine body comportment generate a restricted spatiality in women as well, a sense that the body is positioned within invisible spatial barriers. (Ibid., pp. 34–5)[4]

Women are alienated from the workplace, from their culture, from their bodies, their sexuality and ultimately from their innermost selves. Elsewhere in the same study Bartky explores psychological oppression and comes to the conclusion that psychic alienation is very similar to the Marxist alienation of labour, causing fragmentation and impoverishment in the individual. Also, and this is very important to her thesis and also to our understanding of Hyvrard's work, alienation does not come upon people accidentally, nor do they bring it upon themselves. The victim is not to blame; alienation is the result of oppression.

[Alienation] has come both to the victim of psychological oppression and to the alienated worker from without, as a usurpation by
someone else of what is, by rights, *not his to usurp*.[5] Alienation
occurs in each case when activities which not only belong to the
domain of the self but define, in large measure, the proper functioning of this self, fall under the control of others. To be a victim
of alienation is to have a part of one's being stolen by another.
(Ibid., p. 32)

Not only is such treatment damaging and dehumanising, the results are
chronic and, in Western society, treated far too lightly:

Those who claim that any woman can reprogram her consciousness
if only she is sufficiently determined hold a shallow view of the
nature of patriarchal oppression. Anything done can be undone, it is
implied; nothing has been permanently damaged, nothing irretriev-
ably lost. But this is tragically false. One of the evils of a system of
oppression is that it may damage people in ways that cannot always
be undone. Patriarchy invades the intimate recesses of personality
where it may maim and cripple the spirit forever. No political
movement, even a movement with a highly developed analysis of
sexual oppression, can promise an end to sexual alienation or a cure
for sexual dysfunction. Many human beings ... may have to live
with a degree of psychic damage that can never be fully healed.
(pp. 57–8)[6]

Hyvrard makes similar statements in *La Pensée corps*. Under the entry
'Denial of existence' she writes; 'Woman is not considered a human
being', and proceeds to elaborate on the levels and kinds of oppression:

It is difficult to know whether the bad treatment she puts up with
is the cause or the consequence. Second class citizen, her legal and
customary possibilities are less than man's. Discriminated against in
the labour market, she supplies as a matter of course supplementary
free work, tasks always required but never acknowledged. Forbidden
humanity she is neither the object not the subject of humanist
aspirations. In the *fusional* state, she is reduced to the *magma* of her
physical and psychic utility and sold bit by bit. If racism recognizes
the other and when necessary creates and affirms his intrinsic

inferiority the same is not true of sexism which denies him and imprisons him in fusion.[7]

Under 'Power', her presentation is more personal:

Power
In the beginning, I didn't know what to call what you inflicted on me. Your discourse stuck to my being like your hand over my mouth. What you said about me was not what I felt.

I was not aware of the *information*, the *formatting* and the *predatoriness*. I hadn't discovered *logarchy* or inception. But I was already living all the devouring.

Identity meant together similarity and difference. The contradiction was only apparent. Your power came of my remaining in fusion. You forbad my being to assert yourselves, to enclose yourselves as the sole thinking subject.

But your *ontology* wasn't universal. It could only function in *denial* of the other. The existing grid could not account for what was happening. The language of the swamp helped me make it through.
Read also: Obstacle, acquire, action, scapegoat, captation, conditioning, disidentity, being, madness, out, individuation, formless, mother, Oedipus, one-in-one, order, lightening conductor, taking, projection, reason, role, round, sacred, separation, sexocide, sign, spider web, wholeness, union.

Thus we see the orientation of her concern: initially silenced, deprived of an identity, she finds a language and an escape into autonomy and personhood.

A site of oppression is a locus of struggle, and the struggle is not for power *per se* but for survival and ultimately for wholeness, the possibility of choice and autonomous action.[8] So psychological oppression is the occasion for a struggle for identity, physical oppression provokes a reclaiming of the body, and cultural oppression causes a repudiation of stereotypes, a refusal of conditioning in order to ensure the survival of an ever evolving sense of self. All these issues are addressed in the 'first cycle' of texts: *Les Prunes de Cythère*, *Mère la mort*, *La Meurtritude*, *Les Doigts du figuier*, plus *La Jeune morte* where Hyvrard returns to the core issue of all these early texts and isolates it for closer analysis. Political and economic oppression require a parallel struggle at the level of the group, a struggle for survival, a means of public expression and autonomy in the teeth of scapegoating, colonisation, racism and exploitation of all kinds. These are the questions raised in the second turn of Hyvrard's literary spiral: *Le Corps défunt de la comédie, Le Silence et l'obscurité, Canal de la Toussaint, La Pensée corps*. The last turn so far has been inaugurated by *Ton nom de végétal* which, connected with the earlier book *Le Cercan*, leads us forward into a devastated world where, as we have seen, all bodies from the individual to the terrestrial are struggling to survive toxic oppression created by the development of an industrialised economy.

These divisions are expedient and in no way exclusive. They refer to a shift of emphasis in Hyvrard's writing rather than to a change of topic. An optic that encompasses more and more perhaps, as the narrative perspective of the third major section of *Ton nom* gradually leaves the surface of the earth and soars higher and higher above what is being described, following the trajectory of the condor in the text. But even that is not accurate, because in her very first book, *Les Prunes*, Hyvrard, writing an indictment of colonisation, begins with the blood pouring from her narrator's womb – a miscarriage, botched development, exploited means of reproduction, alienated labour – choose your metaphor. The link between the woman and the colony is established and from then on the continuum of oppression, violence, exploitation and unruliness links woman, the earth, and 'natural chaos' throughout Hyvrard's writing.

Always oppression, always survival; Hyvrard writes in 'contrarations'.[9] Hence, much as in the old Chain of Being where the Moon, Virgin Mary, Queen, Rose, Silver *et al* were interconnected in such a way that each always hovered in the background of a reference to the other, when Hyvrard situates her narrative in the narrator's body, the body becomes generalised into the body politic. Likewise the colony is particularised into the body of its citizen: the narrator's mother is also Mother Death, Mother Africa, Mother Anguish, Virgin Mother, the Great All, and so on. Networks of connection, fields of energy, fractal geometry with its layers of self-similarity. How clearly can the issues be teased out without destroying or denying what Hyvrard is doing – without alienating her from her labour?

And without alienating the narrator from her body, which is part of that vision of women's labour.[10] The root of Hyvrard's political philosophy is in her relation to her own body – miscarriage, birth, cancer –

extrapolated out to her and other women's relations with the world of patriarchy and capitalism which all women experience in their bodies. Maria Mies writes:

> Body politics implies a struggle against all forms of direct violence against women (rape, woman-beating, clitoridectomy, dowry-killings, the molestation of women), and against all forms of indirect or structural violence against women embedded in other exploitative and oppressive relations, like class and imperialist relations, as well as patriarchal institutions like the family, medicine, and the educational systems. Within this sphere of *body politics*, there is unity among women about the central goal of their struggles. This is ultimately the insistence on the human essence of women, on their dignity, integrity and inviolability as human beings, and a rejection of their being made into *objects* or into natural resources for others.[11]

Survival of the female spirit and of human dignity for women come through respect for each woman as an embodied human being. Oppression comes from physical violence against the body, objectification and dehumanisation expressed in attitudes towards and direct treatment of the body, which produce 'em-bonsai-sation' – drastic reduction of potential and capacity for life. Also oppression from without teaches the victim shame and the perpetration of the abuse from within as self-abuse.[12]

The narrator of *Les Prunes* is given the model of 'dead' fairy-tale princesses; the narrator of *La Jeune morte* is shown a china doll in a wooden box. In both cases the 'logarchy', embodied particularly in the narrator's mother, tries to repress all life in her daughter in order to feminise her and make her acceptable. (Just as the French administration suppresses all local energy in Martinique.) Both books depict the survival of an increasingly aware and autonomous self.

Les Prunes, like all first books of authors who turn out to have a lot of interesting things to say, is a novel overflowing with material which will be used in more developed fashion later. It is truly a chaotic text and this is so because Hyvrard had never before combined political observations and economic reflections in one written process. The voices pour out like a stream-of-consciousness chorus.

All the networks of information are anchored to four major points of reference: colonisation and madness, school and mother. Colonisation and madness are two clearly demarcated modes of alienation and are echoes of each other on different scales. Likewise the school system and the narrator's mother are agents of the oppressive force creating the alienation and they, too, echo and reinforce each other's strategies and requirements.

The victims of oppression are the people of Martinique, past and present, and Jeanne the narrator. She refuses to be conditioned into acceptability. As we have seen, she is unruly in her behaviour and above all in her thoughts. For her the world is dynamic and complex; questions are multi-faceted, words have shifting meanings, and she is confused by the binary oppositions, one-dimensional definitions and linear logic others try to force upon her. Her view of Martinique incorporates not only her own voice and perceptions but those of a child other than herself, her mother, her grandmother, her black nanny and sundry historic rebels against the French. Her perceptions are more complex than she can or is allowed to express in 'correct' language.

Language is identified as her chief obstacle. It is the main tool used by the agents of psychological and material subordination and as a means of survival it is deficient and inflexible, lacking the necessary vocabulary and grammatical modes to transmit Jeanne's view. When she does finally speak she speaks *patois* and will not write French correctly. School and mother join forces against her constantly:

> I will save you from words. Everything is clear. Speak. Be quiet. Not those words. Your sentence is not correct. One does not say. One says. Language is an instrument. Words have an exact meaning. (*Les Prunes*, p. 28)

The acquisition of the 'right' kind of language is clearly an initiation into the 'right' role. For the colonised population it is that of the imitation-white-man; for Jeanne it is femininity and marriageability:

> I must say I've rarely seen anyone as aggressive as you are. You realise that if you go on like that you'll never manage to get married. You'll stay an old maid. Make an effort. Come on, speak quietly now. Your father is about to come home *I* put fresh rouge and powder on [. . .] Not that dress, it's not your style. You're like me, see. You're wide from here. (p. 17)

The one who looks best, speaks best and is the most docile is the preferred one. Hyvrard spells it out clearly. Jeanne's upbringing is described non-metaphorically as deliberate and progressive mutilation. Her legs are cut off, she is deprived of her hands and arms then her mouth, tongue and womb. Her voice is silenced. The agent of destruction is her mother. Frustrated and deprived in her own development, she has taken the responsibility of shaping her daughter to the needs of the patriarchal coloniser. The metaphor is violent and graphic:

> Then she lay on top of me and stuffed her phallus into my mouth. Stop, mother, I'm not hungry any more. I don't want any more of the sperm of your love that's choking me. (p. 46)

Jeanne struggles for survival from birth in a description that fuses child with mother:

> I can't manage to be born. I don't want to be born, I don't want to let her be born. I am you. I am this body which contracts so strongly that she is stifling from it. My body squeezes in to embrace you, to stifle you, so that you die sooner than escape me. (p. 73)

She is not allowed a voice. Her body is forbidden to her; she is not allowed to touch it, feed it, dress it as she wishes and above all, she is not allowed to talk about it:

> I have my festivities, she would say then as she went to sleep happy at the dampness between her thighs. One doesn't talk about such things girl. You have your affairs, she asks, ready to mark the calendar. Shh, that isn't talked about. But mother why not parade your great joy? Why not flood the sheets with this happy blood? Daughter, you're dirty. You will be ashamed of your body, of your sex-blood.
> And I am dead. (p. 21)

Jeanne sees her body and her sexuality as sources of joy and energy, but she comes to learn that her sexuality is another potential means of control by silencing and violence: rape and all its concomitant taboos:

> The man with the motorcycle goes away leaving her in the grass.

Tell me Mummy how can genitals bleed? Come now, little daughter, we don't talk about that. The man goes away buttoning his
trousers. How can genitals hurt? Ask your mother [. . .]

The man puts his hands on her breasts. She's frightened. She will
never speak again. But you're at your most beautiful like that. The
soldiers cover the body on the stretcher. Do you understand why
anyone would jump out of a window. (pp. 116–17)

Proud blood or shameful blood? *Les Prunes* is full of blood: blood that
offers life and blood that brings death. Birth and miscarriage, menstruation and rape, the killing of masters and the whipping of slaves, accident
and mutilation. Blood shed by violent control. Women's blood so dangerous that any mention of it is taboo. This blood cannot be restricted
to one definition and function. Its symbolic energy constantly links
oppressors to victims, survivors to suffering in ever-shifting patterns of
significance.

'Death' serves a similar function. The opening sentences of the novel
declare:

Why pretend to be continuing to live. Why behave as if I were
going to be cured. As if I weren't already dead [. . .] (p. 9)

and the last ones are:

I shall have become like you all. You will be pleased with me. They
will say, she's finally become reasonable. And I shall be completely
dead. (p. 238)

Between these two Hyvrard has made it quite evident that all the choices
open to her narrator lead to 'death'. The conditioning her mother and
society impose on Jeanne leads to numerous potential deaths (some of
which we have seen in the above quotations) and ultimately to:

Cinderella and Monroe united [. . .] Red Riding Hood going
through the wood. Sleeping Beauty waiting for the charming
prince. Snow White doing housework. (p. 233)

They are all heading for death or are in a state of living death when
chosen by their future husbands.[13] (Remember the rapist? 'She will never

speak again. But you're at your most beautiful like that.') Hyvrard continues in a long list that goes from 'future exemplary mothers, killing ourselves in the attempt', through adulterous and betrayed wives, virgins, prostitutes, a 'woman who was beautiful when she was young', 'social worker whose work is so feminine' to a 'shampooer of our aborted desires' and 'maid of all work'.

Sexual intercourse brings death (as in Genesis) and so does reproduction within such a system. *Les Prunes* opens with a miscarriage. Alternatively, for the female baby born to a traumatised and self-oppressive mother, life is a living death, an experience of increasing restriction and abuse which has as its purpose the creation of more of the alienated women listed above.

Marriage is death, femininity is death. Madness is also death and the psychiatric hospital is the 'city of the dead'. Death is also slavery; being under someone else's control, vulnerable to violence and torture, be it by electric shock treatment, rape, whipping or by garments that prevent action, and education that impedes thought. Jeanne is socially dead because she refuses to be acceptable, but those who play the game are dead too – dolls playing at being alive.

> Femininity [then] has a vocabulary of repression, of stereotype and of victimization. Social representations of the female body do not coincide with a woman character's perception of her body and its possibilities. In fact the two are usually entirely at odds.[14]

The breakthrough comes when Jeanne recognises the language reversals built into the repressive system in order to maintain the power imbalance:

> But you don't know that women are death. Mother death. Between our thighs they are trying to talk to you. They are so afraid that they say we are life. As if they want to ward you off. (*Les Prunes*, p. 94)

Men believe that women have the power of death. To exorcise their own fear they reduce women to a state of living death and reverse the truth, so that women will be rendered materially powerless and also confused by the discrepancy between what they hear and what they experience in their bodies.[15] In her chapter 'On Psychological Oppression' Bartky remarks that: 'It is in itself psychologically oppressive to believe and at the same time not to believe that one is inferior – in other words, to believe a contradiction.'[16] Hyvrard's narrator is put into that position all the time. She is measured against stereotypes for every possible measure of acceptability and she is measured by and against her mother. Sometimes she is like her (both have broad hips) but usually she does not measure up to her mother's expectations and that is because she refuses to do so. Her mother is 'killing' her, working for the oppressor instead of supporting her daughter and teaching her what she needs to know in order to survive. Yet everyone around her claims that a 'mother' can do only good for her child. This is not Jeanne's experience and this paradox lies at the root of her 'madness'. For her the word mother has a complexity similar to that of blood or death. Mother is the source of all that is negative and positive. She forces her daughter to submit to her control. She shapes, clothes, ignores and silences her. She is the ultimate threat. She is also the giver of life, the ultimate haven, the womb Jeanne wants to go back to. The struggle is between rule and experience, rationality and a holistic mode of thought labelled 'madness'.

Hyvrard makes Jeanne's salvation possible when she recognises how the oppressive system works and realises that power is there for women to take once they step outside their conditioning:

> [. . .] Yes, my beloveds, I will reunite you. [. . .] For I am One. For we are one. Mother and daughter of ourselves. Endlessly. In the blood running from our vaginas [. . .] In the love we make to ourselves when we give birth [. . .]
>
> [. . .] I will stifle you so that you will join us again, for we are the world matrix.
>
> You are alive, says man to Death. (p. 189)

She situates the power in a female genealogy, in sexuality, in motherhood and in the reclaiming of language:

> I won't let them colonise me anymore because I am freed. My endless captivity. My self rising out of the great Magma. My deliverance through words [. . .] They will no longer be able to appropriate me, take me, or name me [. . .] Now I know the verbiage they take for speech. The learned lessons they call thought. The words they chant to annex me [. . .] I escape them for ever in my invented words. (pp. 209–10)

Thus Hyvrard problematises all aspects of the identity, treatment and situation of women in contemporary society, showing clearly the controlling metanarratives and power structures and also the agents of oppression. Her understanding of the system and reclaiming of language takes one form if we follow the works chronologically and another if we recognise that oppression of the daughter by her mother is the emotional core of Hyvrard's work. Then *La Jeune morte* becomes either a detailed rewriting of parts of *Les Prunes* or an explanatory appendix to it.

In brief (and looking at the works chronologically), Jeanne remains the narrator of *Mère la mort* and *La Meurtritude*. As I wrote in Chapter 2, the main thrust of these novels is her search to reconstitute or find an equivalent for the 'lost' language that she feels transmitted women's wisdom and experience before male-centred rationality became dominant and the logarchy overran all other systems. *Les Doigts du figuier* is an early attempt at the linguistic formulation of this 'fusional' or 'round' thinking rooted in the cycles of female life and labour. (Hyvrard finally achieves an elegant and sophisticated form of non-cause-and-effect syntax in *Canal de la Toussaint*, which is a triumph of 'chaos' writing.)

The oppression of Jeanne continues throughout the first three novels. Psychological oppression through language: constant demand that she conform to the order of a world defined by her captors; constant confusion created by the incompatibility of her perspective and the one imposed on her; constant struggle for expression through and against the forms of the language at her disposal. Physical oppression through her violent treatment in a psychiatric hospital, compared directly and indirectly to the torture and deprivation of life in a concentration camp. The agents are now her mother (the woman in mauve) and the psychiatric system. Hyvrard explains in *La Pensée corps*:

Madness

Madness is excluded by confining it or curing it, which is no longer only pushing it to one side, but denying it. As long as the language and the logic of the swamp will not be accepted, what the mad manage so painfully to say will remain misunderstood and considered stripped of meaning.

Madness is considered delirium and not speech, disorder and not an other order, an anomaly and not a *cultural objection*, which it is, however. It is a priori put *out*, whereas it is fundamentally *in*.

The problematics of the exchange can not take it into account. It is structured around separation. The mad are the ones for whom it is fatal. The misunderstanding and failure are complete, since the mad are put a priori in a state of separation whereas their universe is one of non-exclusion.

Madness is the place without boundaries. That of the infinite cosmos and of *chaorganising* life. It is thinkable in rational terms. (p. 86)

(Hyvrard then lists over seventy cross-referenced entries.) This quotation is crucial to the understanding of Hyvrard's view of the world and to the structure and voice of her early novels. It shows the underpinning of all sense of fusional thought and also makes clear how alien non-separation is to the official and acknowledged forms of consciousness in the Western tradition.

To be shut in, her existence denied, is the fate of the goddess-woman-female principle in *Les Doigts du figuier*. The poem is the epic of the overthrow of round thought and chaos understanding by reason, of a female pre-Creation consciousness by a male separational (logical) order. Cast in terms of the female womb-like fig and the grapes of reason, the poem uses the biblical parable of Christ cursing the fig-tree. Of course, this inevitably opens the way to a reading of the text as a commentary on the Christian oppression of women and the historic overthrow of goddess worship by Judaism and Christianity.

> A misfortune happened
> They walled her up in the wine press . . . (p. 8)

> It seems a man cursed her
> One day as he went by [. . .]
> A man who said I am the son of the vine grower

> He just did not care for figs [. . .]
> Round figs like women's bellies [. . .]
> A man cursed her
> He just did not care for women
> He did not care for their hollow round bellies
> He did not care for their open bellies
> Their bellies of blood . . . (p. 10)

He was afraid of that fathomless belly . . . (p. 11)

He did not care for women
He did not care for the seasons
He did not care for the earth
A man cursed her as he went by
He separates
He shatters the order in the world
He is the desiccator.

In this short extract we see all the elements we have met before: the repression of the woman as woman, denial of her body, experience and sexuality, refusal of her way of being in the world, the violence done to silence her, the suggestion of economic motives and the male rationality which imposes an organisation on the natural order of woman and earth, body and terrestrial body. *Les Doigts du figuier* is a generic description of systemic gender discrimination and a metaphoric defence of a system of thought different from Western logical rationality and objectivity. The woman is walled up and presumed dead, but she is dead as the narrator of the novels is 'dead' – denied, excluded, labelled 'mad' – that is, not rational, not part of the accepted order.

Not only is Hyvrard attempting to express the overwhelming extent of oppression in the world and the violence of women's struggle to survive in an extremely hostile environment, but as an author with a female perspective, she is struggling to forge a form and language within an alien context. Françoise Lionnet discusses the situation:

The female writer who struggles to articulate a personal vision and to verbalize the vast areas of feminine experience that have remained unexpressed, if not repressed, is engaged in an attempt to excavate those elements of the female self which have been buried under the cultural and patriarchal myths of selfhood. She perceives these myths as alienating and radically *other*, and her aim is often the retrieval of a more authentic image, one that may not be ostensibly 'true' or 'familiar' at first, since our ways of perceiving are so subtly conditioned by our social and historical circumstance and since our collective imagination is so overwhelmingly nonfemale. Having no literary tradition that empowers her to speak, she seeks to elaborate discursive patterns that will both reveal the 'hidden face of Eve' and displace the traditional distinctions of rigidly defined literary genres.[17]

In these early books Hyvrard uses the 'traditional' link between woman and madness to establish her metaphor of women's condition and within that framework challenges, deconstructs or reconstitutes many other myths, stereotypes and fairy tales. The technique is interesting in that, although the 'mad' narrator is individual, because she is not set in static and definable circumstances and because the people around her are not rendered particular either, the result is a generic situation. The problem is that this generic situation could be read as a traditionally feminine dilemma (a fairy-tale structure) if it were not for the very evident analysis of oppression which emerges from the juxtapositions within the text. Hyvrard's cross-referential metaphors extend the situation from the personal into the general and political. Yet this generic narration remains intensely particular to any individual woman because it is told with constant reference to the cares and travails of a woman's body and a woman's mind with all their links to the female condition in a sexist culture.

La Jeune morte is a text of a very different kind, yet it is intensely and utterly generic in the same kinds of way. It is the story of a bad mother-daughter relationship, totally culture and class specific in its details, and devoid of any political or economic metaphors, yet when Hyvrard herself speaks of the relationship as a metaphor of a cannibalistic economy, of the effects of the television sapping its audience of all other values, and of the effects of chemotherapy infiltrating the host body in order to annihilate, 'nullify' and kill, then I find that the resonance and equivalence across scale make it quite possible for me to accept Hyvrard's analysis and read the book as a microcosmic version of a phenomenon that recurs throughout advanced Western capitalism.[18] The economic predator devours his human prey as the mother in *La Jeune morte* attempts to absorb her daughter's individuality and life force, while the daughter struggles for survival.

The book is a perfect illustration of the condition which Kristeva theorises as abjection. Abjection is caused by 'what disturbs identity, system, order. What does not respect borders, positions, rules',[19] and it flourishes in a bad mother-daughter relationship where the mother herself, feeling powerless in a symbolic realm centred on the phallus, uses her child for her own authentication. (The narrator's mother in *La Jeune morte* never says 'I am', thus authenticating herself as subject-being, but always 'I have [three children]'.) In such a situation 'there is, however, hardly any reason for her [the mother] to serve as go-between for it [the child] to become autonomous and authentic in its turn' (Kristeva, p. 13). The ensuing struggle is chronicled in Hyvrard's text.

Annie, the narrator, is trying to see, understand and document what is happening to her that makes her feel as though she has no existence of her own linked solidly to the world of other people. The apparent confusion of Jeanne is no longer present. Annie observes her mother and herself clearly and precisely. She tells what she sees and lays out her reflections in short segments – sometimes a single line, never more than three short pages – succinct anecdotes or commentary poignant with the pain, anger and courage of the little girl (her age varies from about four to about fifteen) trying desperately to understand the nature of the destructive force she is up against that nullifies all her efforts. And, 'de-maddened' by the process of understanding, she discovers her own identity in spite of the conscious or unconscious efforts of her mother who seems to want to prevent her daughter from separating from her in any way.

The mother has no sense of herself as an acting subject in the world. (Annie describes her as behaving like a child, at a loss for what to do next when, for some reason, the father is delayed.) And having no sense of self, she is unable to give that sense to her daughter. Jessica Benjamin describes the psychological impasse in *The Bonds of Love, Psychoanalysis, Feminism and the Problem of Domestication*:

> Only a mother who feels entitled to be a person in her own right can ever be seen as such by her child, and only such a mother can appreciate and set limits to the inevitable aggression and anxiety that accompany a child's growing independence. Only someone who fully achieves subjectivity can survive destruction and permit full differentiation.[20]

A mother who has not got a sense of herself as subject cannot achieve a balance with her child. She is dependent on that child to supply a sense of herself-as-mother but she denies that dependency to herself and dominates the child to prove her own power.

In order to exist for oneself, one has to exist for another. It would seem there is no way out of this dependency. If I destroy the other, there is no one to recognize me, for if I allow him no independent consciousness, I become enmeshed with a dead, not-conscious being. If the other denies me recognition, my acts have no meaning; if he is so far above me that nothing I do can alter his attitude toward me, I can only submit. My desire and agency can find no outlet, except in the form of obedience.

We might call this the dialectic of control: If I completely control the other, then the other ceases to exist, and if the other completely controls me, then I cease to exist. A condition of our own independent existence is recognizing the other. True independence means sustaining the essential tension of these contradictory impulses; that is, both asserting the self and recognizing the other. Domination is the consequence of refusing this condition. (Ibid., p. 53)

Hyvrard's book is a total example of Benjamin's premise.

The principal parameters are established on the first page of the novel. Indifference: the only emotion the mother allows in herself. The disappointment the daughter thinks her mother feels about her. The first statement of the mother's main strategy ('Neither denial, nor negation nor cancellation. There's not.'). Absence, in the mother, of any understanding of the nature of identity and presence of a highly developed sense of power and possession:

> . . . since her relation to the world doesn't allow the use of the verb to be. She doesn't say 'You are my daughter', but 'I have three children'. (*The Dead Girl*, p. 7)

(This interplay between being and having, which is present already in *Mother Death*, is a major theme throughout the novel – and a major headache for the translators.) Finally, the image of death, established already in the title, is linked to the question of language:

> There's not. That's the phrase she throws at me, a shovelful of earth to seal a tomb or more precisely a grave . . . (p. 7)

The title, *The Dead Girl in a Lace Dress*, and this first image of death take on their full significance a little later when the narrator describes herself as a doll and compares herself to the real one:

I'm the rag doll she plays mummy with. The other one mustn't be damaged, the real one, the china one. She's asleep in the large wooden box her father made.

We girls don't have the right to touch it. Only to look at it when, from time to time, our mother ceremoniously lifts the lid. (pp. 20–1)

It seems evident that the china doll is the dead girl, offered as an ideal model to the daughter who is 'a fraction of her three children. The weak part which crumbles, bridles and does not keep its shape' (p. 16). The double message Annie receives and her anguished situation are underlined by the repeat of the metaphor, 'I am her glowing little doll whose arm she pulls off now and then to persuade herself that it's not happening to her . . . (p. 55), followed immediately in the same section by words where we see the tension and play between what we recognise immediately as the internalised words of the mother and Annie's resentment:

I am very lucky to have a mummy who has sacrificed herself for us, her three children. Not all children have that. Some have been adopted. They have only a mother who looks after them, but they don't have a mummy. *I* am very lucky. When you are so lucky it's normal to stay beside your mummy. Whatever your age, whatever you have to do. Above all whatever little pile of ashes she makes you into: it's normal, she has sacrificed herself for you! I *would be very ungrateful to want to live for myself, after all she's done for us.* (pp. 55–6, my emphasis)

Annie is 'invaded' by her mother's will, forced to struggle with two conflicting 'truths': if her mother is right, there must be something inherently wrong with Annie. If Annie is right, then she must face the fact that she is being abused by the person she depends on for love and security. But before she can decide that she is right, she must achieve a solid sense of self:

Like the psychologically disturbed, the psychologically oppressed often lack a viable identity. Frequently we are unable to make sense of our own impulses or feelings, not only because our drama of fragmentation gets played out on an inner psychic stage, but because we are forced to find our way about in a world which presents itself to us in a masked and deceptive fashion.[21]

Annie sets out to discover exactly why she does not have a sense of self and connection to others. She comes to the conclusion that her mother 'subjects [her] to disappearance' (p. 70). Her mother's aim is to eliminate all distance between herself and her daughter in every way and on every level possible and imaginable. Annie says that mummy is 'gluey stuff' that gets into everything. Her mother is a monster of invasiveness and control. Annie is not allowed to have friends, not allowed to go out without her mother, not allowed to move around freely in the apartment. Her mother is between her and the world all the time:

> She settles into me like a necrophagous insect feeding on my putrefaction. I must not be, so that a hand could not be put between her and me. She assimilates me for herself. She makes me her. She mehers. [*sic*] She loves me.
>
> If there really is no Annie, how is it that she is so good at preventing me from growing? [. . .]
>
> She cultivates me in a pot.
>
> I can't free myself of my fascination for the mistletoe smothering the apple-tree in the meadow. I don't know the word parasite.
>
> The mistletoe loves the apple-tree. (p. 40)

Not only does the mother control Annie's relations with the outside world, she also exercises her power over Annie's body, both the outside and the inside. Watch the strategy. First she imposes her choice of clothes:

> We always choose what she wants. No means of doing otherwise. She knows what's necessary for me. I am like her, broad-hipped. (p. 16)

Next she takes over Annie's clothes and in a process which annihilates any self-esteem Annie might have managed to acquire:

> As soon as we are home, she undertakes to put the finishing touches to the garment she has just bought me. [. . .] Whatever the size, it must be too small for me.

She always makes a third between my clothes and me. (p. 17)

Finally, Annie realises that her body doesn't belong to her either:

She doesn't say 'Your skirt pulls on your buttocks,' but 'It pulls here'. Besides it's not 'my' skirt but hers, and they are our buttocks. (p. 61)

Annie's inside is subject to an analogous treatment. Her mother uses food as a weapon of conquest and occupation. The stages of the war are as follows:

Control:

She asks me what I want to eat. Not to cook it for me but to explain to me that it isn't good. (p. 8)

Elimination of pleasure:

Food should have no other taste than that of there's not. (p. 9)

Refusal of differentiation:

There's no question of telling her one has had enough. That would imply that there could be some distance between her hand and our mouth, when in fact there is none. (p. 10)

Abuse of power:

– I'm going to put you on a diet.

At last, she sees the possibility of controlling everything that goes into me, of abolishing this freedom I have left to guzzle and destroy myself rather than submit. (p. 27)

In this passage Annie shows her mother's intentions and also the oppressive results which are revealed through her choice of language:

– I'm going to put you on a diet, she says avidly.

Not 'you must' or 'you should go on a diet'. It's neither an order nor a piece of advice, but an administrative measure she takes.

She is thinking aloud. She talks about me as though I were not there. It's the 'you' that creates the uneasiness. One can't say you to someone who isn't there. [. . .]

She talks to me as she would to her doll. I am the substitute for an absence. An absence incarnate – a non-body. (p. 27)

Annie is and feels totally invaded:

She can't bear there to be space between her and me. She stretches full out in my digestive tube. She is at home there, from the kitchen of my mouth to the WC of my anus. She does the housework there [. . .] (p. 60)

We can see from Annie's words that her head has been occupied too. Much of what she says has come directly from her mother's lips; we can hear the different voices. All of Annie's energy is occupied in defending herself from constant and wholesale attack. Her mother establishes all norms and values, passes all judgements. She tries to eliminate or deny all feelings, she discounts all Annie's emotions, devalues all her thoughts, filters and perverts all information. Her aim is to prevent Annie from being capable of living for herself.

Annie doesn't even have a name of her own. Her elder sister's name is Françoise-Annie and her mother uses the names indiscriminately for both the girls. Not only does her mother deny her an identity by depriving her of her name, she also tells family stories about the past without ever being able to remember which of the girls the story was about. And, as the ultimate nullification, the mother repeats as leitmotifs, 'Three children, it's too many', 'If I hadn't had three children . . .'. Annie muses:

We don't know what she would have done exactly. We just have the impression that we shouldn't be here. Especially me. 'Three children, it's too much', she tells me, me, the last one. (p. 45)

Annie's awareness of being unwanted is present from the book's opening:

I don't know what use I am to her. [. . .] I am rather that piece of dirt which absolutely must be eliminated for the world to be nice and clean. (p. 8)

So are her anxiety and insecurity:

I constantly have the feeling that she wants to get rid of me. I make desperate efforts to please her. I live only the absolute minimum with the idea that she will make up her mind to keep me anyway. (p. 55)

Her sense of the unfairness of life recurs as she realises she is always the wrong size for everything: too big to sit on her mother's lap, too small to go to the theatre. Gradually this feeling of being oppressed becomes clearer but, as she has only her own experience to judge by, she has no way of measuring whether or not her feeling is appropriate to her circumstances. Then comes the day her mother does something concrete, something that leaves a proof of her action that can be checked against the world outside. She tears pages out of the book Annie is reading:

I do not know the expression 'a demurrer' but I understand it intuitively. The empty space she has created here is forever the site of negation. Here, where she says there's not, I know that there used to be, and that in ten thousand other copies, there is. (pp. 82–3)

Annie challenges her mother and, for once, receives an unambiguous reply: 'It didn't tally with my philosophy of life.'
    At last Annie sees her enemy and can acknowledge that the misery she has undergone is no less real for being elusive and intangible. From this moment she begins to create between herself and her mother that space she could only previously feel by its absence:

How do you say the opposite of a mouth that doesn't want to let go of the breast?

    Be that as it may, one of these days I shall have to make up my mind to wean her. (p. 90)

Hyvrard forges weapons for Annie in the material used by Annie's mother: language. First Annie protects herself: 'To set up, around her sentences, the cordon sanitaire of inverted commas' (p. 90). The separation is beginning. Then she thinks in terms of revenge: 'To do to her what she has done to me: to erase all traces of her' (p. 91). Her strategy is writing. 'Mother spots come off with a bit of writing' (p.91) she notes, reminding us of earlier scenes where her mother cleaned spots off her clothes. Finally she dares to write 'There is no more mummy' (p. 92).

The enemy has been eliminated. Annie's means of thought and expression have been liberated and her relationship with her mother has shifted: 'I have broken her toy. I am jubilant' (p. 92). The doll metaphor is emptied of its content: 'The imputrescible wooden coffin floats empty on the surface of the words' (p. 93) and Annie takes charge of her views and their expressions. 'It is not true that language cannot tell what she does to me' (p. 93) she writes, and proceeds to indict her mother's dominance, parasitic love and possessiveness. Finally, on the last page of the novel, she claims her name and her memories – her identity. The dead girl has gone. The narrator has survived.

The book is not entirely negative and therein lies much of the poignant intensity that underlies the ultra-lucid depiction of the psychological oppression. Annie loves her mother and there are moments of joy, anecdotes of happiness that make visible the pain of the relationship gone wrong. Annie is caught in a double bind. Her mother is her love object and her potential murderer. Her mother gives her positive messages just often enough to keep her in a state of confusion. Bartky explains:

> [. . .] to be psychologically oppressed is to be caught in the double bind of a society which both affirms my human status and at the same time bars me from the exercise of many of those typically human functions that bestow this status. To be denied an autonomous choice of self, forbidden cultural expression, and condemned to the immanence of mere bodily being is to be cut off from the sorts of activities that define what it is to be human. A person whose being has been subjected to these cleavages may be described as 'alienated.' Alienation in any form causes a rupture within the human person, an estrangement from self . . .[22]

Annie is torn. If she does not struggle for an identity, she will not survive as a whole human being, yet her survival requires that she vanquish her mother, eliminate her. This is a female Oedipus myth and Hyvrard sees the act of writing the book as a transgression of similar mythic dimensions. She said, during the course of one of our discussions of *La Jeune morte*:

> I don't think that any daughter has been as far as this in the analysis and structuring of the horror that can exist between a daughter and her mother when it's going badly . . . a sort of horrible, fundamental cannibalism.
>
> I would say that, perhaps for the first time, I have the impression that I've done something useful in the sense that now no daughter, no psychiatrist at the other end of the horror, will be totally unequipped in the face of this abomination [. . .] Before we didn't know what happened in the production of madness [. . .] But this is the grammar of how the mother drives the daughter mad in order to devour her when she no longer has the means to defend herself because she has gone mad. Now we have the tools.[23]

Apparently personal though *La Jeune morte* is, it is a detailed and lucid explication and demonstration of the workings of oppression which may be applied to the individual or the group. The novel not only throws light on Hyvrard's first four books but provides a tool for the psychological examination of family relationships and a metaphor for a variety of modes of social oppression, as Hyvrard herself has suggested. She proposes the book as a 'grammar of nazism',[24] and by this statement connects *La Jeune morte* with her increasing interest in the philosophers of the Holocaust such as Levinas. Hyvrard herself certainly thinks of the text as an important act of witness to a form of oppression that usually remains unspoken and taboo.

Chapter 6

MODES OF ECONOMIC OPPRESSION

La Jeune morte is the most detailed examination of the strategies of oppression used by a totalitarian regime and the techniques of survival of a victim, but it is not the only one of the books to focus on this struggle. *Les Doigts du figuier, Le Silence et l'obscurité, réquiem littoral pour corps polonais*, and *Le Cercan* are all texts of direct protest in which the writing itself is a political act more directly visible than in the other works.

'The wild hope that the book, all by itself, can make murder unnecessary' writes Hyvrard in *La Jeune morte*, but freedom of speech is always the first thing to be constrained or suppressed in circumstances of struggle.

In *Les Doigts du figuier* the female is imprisoned and silenced. She represents all forms of thought and expression other than post-Adamic naming, separation and linear rationality. *Les Doigts* is a declaration of the right to see the world other-wise; from the perspective of the Other, from a woman's perspective because, as Simone de Beauvoir spelled out so clearly in *The Second Sex*, woman is always man's other.[1] He takes for himself action, transcendence, reason, right and all monuments. He takes himself for the norm. To the woman he ascribes all the tasks and attributes that are not useful to his view of the way things are and should be. Woman should always be at man's disposal to meet his needs – so the fig-tree which had no figs when the man was hungry was cursed and killed, even though it was not the season for figs. An unreasonable demand, a totalitarian act, and a book of protest on the mythic plane.

Observation of the workings of oppression on the political plane resulted in *Le Silence et l'obscurité*. This is a book-length epic poem also; it is the tale of the clash between Solidarity and the Polish government in December 1981, from a woman's point of view. The importance of language and freedom of expression is made evident here again. The first death in the poem is that of Jerzy Zielenski, the editor of *Solidarity*, and Hyvrard refers to him constantly as 'the body of words'. This is the chronicle of a people rising up against an oppressive regime, a people who (like Annie) have nothing to lose because life, as defined by the oppressor, is nothing but a living death.

The tanks moving forward on the people
Who do not disperse
There is no longer anything to lose they believe

But life
And life they have already lost
Since it is being denied
Suicidal are being called those who cannot live
Unless in dignity with themselves
(*Le Silence et l'obscurité*, p. 52)

Just as she catalogues the strategies of Annie's mother, so here, day by day Hyvrard lists the retaliatory actions of the government: army, tanks, paralysing gas, disappearance, flooding of mines, deportation, torture, death. Just as Annie is reduced to her indestructible core – 'An unknown matter: some refractory annie, hardening in the fire' (*The Dead Girl*, p. 85) – so the Polish people were brought to that place where nothing is left but the determination to survive.

How does one say this primal life
When it no longer is
But the relentlessness of repelling death from the body
And that one says to oneself
That concerning the soul we'll see later
For the rest one learns not to think
Seeing indifference spreading itself and accepting it
Because it means choosing between indifference and abandonment
And that abandonment means death

How does one say
This relentlessness to survive
Extreme situation
Dead-end situation

Where the passing of the day
Is no longer anything but terror and exhaustion
And this obsession in the mind
To hold on
To hold on
To hold on
Without pursuing anything else
But the terms of survival
The hours thus
The days thus
The weeks thus
The months thus
The years thus
When one looks back
And one realises
Astonished that one has resisted
(*Le Silence et l'obscurité*, pp. 86–7)

This determination to survive in the face of an invasive, controlling and destructive dehumanising force is the focus of *Le Cercan* also. On another plane the same battle is waged here; this time between chemotherapy patients and the medical establishment. The patients want to sustain their humanity fully: information, discussion, understanding, consultation, choice, dignity and right of expression. To speak, to be heard, to be taken into account and not rendered invisible by the official discourse (as Annie is by her mother's use of pronouns). The doctors want to invade the body, conquer its unruliness, re-establish order, and they take no account of the level of destruction or number of casualties along the way. When the narrative 'I' complains to the medical 'You' of certain symptoms and discomforts clearly caused by the chemotherapy, her experience is flatly denied. Ultimately the doctor says that until recently not enough people have survived the therapy for the doctors to concern themselves with side effects. The description of the colonisation of Africa in *Le Corps défunt* bears witness to a similar attitude amongst the colonising nations.

Totalitarianism recurs on all scales from the individual to the global. Hyvrard bears witness to what she experiences and observes; the state of affairs she depicts is one in which individuals without power – women, immigrants, men who are outside the dominant paradigm – are oppressed and progressively dehumanised by institutions of all kinds, from schools and hospitals to multi-national corporations. Increasingly, human beings in the non-dominant groups are treated as objects, as possessions, as commodities and have to fight for survival.

In a paper entitled 'On the Concept of Nature and Society in Capitalism', Claudia von Werlhof raises the pertinent question:

> Why are women as well as the largest purportedly 'Third' part of the world regarded as 'nature' and treated as objects to be appropriated, exploited and destroyed? And why does such behavior incur no penalty, as if it were merely a minor misdemeanor? Why does the smaller part of the world, the so-called 'First' world and these petty offenders, men in general and white men in particular count as 'society,' subjects, real 'people'? What does this seemingly natural – that is biological and geographical – counterposition of 'black' and 'white,' 'man' and 'woman,' First World and Third World mean? (p. 96)[2]

She goes on to define the concept of nature as one determined by economics. 'Nature' is everything the dominant group (white, male, manager . . .) can avoid paying for or get very cheaply – resources of all kinds:

> . . . at any given historical instant, nature is what the economic process consumes as 'inputs'; this embraces the land and the soil, the products of the soil, mineral resources, the products of industry and handicrafts, services and – first and foremost – the people to work and produce them . . . The 'what' of nature is, therefore, ultimately a *who*. (Werlhof, p. 97)

Historically men have established a monopoly over land and women. Increase in monopolisation has therefore extended the same behaviour to everything else – as if these things were women or land.

We see now how Hyvrard's metaphoric exchange in *Les Prunes*, between the female narrator, Mother Africa, Mother Earth and the colonised population was instinctive, effective and not unexpected in an author trained as a Marxist economist.

Women have to be assigned to 'nature' precisely because they have

been deprived of their nature, because, un-naturally, they are not to
be permitted to control their natural capabilities. The universal
drive to turn women into 'nature' is the absolute economic pre-con-
dition of our present-day mode of production . . . (Werlhof, p. 103)

We see also the flaw in the system: land only has to be seized once, but
women are people and do not submit to being the object of monopoly.

Control over people, the monopoly of force and robbery over them,
has to be permanently established maintained and imposed in the
face of resistance . . . Although this new form of violence is quite
evident, it is also clear that the old form continues as a complement
to it . . . in the family, school, in the armed forces, in prisons, at con-
fession, at the doctor's surgery – in short, direct force, both psychic
and physical is applied in all institutions of instruction and healing.
(Werlhof, p. 103)

This is the world of Hyvrard's fictions (her 'realities', she says), a world
where violence is directed constantly against her female narrator on all
possible levels and, through her, directed at all people excluded from
'society' and at the planet itself.

The progressive extension of the concept of nature to embrace all
humans and their labour, whilst the concept of society extends to
everything which can become or be transformed into a commodity
– a thing – including people and their relationship as well as nature,
is the foundation for the contempt for nature and people which
characterizes this system. This is a standpoint from which even the
exploited cannot detach themselves; anyone wanting to be 'human'
within this system must learn to despise nature and other humans,
especially those exploited, those who have even less of 'society,' of
commodities and money. They must, therefore, come to despise
the poor, women, blacks, the old, children, the 'a-social'. (Werlhof,
p. 108)

Hyvrard's first books focus on woman as the central metaphor; next she
claims a public voice and begins to comment directly on economic
exploitation, without abandoning the women. And, stark proof of what
she had already written, her editor at the Editions de Minuit refused to

publish *Le Corps défunt de la comédie*, advising her to put the manuscript in a drawer, forget it and write more 'mad' monologues. He had reached his comfort or tolerance level – and he spoke for the 'centre'. A woman writer can be allowed to be unruly within the context of traditionally defined and constrained unruliness; the voice of a mad narrator is acceptable. She may not claim her right to public expression and voice unveiled criticism of the dominant power structure. At this point she must be suppressed.[3] Hyvrard promptly took her manuscript elsewhere, but since *Le Corps défunt* she has not been published by a male-directed publishing house.

Le Corps défunt opens with a series of 'lessons' on the history of the invasion and exploitation of Africa, lessons in which perspectives previously discreetly ignored by the proponents of the dominant power group are given a voice and place in the description of events. (See pp. 51–3 above for extracts from the first five sections.)

Sixth paragraph: Aid.

Collaborators. Dictators. Tyrants. Kings. Emperors. Majordomos. Lackeys. Servants. Straw men maintaining order for the benefit of their masters. Straw men made and unmade at the whim of the wind. Yea yea the Under Fired Pot manipulates the world, he twists it. Yea yea we are in trouble. Peoples dying of hunger. Tyrants edged with ermine. That threadbare tyrant. That tyrant must be changed. French paratroopers carrying out orders. French paratroopers overturning dictators at the whim of white tempers. French paratroopers carrying off the archives of the plundered empire. Yea yea comrade, when you are conquered you eat shit. . . . (*Le Corps défunt*, p. 21)

We see how the voices of the colonised infiltrate the dominant narrative, calling into question the basic assumptions of capitalist exploitation, rendering present the excluded, showing the flaws in the system, destroying the metanarrative that consolidates and normalises the controlling structure of the dominant group. This metanarrative is constructed on the separation and isolation of the elements to be controlled, just as Annie was isolated so that she had no firm basis for comparison whereby she could measure the abuses heaped upon her. The concept of separation is essential to traditional economic and political thought. It is the root of all forms of control. It depends on the Cartesian dichotomy which is central to the rationale behind the whole French system, be it education, colonial administration or language usage. To challenge the concepts of control and separation is to challenge the underpinnings not only of the Newtonian world view but of the development of modern France. *'The revolutionary view would be to propose that the control is a chimera and the desire for it induced by the illusion that we are separate from the world and each other'* (my emphasis).[4]

Le Corps défunt is this revolutionary view expressed within the old view and, by its structure and language, bringing about the destruction of the old in ways similar to Wittig's *Les Guérillères*.[5] In both texts the notion of revolutionary takes both its meanings, referring to political revolution and dynamic circularity. In both texts all traditional notions of male-linear-rational narration are jettisoned in favour of cyclical time, circular space, multiple voices, non-white and non-male, in pluri-level symbolism (echoes, leitmotifs), non-hierarchical interconnectedness, evocative and provocative juxtaposition, elimination of cause-and-effect reasoning.

There is much less control over the reader here than in 'traditional' novels. Each reader weaves her own network of priorities and significance to arrive at her own understanding. There is, however, no less control over the text. Gregory Bateson offers a useful definition (though his concerns conversation):

> A metalogue is a conversation about some problematic subject. The conversation should be such that not only do the participants discuss the problem but the structure of the conversation as a whole is also relevant to the same subject.[6]

The problematic subject of *Le Corps défunt de la comédie: Traité d'économie politique* lies in the title: The Corpse (defunct body) of the Comedy: Treatise on Political Economy. This is the dead girl of *La Jeune morte* transposed to a national level. The comedy is the human comedy that ran from Dante via Balzac to Malraux, from the condemnation of the grasping exploiter (be he king, pope or Judas Iscariot) via the triumph of the capitalist bourgeois (Père Goriot or Père Grandet) to colonial destruction (Malraux uses Indo-China), and it is now over. The individualist political economy of the Western World since the Renaissance is defunct. Hyvrard's text, including the very words of a requiem mass, is its death-knell.

Like Dante (the avant-garde thinker of his era), Hyvrard constructs her text in a series of inter-reflecting spirals. As in *La Meurtritude*, she offers the reader an ancient system, devalued in the modern world, as a key to her structure. This time she uses the Royal Game of Goose, which was considered a serious way of foretelling events until well into the eighteenth century, when it became what it is now, a board game for children. (See Fig. 2.) In other words the game lost its significance as reason gained in importance. The board, on which the game is played

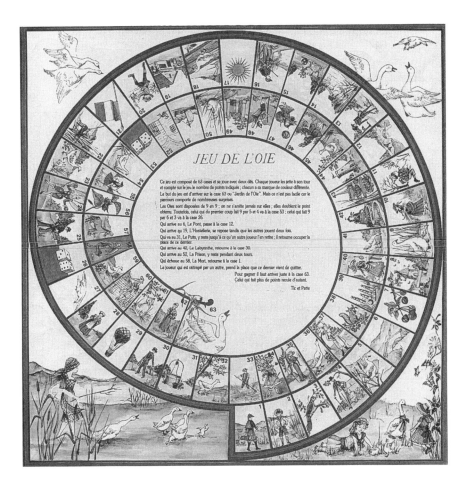

Fig. 2
Board on which the Royal Game of Goose is played.
(Jeu de l'oie. Tic et Patte.)

with two dice, shows a spiral path divided into sixty-three squares, some
of which are blank, some printed with geese. Seven others bear images
of the principal stages along the way: a bridge, a hostelry, a well, a
labyrinth, a prison, death and finally, in the centre, a clump of trees.
Seven stages and two voices is the structure of *La Meurtritude* and the
seven symbols, if we substitute a hospital for the hostelry and a wash-
house for the well, give the essential elements of the symbolic world of
Hyvrard's texts in her first phase. Unchanged, they also give important
keys for the reading of *Le Corps*.[7] Primarily, however, the Royal Game of
Goose acts as an indication of the shape of *Le Corps* and the arbitrary
nature of the reader's journey through it, a commentary on its function
as a foretelling that will not be taken seriously, and a taxonomy of the
elements of another level of the text.

If we return to the 'story' of *Le Corps*, we find a brief history of colonial exploitation followed by a crash course in contemporary economics.
The lessons are:

Under-development:
   Origins,
   Colonisation,
   African song,
   Natural resources,
   Multinational companies,
   Aid

– all of which we have seen already. They are followed by:

Cantata to the Blacksmith King:
   Requiem in steel-making minor
   Women
   The Press
   Pollution
   Petroleum
   Industrial accidents
   Unemployment
   Unemployment [*sic*]
   The Automobile
   Aerospace
   Money

Market rates of raw materials
Armament
Continuing education
Publicity
Nuclear energy
The Labour Force
Prayer for the Dying:
Grief
Treatise on political economy:
Conclusion

The spiral goes from suffering to resistance and defiance. The stages are: 1) the coming of the white man, 2) industrialisation, 3) modern industry and its ills, 4) money and the trade in commodities including information, media, words and images, 5) suffering, 6) denunciation of the system. This provides the first circle, the one that supplies the context. Each 'lesson' slides from a listing of 'typical' economic problems to those physical and emotional effects which are usually left out of economic studies. And what we see in this history of ever-increasing exploitation is that there is a two-way movement: first, white men invade Africa for their own gain, then Africans 'invade' France as slaves and exiles, forced to seek survival in the economy that has destroyed their own. The poorest people on the descending spiral are the immigrants from Mali, which is now the poorest ex-colony in a much abused continent, yet it was the most prosperous centre of trade in West Africa in the Middle Ages.

The next circle (the order of this list is mine and is more or less arbitrary) is a double temporal cycle which reflects both the natural cycles of the earth and the interminable round of a Paris worker. Information about people in the text – which is as near as Hyvrard gets to telling a story – moves round a year marked by the suffering and oppression of Arab and African immigrants in Paris and through the day from rush hour to rush hour.

The form of the Game of Goose is echoed again by the topology of Paris, as the references to the sub-structure of the city – metro and canals – spiral from the workers' quarters at the Porte de Lilas to the Marais, the rich Renaissance heart of the city, in a movement that underlines the economic divisions of Paris society.

So far the spirals are not unexpected, though the juxtapositions are rich with implications, but it is here that the structure becomes wonderfully inventive and ironic. In the middle of the book, in lesson 14: Continuing education (note the title), the reader comes across a command 'Read the rule of the game' (p. 89) and then finds more instructions in a context that seems to offer a key:

A game. Only a game. The keyboard. The screen. The list of programmes. Marie. Marianne. Marienbad. Read the rule of the game. This cathode tube. The green light. The same language. Nothing is lost. (*Le Corps défunt*, p. 89)

Last Year at Marienbad on the television seems obvious enough. The same language is in the film. Throughout her work Hyvrard's narrators have been trying to regain lost memory and survive: 'The woman in the ditch. Learn the saving action.[8] Memory. The rule of the game' (p. 89). The question is, 'What memory is she transmitting'? The possible reply appears also in the text:

Yes, remember. Last year. Marienbad. When the deconstructed language began to fuse forever. When the images and words disconnected. Another speech. Another world. (p. 89)

Indeed in *Last Year at Marienbad* image and language are disconnected.[9] The curiosity lies in the fact that the film is not obviously referred to elsewhere in *Le Corps défunt* yet, the more the book and the film are compared, the more snatches of the film become visible in Hyvrard's text. Also, just as Hyvrard keeps writing about the missing piece ('la pièce qui manque') so *Marienbad* is built around a missing piece of information. And 'curiouser and curiouser' as Alice would say, behind *Marienbad* is another famous French film, *The Rule of the Game*,[10] which was lost during the 1939–45 war, and the only copy extant has a scene missing, presumably gone for ever.

Le Corps défunt claims to be the corpse of a collapsed world. Likewise the people in Marienbad are the living dead, relics of the world of *The Rule of the Game* – an aristocratic comedy in the old tradition. The spirals of Hyvrard's text lead, not to the moral judgements and possibility of eventual paradise of Dante, but to a hole in her text which leads us to a parallel criticism of the same society in another medium and on another plane, through which we slip, if we follow Hyvrard's instructions, back into an earlier depiction (as a comedy) of that same degenerating society, and again there is a hole. 'The new world which appears in the break mixing everything to share it out otherwise' (*Le Corps défunt*, p. 50).

Let me avail myself of Hyvrard's invitation and take a diversionary path through the films, the better to look at her world.

Le Corps défunt de la comédie, by its very title, is a comment on the class-ridden society depicted as comedy in *The Rule of the Game* and as an exercise for the walking dead in *Last Year at Marienbad*. Indeed we might say that *The Rule of the Game* is the comedy of which *Marienbad* is the 'defunct body'. In the book and in the film we are presented with a male-dominated society in which each person is playing games. The men know the rules, and he who knows them best appears to win. Male voices and presences predominate. It is the men who impose rules and roles on the women; they pursue the women in the name of love and force the women to respond to their demands in their terms.

In all three works it is clear that the women have values of their own which are constantly suppressed. In sum they are victims. In *Marienbad* the discrepancy comes out most clearly in the interpretation of the statue. The man says that the male form wanted to stop the female form from moving forward whereas the woman claims that the female has seen something wonderful. At this the man offers a compromise re-interpretation that the female is gazing at the sea in the distance and the male is preventing her from falling over a cliff. For good or ill, he impedes her advance. Remember that A tries to leave the paths laid out in the garden but never manages to escape the pattern. And Hyvrard's woman is carried dying up out of a ravine.

That woman is man's victim is made symbolically clear in the shooting scenes: the extensive hunt in *Rule*, which becomes fragmented into the precision pistol-shooting scene and the apparent shooting of A in the bedroom in *Marienbad*. All the fights and the final killing in *Rule* are over women and, in their attempts to win, the men break their own rules. Again in *Marienbad* the information is the same but the form much more symbolic. The game the men lay out with matchsticks or cards, A lays out with identical photographs of herself.

The Marquis in *Rule* collects mechanical toys, including a stylised black woman as a musical doll. This is in itself a comment on accepted attitudes to colonisation and a reminder of the status and sufferings of the immigrants in *Le Corps défunt*. It is also a reflection on the theme of mechanisation and an ironic comment on the characters in the film. If we look at the two films together, we realise that the characters in *Rule* have become mechanical dolls in *Marienbad*. They move stiffly, speak in a fragmented manner, and all the rules of the game have become more obvious and more rigid: male domination, class distinction, power and wealth, competition, games, rules, women as victims of the system and alien to it. The building and the social system appropriate to the game subsist but the people are trapped in the system. There is no life in them: everyone is maintaining appearance. Only the shell of the lifestyle remains.

Marienbad provides an ironic, destructive and deconstructive comment on *The Rule of the Game*. Scenes, roles and language are fragmented so that meaning of the usual kind disappears. As Hyvrard states in the passage quoted earlier, there is no direct connection between word and image in the film and, in the resultant relativity of information, we see society with new eyes – a new world and a new language break through the cracks as the old order weakens. As *Marienbad* grows out of the destruction of *The Rule of the Game*, so Hyvrard's writing grows out of a parallel criticism of the economic and political rules and theories of a previous age that are still being applied mechanically today by people who are as far from real life as are the characters in *Marienbad*.

If we follow our analogy and assume that *Marienbad* offers the plan of *Le Corps défunt* 'mis en abîme' within the text, then we see that, like the hotel, the book has a wandering structure which does finally reveal within itself its own plan. The main path leads from the origins of the exploitation of Africa to the disastrous situation in the world today. And I find that, in another link with the film, the short divisions of the text resemble the baroque panels on the corridor walls of *Marienbad*. Each bears an extremely intricate design made up of known elements in unexpected combinations, each is a variant of the previous ones, each contains so much information that it becomes difficult to absorb the whole. According to their habits of mind, readers tend either to grasp the outline and remember none of the detail or to focus on the detail and not even recognise that there is a pattern.

> Pile up the facts. The words. The phrases. The gestures. Pile up everything that can permit understanding. (*Le Corps défunt*, p. 45)

This is precisely what Jeanne Hyvrard does as she leads her reader through the apparent labyrinth of *Le Corps défunt de la comédie*. Nevertheless, carefully placed signposts become particularly meaningful to the reader once an awareness of the underlying importance of the films in the structure of this treatise on political economy is established.

That power and money, games and play, truth and falsehood, reality and the unreal, form the basis of the text is evident from the very beginning. People say one thing while they do or mean something quite different. It is this game-playing, this tampering with the truth and reality which must, according to Hyvrard, be destroyed. Weaving references and images from the two films (both of which focus on game-playing, the power that arises from winning, and the 'lie' which is an integral part in the art of playing to win) carefully into the text, Hyvrard tries to help her reader understand the hypocrisy and falsity of most information available to ordinary people.

A detailed examination of the facts, words, phrases and gestures contained in each lesson of the book reveals just how extensively *Marienbad* and *Rule* exemplify the anachronistic, but oh so present, world of oppression and exploitation, the world of power game-playing where men know the rules and win, to the obvious disadvantage of women. Both films depict a way of life, the values of which are no longer acceptable, and against which Hyvrard is protesting. If the world is to survive, a new value system must replace the old.

The defunct body of the title is the social body, the body of the earth and the body of the woman in the text, as usual:

> My body of words disfigured by lies. My body of disunion cemented
> by anguish. My body of scandal stifled by fear . . . My economic
> body started up again by armament. My body of revolt stifled by
> misfortune. My body of unemployment reabsorbed by war . . .
> My body of convulsions beside the cemetery. My body of agitation
> trying to give warning. My body of confusion ill from being torn.
> (*Le Corps défunt*, pp. 10–11)

This body is struggling against the lies and silences, the voices and suppressions of power. Take for example the sinking of the Alexander Keilland oil rig, 'an inexplicable accident' (p. 37), 'such an accident can't happen in France' (p. 78), 'Accident technically impossible. It can't happen so it hasn't happened' (p. 97).

The narrator's intention is to find the sense of what is happening, to find her way through the labyrinth of lies and break out of the imposed silences.

> I fight to the full power of the pen/mask, cinema, circus, curses, theatre, comedy, to the full power of all you say: 'If you go on like that . . .' Then what? I fight so that life won't die. (*Le Corps défunt*, p. 143)

The book is a shout of survival and a cry of agony for all that has been lost: the people dead and dying; the rights of the oppressed; mother earth; mother lands; language and hope. It is a critical history and indictment of colonisation, industrialisation and capitalism, a portrait of alienation, deprivation and exile. It is a requiem for a dying world and the stubborn affirmation of a new order:

> Whosoever come through the night will know the morning
> Whosoever lose their reason will see the world upside-down
> Whosoever lose the objective will find the meaning
> Whosoever die for themselves will be reborn one day.
> (*Le Corps défunt*, p. 152)

Le Corps défunt is a portrait of the present.

In *Canal de la Toussaint*, published three years later, Hyvrard traces the exploitative and dominating attitudes and actions prevalent in Western Europe since the Renaissance, while creating simultaneously a parable for the future. The book is in two parts: 'Treatise of Disorder', in which the author lays out her own theory of chaos, and 'Terra Incognita' which, in a fragmentary fashion through a complex weave of other themes, tells the story of Magellan's voyage from Seville to the Straits of Magellan, which he named All Saints Canal – *Canal de la Toussaint*.

Magellan's voyage is of interest because it incorporates issues of global thinking, global power, exploitation and trade. I suppose that, in his way, the pope was the first multi-national. Certainly the pope in Magellan's day had pretensions to world power (not global, he thought the world was flat) because by the Treaty of Tordesillas he divided the known and unknown material world between the king of Spain and the king of Portugal, giving the one all territory to the east of Europe, to the other all territory to the west. Hyvrard uses the action as an example of linear thinking in a non-linear world: 'Tordesillas, sharing of the world. How is that possible since at the Moluccas East and West are indistinguishable? Absurd treaty' (*Canal*, p. 186–7).

Magellan is obsessed with the belief that the world is spherical. To finance his voyage he is prepared to propose the eastern route to the Spice Islands to one king, the western route to the other. Like all explorers and researchers he exploits his financiers' competitive desire for monopoly and gain to finance his obsession, his research, his adventure. Magellan does not think like most of the men of his time:

The earth is round. Water does not fall on the globe of the world. The Incognita map. Woman-thought. Other thought. World-thought. White thought. The sea falls. (*Canal*, p. 109)

He is able to think differently, writes Hyvrard, because his body is different from that of other men. He has a limp and as a result does not naturally move in a linear fashion. His walk is curved so his thought is curved also, with the result that instead of calculating straight lines on flat maps, he is able to navigate across the curved surface of the globe. 'La pensée corps – la pensée courbe' (body-thought, curved thought): Magellan's thought is revolutionary, his voyage will be a revolution also – but he will not evolve fast enough to complete it himself.

Revolution, the circumnavigation.
Revolution, the planets around the light.
Revolution the globalisation.
(*Canal*, p. 122)

The circumnavigation, which will change the thought processes and trade patterns in its time, finds a parallel in contemporary globalisation. Throughout the book Hyvrard juxtaposes and links commerce, travel and economic shifts in different periods and different parts of the world. The networks she establishes draw sweeping curves across the globe, curves and connections which are made plain by the structuring motifs of the text: ellipse/ellipsis, parabola/parable, hyperbola/hyperbole. (In French the mathematical and literary terminology is identical.) The mathematics and poetry of round thought – words and numbers, writing and economics.

The desperate effort of the text to tell the world in motion. On the human scale. For the first time. Acceleration. (*Canal*, p. 188)

This paragraph sits in the middle of several others which together describe the project of the whole book Hyvrard-fashion:

The world is no longer anything other than this shortcoming, the effort to bring the miraculous cargo to port. A billion starving people in the hold of the World boat. Economics.

Disorder. Disorder of History and Geography. Empty and concentric writing. Chaos.

The desperate effort of the text to tell the world in motion. On the human scale. For the first time. Acceleration.

Concentric bodies thrown into the sea. Abandoned food. Desertification, Massacres. Debt.

Disorder of all sorts. Sand escaping between History and Geography. My hunger running through the fingers of the words.

Man cannot think fusion. He does not take hunger into account.

Woman cannot tell fusion for born of Woman, she cannot get used to famine. Meal.

And how could woman organise what man does not want? Geonomics. Death of his power. Return of sense. (*Canal*, p. 188)

The book is full of boats and cargo: Magellan's European trinkets for the natives on his route, the proposed spices and other luxuries he is to bring back, the wrecked boats of Magellan's fleet with the cargo of food and necessities lost, and the oil-tankers in the Persian Gulf lost in the war between Iran and Iraq. Then there is the human cargo: the Patagonians Magellan kidnaps and keeps in the hold to bring home as exotic loot, the slaves shipped from Africa to the New World who die by the hundred on the way, the stowaways in the contemporary vessel, the Garyfallia, who, fleeing starvation in Africa, are thrown into the Indian

Ocean as food for sharks. Disposable human beings and abusive ships' captains, 'starving people in the hold of the world boat'. Not only sea-cargo either. Hyvrard juxtaposes the gold of the ancient Kingdom of Mali, exchanged for salt and carried across the Sahara to the Arab world and Europe, with the black gold brought from the Middle Eastern deserts to fuel Europe. The movement of trade and the shifts of prosperity over time that are caused by the disorders of geography – the growth of the Sahara for example – and of history – war and colonisation.

Hyvrard follows Magellan's journey as recounted by Pigafetta.[11] Events and places on his journey are starting points for her philosophy and economic commentary. He travels down the west coast of Africa and the east coast of South America:

> Always slavery. Zanzibar and Gorée. The Berbers. The Arabs. The Portuguese. Change of masters in what he calls History . . .

> Change of masters in what you call history. The Negroes do not notice.

> Women do not notice. Their fate is always the same. Booty. (*Canal*, pp. 198–9)

Having described the rich civilisation that existed in certain places, she continues with the arrival of the Europeans:

> West. West that voice, coming along the Barbary coast to go down to the land of the Negroes. Salt for gold. Slaves for copper. Trinkets for food.

> . . . He calls extortion development.

> The world is no longer anything but this shortcoming, understanding by what disorganisation a whole continent is dying of hunger. (*Canal*, p. 203)

Famine, hunger – the two words occur again and again. Hyvrard shifts from the exploitations in West Africa to the flaws in contemporary development in South America where the results are the same. The supposed order of commercial exchange is a monstrous disorder which leaves a trail of havoc, destruction, exploitation, starvation.

Here the issue is aid. First the financial hypocrisy and machinations:

6 June. Ecuador obtains suspension of credit. Peru before the Club of Paris. Brazil rejects the moratorium. Nicaragua in difficulty. Four presidents write to the heads of government of the industrialised countries. Correspondence.

The absurdity of believing in reimbursement. He has taken the extension of chaos for development.

8 June. Peru obtains from the Club of Paris a reorganisation of payments of its public debt.

The world is no longer anything other than this failure, the effort of the continents to invent payment of non-payment. And how could it do it, since it believes that one thing can not be in itself its own opposite? And yet. Financing. Refinancing. Consolidation.

Absurdity. The seven reunited in London trying to find how to solve insolvency. Liquidity.

The world is now only this failure, the invention of a system transforming lies into low-performance assets.

The world is now only this failure, the effort of a system to transform low-performance assets into losses, without touching lies. (*Canal*, p. 277)

That is at the governmental level: power play, politics and economic sleight of hand. Then Hyvrard describes the effect of the aid, using Brazil as an example (a more extended quotation is in Chapter 3):

Fragmentary and concentric, the thousand homes of despair. The nameless woman in the brazilled house. Without water. Without food. Rotting carcasses of long dead cattle. (*Canal*, p. 278)

'Aid' is revealed as a euphemism for exploitation, corruption, violence and abuse at all levels, from the international to the local and individual.

Always certain people with exploring minds and a taste for adventure are pushing forward to new discoveries, which again transform the economy and cause revolutions in attitude which seem, always, to end in the exploitation of human beings and of women in particular:

> The species' body, fragmented and concentric. The species' body in the process of organisation. The same organs for several successive individuals. Perdition. Recycling. Foetus. Bank. (*Canal*, p. 312)

Cybernetics and biotechnology; the economics of exploitation and the dehumanisation of the species, which is the equivalent, on the global level, of the abuse Annie suffers at the hands of her mother, Jeanne in the hands of her society.

Magellan stands as a metaphor of progress: passion, obsessiveness, money, secrecy, power, ruthlessness. He is flawed. He thinks 'other', his thought is 'woman-thought', 'round thought', but he is not a woman. He is a man who can no longer be a soldier, a wounded man but a man who cannot give up his old habits and behaviours even if he can envisage a different world. Unable to turn his back totally on Europe – on linear logic, capitalism, individual power and gain – he is not ready to move into the Pacific, which in Hyvrard's juxtapositional writing becomes the site of interconnectedness, of 'world-thought':

> World-thought is that of the world in motion. It cannot think itself in terms of *out* for it integrates. Its *disorder* is only superficial. The logarch's order disintegrates, not the world's organisation. It makes itself. It is the fiction of order that makes water, not perpetual creation, recreation. It is the myth of control that erodes, letting come up, in the *rifts*, the memory of *unity*: all the logarch has repressed, all he can not conceive of by proclaiming himself out, all that she can inceive of by gestating in. (*La Pensée corps*, p. 172)

For Magellan to leave the Atlantic, to turn his back definitively on Europe, would signify a refusal of the 'myth of mastery' which is expressed in logarchical thought (logic, separation, hierarchy, domination) and an acceptance of an-Other order, hence the realm of the Other, hence disorder:

Disorder

The logarch calls disorder the *order* it can not conceive of, that of the *other*. In logonomics there is only room for one order. The beings who inhabit its territory cannot be beings-in-themselves, not that the logarch does not regard them as peers, but, in his frame of mind, he cannot conceive them. Hence the permanent gamble called power. It does not come from an intrinsic taste for power, but of a necessity to make function an order of which the essence is control of the environment. Technical thought.

Read also: Chaos, environment, log—, obstacle, *power*. (*La Pensée corps*, p. 56)

The Atlantic is the male domain, the Pacific potentially the female. Magellan is a transitional being, caught between two world views. Hyvrard, in mid-sentence (to show his predicament and perhaps hers too), abandons him in the Straits of Magellan with a Patagonian mocking bird overhead: 'Above the fleet scattered among the rocks, the Patagonian mocking bird whose   [*sic*]' (*Canal*, p. 356).

Canal de la Toussaint is a study of the thought process, attitudes and behaviour of the dominant white occidental male and of the concomitant economic 'behaviour'. 'Commerce. Peaceful invasion. Peoples caught in the trap' (p. 220). The result is an indictment of the ways of the First World, its greed and its flagrant disregard for human life. The urge for progress is not sustained by any moral sense or even sense of the ultimate survival of human life on the planet. Development creates famine. Reason leads to dehumanisation and death. The economic 'progress' of the developed Western nations oppresses most of the world – including many of the citizens of those same nations.

As counterbalance to this dominant mode, Hyvrard offers chaos, interconnection and round thinking. This is the way of thinking of the woman who appears regularly throughout the text. She is the woman who coincides with Hyvrard's definition of her feminism as the tragic memory of the world resisting modernisation and 'a femininity in process of extermination'. The problem is that she is the woman Magellan has left at home in Seville, her hands in the sink. She is the energy pulling against Magellan's apparent advance but she is not in any position to modify his view of the world. His revolution is a male revolution and she has no part in it. Her thought process is private and has no expression in the public domain. She survives but changes nothing. He initiates change which will bring exploitation and destruction. His limp is sufficient to move him out of the old ways of seeing the world but not sufficient for him to transmit his beliefs to other men. Hyvrard leaves him stalled between two worlds.

Hyvrard's most recent book – *Ton nom de végétal*[12] – is also a book about oppression and exploitation but not in the way of the ones immediately preceding it. The angle of perception has shifted in some ways back towards that of the early novels and of *Le Silence et l'obscurité*. *Ton nom* is primarily concerned with survival, the survival of the individual and of the human species in a hostile environment, but even more than before Hyvrard refuses easy separations between the negative and positive. The distinction between what heals and what kills is always at issue at all levels, from the individual to the global.[13]

The three central sections of the book, 'Récit' (Tale), 'Paradis-fiction' (Paradise-Fiction) and 'Roman' (Novel), are narrations on different planes of the experience of chemotherapy. The first is a woman's chronicle of the physical horrors she suffers and of the attitudes and professional opinions of the doctors. The second is the story, told by the same narrator, of the relations between her and 'you', a male partner, and how he struggles to force her to make the effort to live, feel and think again. The third is set in a world where glaciers and volcanoes create upheaval; a number of abstract human forms cross this chaotic geography and the description is puncuated by textbook-style descriptions and classifications of various families of plants, reptiles, minerals and chemical processes.

It seems to me that what Hyvrard is proposing is body, spirit and mind struggling to come to terms with chemical devastation. This utterly invasive process breaks down all the life-sustaining organisation within the organism, pours poison into the system and is described as a cure. (Not very different from Annie's life in *La Jeune morte*, either, though in a different mode.) The links between chemotherapy, totalitarianism, colonisation and ecological devastation are evident: this is a totally oppressive procedure and the attitudes of the doctors make it clear to the reader that the patient is the victim of psychological oppression also.

> I admit everything you want. To have turned the name you gave me into a Mastosis, the object of your pleasure into a nodule, the milk that I should secrete into a tumour. I admit having contracted the totaliarian disease, cellular anarchy, biological and cultural

irredentism. I admit everything you want as you have all the proof in hand.

The corridor of the condemned to death. Appeal to the Supreme Court. Whereas it is exact that . . . How I hate you now with all the flowers of my flesh that I throw in your face to tell you how much I prefer Her, the goddess queen, the flesh mother, the all powerful. [. . .]¹⁴

I have had.

I have had this battering of all my living self. [. . .]

One day you punched me, because I did not turn my head quickly enough to be positioned correctly under the machine. You looked at my swollen arm and you said *if your breast had been removed this wouldn't have happened!* What a lie you told then and what a horrible thing to say. How you despised me to think that I could believe what you had said then . . .

I watched what you did. I had no superior to tell. No statistics to calculate. No thesis to finish. No cure to patent. No scientific paper to write. No article to publish. No seminars to give. No treatise to treat. Not on ethnology. Nor on aetiology. I was only living matter over which you had total rights. I watched you, paralysed with horror, contemplating the dawn of the coming century. (*Ton nom de végétal*, ms, pp. 27–8)

Body, spirit, mind and also individual, group and planet. The individual can stay alive physically but there is no human-ness without exchange, no desire, no love nor sexuality, no creativity nor expression. The individual's survival is set into context in 'Roman', the fourth section of the book. This is a struggle between two modes of understanding, two paradigms (the two described in Chapter 2).¹⁵ The struggle is there in the very writing of the text. On the one hand there is the separative and analytic 'scientific' way of knowing, which is exemplified in Hyvrard's taxonomy of life forms and transformative processes.

0805. – Arsenic, from the Greek arsenikos: viril. Body solid at ordinary temperature, iron grey in colour with a metallic sheen. The density of arsenic is 5.7. It sublimes at 400°. Projected on to hot coals, it vaporises giving off a strong smell of garlic. Not poisonous in itself, it becomes so by oxidation. The antidote is milk.

1107. – The family of Crinoidea has a body in the shape of a cup or of a flower with jagged petals, divided into branches, finely articulated and more or less forked and branching [. . .]

0806. – To classify is one of the essential functions of human intelligence . . . (*Ton nom*, ms, pp. 272–3)

The other way is chaos (as in chaos theory) accepted as a hypothetical description of the way the natural world organises itself.

2 – Matter animated by the desire to survive would call itself breath and yet not even yet for it would need movement, and the will to make sense. And what to call this simple attempt to escape from a fragmentation still more fragmentary, except to call breath this effort to rejoin the polar world?

The glacier moves forward under the weight of its own weight. But how can this dome of ice stay stored light on the summit, when the very weight condemns it to melting. Indeed it would melt if it were not for the altitude and the binding material that keeps it attached to the volcano, this white matrix holding in its breast this thing already resigned to its dispersal. (*Ton nom*, ms, p. 174)

This is one of a long series of variations on the theme of the breath of Creation that structure this section of the book.

Taxonomy is all very neat and tidy and reassuring; the problem is that on the whole the life forms to be categorised and classified are not. Hyvrard generates wonderful lists, numbered by group and scattered through the text. For example 02 is the Explorer, so his appearances are identifiable: 0208 being the eighth mention of him in the text; 07 is iron, 0701 steel and then on through chemical variants and properties of iron; 10 is a category of reptiles, or so it seems, until after 1001 chameleon. . . 1003 iguana. . . 1005 dragon. . . 1008 turtle. . . 1009 crocodile. . . we arrive at 1012 human being.

This connects us directly to the description of the Creation which opens *Ton nom*. In it the Creator, having created birds and having created reptiles, does not know what to do with the human species.

He did not want to settle him in the birds' kingdom, for man did not want to remember that he was born of Her, the great chaotic all, the mother of seraphim, bearers of wings and song.[16] Nor could he settle him in the snake's kingdom since he constantly fought with it over the mastery of all the other beings.

He decided that he would keep him in the big white garden with him.

Let the day break and the world begin! (*Ton nom*, ms, p. 1).

And it connects directly to the end of the text where a human being crawls out of the sea on to a devastated beach.

Most categories are of chemical reactions: 12 is arable land, its chemical variety and the effects of various fertilisers. A group of creatures that move about in water (like the human foetus) is 11, and the narrator includes herself in this category, with the salmon for whom reproduction brings individual death and survival of the species:

Do some grammar! you said, forgetting to tell me about the pain of the salmon going up towards the spring to die, and making me believe that their jumping over cascades and dams was joyful. The salmon's ascent toward their origin, it was not that, but a slow and painful procession where, in a sacred and inviolable order, the school was labouring heavily against the current, as though on each stroke of a tail depended the links to be passed on and the survival of the species. 1101. And indeed it did depend on it.

(Here and in the previous quotation we see again the connection Hyvrard makes from the origins to the future, tracing the survival of the species from the Great Mother through the bodies of generations of women, a genealogy she now calls sacred (see Chapter 7).)

Many of the lists begin with the anodine and end with the toxic. Category 08 is the one that makes this quite evident: 0801 saxifrage; 0802 arnica; 0805 arsenic; 0806 classification of plants; 0809 poison. The problem, as Hyvrard herself points out, is that it is not always easy to make a clear distinction between the medicinal and the poisonous.

0806. – To classify is one of the essential functions of human intelligence. Confronted by the vegetable world, man, strong in his experience, has learned over time to distinguish the good and bad plants, those which were useful for his nourishment and those synonymous with death which he used as poison for hunting or war. *But, in reality, it is impossible to insert each plant into such a narrow classification.* The vegetable world develops in its breast multiple chemical properties making up its own metabolism. *If a goodly number of the molecules thus formed are favourable to mankind, others, to make up for it, are fatal, because not incorporable into his biological cycle.* (*Ton nom*, ms, p. 273, my emphasis)

The difference can lie in the dosage, in the intention, and sometimes, in some plants, in the season or time of day. Chaos in nature destroys scientific categories.

Ton nom de végétal raises a great number of issues by the provocative juxtaposition of its themes. The most important question, however, seems to be how much a human being and the human species on this planet can survive in the way of chemical change in the personal or public environment. When is transformation beneficial, when polluting, and at what point does it become lethal?

The ambiguities and paradoxes proliferate in an interconnected chaotic system. Hyvrard's narrator speaks of her cancer being her body's way of surviving a deprivation of love. (Hyvrard has published a conversation with her mother on this topic in *Le Cercan*.[17]) In these terms the cancer is seen as curative, yet so is the chemotherapy.

In the final paragraphs of 'Roman' Hyvrard describes the arrival on land of a naked male human being in terms that can serve as a metaphor of birth, a metaphor of re-birth/survival after chemotherapy, or a metaphor of the aftermath of some tremendous cataclysm. Whichever it may be, the prognosis is not encouraging:

When he came out of the womb of the sea, the Implorer had neither clothes, nor vessels, nor swaddling clothes, nor language, nor baggage, nor roads, nor maps, but only before him, between the sky and the earth, the scattered marshes of the vast delta. In the seaweed and the reeds lay the stiff flesh which no one claimed, because it emitted all around a sweet and subtle odour which kept insects and crustaceans at a distance.

The river's mouth abounded with fish and birds come before him into the world and which, since then, had grown and multiplied.

But as he had neither net, nor bow, nor arrows, nor boat, be it a small boat or a raft, he did not have the means to satisfy his hunger and cried against his mother's body, the beach, all cluttered by debris from the shipwreck, cord, chorion, placenta, and all the fetid slimances of the chemical and nuclear waters, matrificial molecules and patroclysmic manipulations.

1012. – As he crawled towards the earth, looking for his food, his diaphanous and obsolete skin was scratched by the dead branches. He had neither scales, nor claws, nor spurs, nor any of those things which allow living and fighting, and outside his mother's body, his flesh was drying out brittle and sharp, like shards of glass. (*Ton nom*, ms, p. 283)

The important shift here is that this is a male who is outside the female reproductive network of survival that Hyvrard has set up elsewhere. His predicament is reminiscent of Magellan's situation at the end of *Canal*. In the last section of *Ton nom*, 'Contemplation', Hyvrard develops the metaphor of birth. Her narrator alternates reflections on the effects on herself of her experience of her mother's womb with reflections on the cybernetic womb and its production. Both are portrayed as systems of control over what is being developed. The situation for the individual and for the group are parallel. The paragraph concerning the mother's womb could be a synopsis of *La Jeune morte*:

She shuts me in the womb, to fertilize me, and make me produce, identically, that which she needs for herself, accomplishment of the program conceived within herself, for herself, reproduction. (*Ton nom*, ms, p. 287)

Similarly, the cybernetic womb takes over every aspect of its public:

In the cybernetic womb, propaganda of abundance and publicity. Without reserve. Without any part reserved for oneself. The abundance of the great overflowing. Consumption without limit, the great burning. (*Ton nom*, ms, p. 287)

Hyvrard brings these two threads of her thought together with two other considerations:

Consumere: to eat, waste, destroy. *Consummare*: make the sum, the total, to finish, accomplish, make perfect. (*Ton nom*, ms, p. 287)

And she arrives at her metaphor of cannibalism once more:

Of the pain, I know nothing, but everything of the devoration. (*Ton nom*, ms, p. 287)

The paramount danger in Hyvrard's work is the danger of being devoured – overwhelmed, infiltrated, eaten up by an act perpetrated by people of the same species. Cannibals come as individuals, groups, nations and in many forms: mothers, chemotherapists, colonisers, multinationals, electronic communication networkers. Like locusts, they devour everything in their path, leaving devastation in their wake. This devastation can be economic, cultural, territorial, physical or emotional and its cause, according to Hyvrard, lies in the experience of being alienated from the place that you rightfully inhabit successfully. On various levels this can be country, class, family or one's own body or sense of identity.

In the womb of death, sowing, proliferation, germination from the other to the identical. The maddenedness. The making of madness.

Madness, alienation, place in oneself taken by someone other than the self, becoming other, being chased out of one's own place, in oneself. [. . .]

Madness, alienation, mental distraction, destitution of the being whose internal order has been dismantled to make it usable without any precautions, in the infinite waste of an infinitely reproducible substance, gratis, gratuitous, given. (*Ton nom*, ms, p. 28)

Thus, at the end of *Ton nom de végétal* Hyvrard comes full circle and connects this text with all that has gone before: the programming of Annie and before her of Jeanne, the link between their personal regimes and other strategies of invasive transformation, be they colonisation, the demands of a consumer society, or psychological modification through the media. Hyvrard's world is one in which the individual human being is constantly under threat of dispossession of self, the victim of a variety of cannibal economies.

Chapter 7

NODES OF THE SACRED

The political economy, trans-national commerce and cybernetic systems of contemporary capitalist society treat human beings, women in particular, as commodities to be traded, slaves to be oppressed, deviants to be homogenised. As we have seen, Hyvrard is very clear about what she describes as a cannibalistic system out to devour everything in its path. Its manifestations are increasingly technical and its effects ever more dehumanising. That her major metaphor for the source of this destruction of all difference, all individuation should be the womb, indicates to me that Hyvrard sees this network of cannibalising economies as the results of 'bad birth'. Just as her understanding of abusive mother power – bad birth at the individual level – produced, as a response, an empowering female genealogy reproducing itself through time (Hyvrard's feminism), so the negative, oppressive systems of the last two chapters are accompanied by a network of elements that Hyvrard designates as sacred.

Even though I have separated these elements of Hyvrard's world picture for the sake of coherence, they actually fit together as 'contrarations' – contrary perceptions of a given word, situation or problem which should not, frequently cannot, be divided from each other. Such non-separation is crucial to the nature of chaos writing and to Hyvrard's 'round thought'. Within it flourish complexity, ambiguity, paradox, dynamic juxtaposition, the constant flow of interconnections and 'enceptual' understanding.

The nodes of the sacred are the strategies of defence or points of resistance Hyvrard gives to her narrators. 'The sacred is what remains of the chaic in a logical universe' she writes in her definition of the sacred in *La Pensée corps*. (Chaic-chaos, logic-logos. The chaic is the order within disorder, the coherence in the irrational.)[1] The full description gives the context of her thought:

Sacred

In the beginning is the enception, the perception one has of the world. The perception of the whole world and the part. The perception of the self and of the relation of the whole and the part. There is no self.

Between the self and the one,* enception. In all places, in all things, relation. Fusional thought reunites there where logical thought separates.

So there is no clear definition and separation here. The self emerges constantly in relation to its context. Everything is interconnected and in process (as opposed to conceptualised, categorised and fixed in place).

A concept is without any relation other than logic. Enception has all the relations of reality. Disorder and movement.

Logical thought separates. It excludes from the beginning all that is not entered into the order it chooses.

The order of the world is predatoriness. Logical thought is from the start exclusion. Predatoriness without enception has no longer any limit, the predator having with his prey no relation other than murder.

Predatoriness is necessary to food. As soon as one kills without eating, the massacre begins. As soon as one concepts without encepting, the perdition begins.

The distinction here is between connective thought, which is in a constant state of adjustment to reality, and thought that separates each piece of what is known and values it according to its place in a system of knowledge rather than in a network of relations. In a system where one species kills another, relatedness brings respect, holistic thinking, ecological responsibility, and spirituality, whereas logical thought divests itself of all connection, empathy and contextual understanding. An extreme example would be the traumatic dissociation of sociopaths.

---

* Translator's note: Hyvrard uses the pronoun 'on' (one) to signify a being partially emerged from the universal magma but not yet sufficiently differentiated from it to have an identity as a person.

Conception and enception are the two movements that lead from the child to the mother, from the future to the past, from time to space.

Conception is closed and turns back towards the subject. Enception is open on the world. A concept can not be perceived in the middle of the world. It isolates a part of the world.

Enception is sacred thought. It thinks, at the same time, the origins and the end. Conception can not do that. It can only link the origins with the end, but it can not think them at the same time, since, from the beginning, it has detached them.

This is the difference between genealogy and taxonomy, between chaos and logos for Hyvrard. Enception is a thought process that the thinker is part of as it happens. There is no separation between the thinking and the act of living that thinking. This is the process of chaos, of the cosmic dance. It is not possible to observe it and to think oneself objective. That is the process of conceptualising. A concept is separated off from both the thinker and what caused the thought; it can be exchanged as a token of possession of knowledge, or used with others to construct order. The sacred can only be understood in the living of it because once analysed it is no longer sacred but a study of the sacred.

Enception is sacred thought and not thought of the sacred. Conception thinks the sacred. Enception is itself of the sacred. They can not agree on the sacred. One separates it and the other does not even perceive it, because it lives it.

In the beginning, he separates the sacred. He isolates it. This separation does not account for the world but for its fantasy. Left is *chaos* which he cannot do anything with. Yet chaos dominates him. Look.

Chaos is the organisation of the world, not its order. The logos is the order he applies to chaos in order to believe that he has mastery over it. He does not succeed. He can at the most conceptualise it and then he loses it.

How could he think what he has lost other than as emptiness? He gets lost with it, since chaos dominates him. Beyond formlessness and the void is not emptiness.

Chaos can not be concepted for it encapsulates everything. It can only be encepted from everything.

The essence of chaos is the chaic. Not chaicity, which separates the object from its nature. Or then logicity would have to be said also.

The chaic is excluded from the computerised world. It still resists in language. By surprise. By mistake. By memory. It comes back in images.

Thinking the sacred is still separating it. In enception and the chaic, it is not separated.

Scientific, logical thought and sacred thought are not compatible. For them to come together, logic and reason will have to be seen once again as sub-sets within a much larger variety of ways of knowing that incorporate dream, madness, mysticism ... and permit a holistic, dynamic understanding of complex process – Chaos (theory of), the organisation of the world. The sacred, for Hyvrard, is whatever remains in today's world that permits a contact, a glimpse, a memory, a re-embodiment of chaotic interconnectedness, of fusion with the whole.

The sacred cannot be thought without reintegrating the logic in the chaic, the part in the totality, the order in the organisation.

The sacred is the dismemberment of chaos after one has started to attempt to concept it. After it is conceptualised, there is nothing left except the beginning of the massacre, ashes and cremation.

The sacred is what remains of the chaic in the universe of logic. The residue. It remembers that it can not be encepted, because it says itself to be unpronounceable. (*La Pensée corps*, pp. 192–4)

The sacred, then, is Hyvrard's term for those places of resistance against further encroachment by the logarchical order. The term signals the realm of the irrational, a space of emotion and reflection and of unsuppressed difference. There is no connection with religion implicit in this sacred; occidental religion is a logarchical system which disseminates the 'myth of mastery' and oppresses women. The sacred, in Hyvrard's writing, tends to be a female domain. Indeed, the struggle between the sacred and the religious could well be another interpretation of the central metaphor of *Les Doigts du figuier*. The sacred is held captive in the wine-press of Christian ritual.

The locus of the sacred, for Hyvrard, is the female body, source of life and of love – but, in the logarchy, this body is not treated with respect,

rather it is abused. Herein lies the tension that permeates the contrarations of the early texts. Sexuality is as likely to be expressed in rape as to
be the expression of love. Conception may lead to birth or to miscarriage
or to abortion. The ideal of how things ought to be, and perhaps once
were long ago, is an elusive image that swirls in Jeanne's confusion and
it is for the clarification of this ideal that she fights so hard. She has the
sense of a lost wisdom, a lost genealogy, a lost language. Knowledge that
should have been passed to her by her mother – but her mother is an
agent of her oppression rather than a source of support. Her mother gave
her life and yet tries to reduce her living to the minimum. It is for the
clarification of this contradiction also that Jeanne maintains her perspective with such a desperation.

Wittig also has this sense of genealogy and lost language and, like
Hyvrard, situates the sacred in the female body. However she avoids the
issue of negative and positive sexuality, bad and good birth altogether. In
Les Guérillères there are no mothers and no stories depicting sexuality.
Breasts and vulva are sacred to the goddess and reflect her light. They
serve as weapons, signs of resistance, of self-esteem and play. The lost
female language is reclaimed through the retelling of myths and stories,
the reconceptualising of prayer and history. It is the work of a community reappropriating its culture not of an individual struggling for
personal survival.

In Hyvrard's texts her women narrators are points of resistance against
the dominant context. They are victims, in no position to actually change
their situation and escape, but they can and do hold their ground, insist-
ing on the rightness of their way of thinking. In *La Pensée corps* this is
described as woman-thought and captive-thought.

Thought

Woman-thought can account for specifically female experience
not because of the sex of the *woman* not even of her gender, but of
the particular place she occupies not only as *fusionary*, but as fus-
ioning *mother* and daughter. Her effort towards individuation is
constantly thwarted by this situation. It is not the same for other
fusionaries who in other contexts may stop being that way. In the
present state of the way things function, woman cannot manage to
escape it.

Captive-thought cannot be expressed in the *terms* and *rules* of
articulation imposed by the *logarchy*. It is expressed in poetry

through feminine metaphor. It does not concern women only, but all categories of dominated people.

It develops in the universe of the in, because of its impossibility of *being-in-itself*. Fusion is imposed on it by the logarch by means of the coercive mental apparatus of logonomy. (*La Pensée corps*, pp. 168–9)

Each woman's protection lies in the resistance that also causes the abuse that falls on her. As we have seen in *Les Prunes*, a woman who does not resist is a mere doll, stereotypical, powerless and 'dead'. A woman who does resist might be constrained and excluded from a society which considers her 'dead' but as long as she is true to her view of the world, her identity has not been destroyed. Her protection is rooted in an awareness that, however secluded she may be, she still remains part of a network whose power is drawn from time, tradition and biology. By her body a woman is connected to her mother, and as a mother (if she is one), to her daughter and so to the female. By her body a woman is connected to her lover and thus (in Hyvrard's world) the male. Hyvrard sacralises sameness in the mother-daughter links in a female genealogy that stretches back to the Great All, chaos, the Mother Goddess before Eden. She sacralises heterosexual love and through it the bond of difference. No other connections have a place in her world.

This is the ordering of a lost era that structures myths and fairy tales. It seems to be a heterosexual world, yet it is totally woman centred and woman embodied. The male lover is necessary in order to permit the procreation of the next generation – which is why fairy tales always end once the woman has married him. He has no other function. Through the union of male and female in sexual intercourse (metaphorically represented by the wedding and 'they lived happily ever after') and their fusion in orgasm, the male represents a remnant of the lost integrated world. As such he allows the woman to live the sacred (and could himself if he situated his function on that plane – but Hyvrard does not see him doing so).

The structure of Hyvrard's texts comes directly from her lived experience; the weaknesses of that structure come from the fact that she does not extend it at all. As a result her books are constructed without any sense of female community. (This may be a culturally inappropriate complaint, given the ubiquity of heterosexual pairing in French social behaviours.) Also the dichotomy between the oppressive patriarchy and the protected male partner could be read as the self-defensive pattern of behaviour of a steadfast heterosexual. Given my interpretation of 'tu' as agent of the sacred, I do not think that this is the case. Let us look more closely at the recurring pattern. The books are constructed with a particular and a general opponent to the narrator and a particular and general supporter:

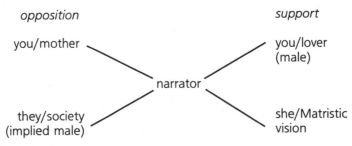

The sides are not symmetrical. The male general 'they' is social and political whereas the female generality is metaphysical. There are no supportive human females in Hyvrard's works, only a multiplicity of sameness, hidden in a female genealogy that has been silenced and fragmented. This genealogy has its good births, which produce live offspring, and its bad births: miscarriage, product of rape and other sexual oppressions, and daughters of oppressed, abject mothers. It seems to me that in Hyvrard's system as sketched above I could, and perhaps should, substitute 'abjection' for 'opposition' and 'sacred' for 'support'. Then the living you/mother and the living male they/society together prevent the development of the narrator while the you/lover and the she/Mother provide glimpses of lost potential – the missing piece for which the narrator strives.

The first development of these pairings is visible in *Mère la mort*: on the one hand the search for the goddess, the Great Mother, and on the other the narrator's male partner patiently excavating and rebuilding the house against the cliff in order to take care of her there.

Mère la mort is a matristic text, in the sense that a matristic writer sees the spirit connected to the entire cosmos in ways which are compatible with Hyvrard's developing concept of fusional thought, round thought, woman-thought. In such a context

> ... the Earth itself is sacred, and [that] since we are an interdependent part of it we are sacred too. In these living systems the Earth

is the Mother, both of life and of death, but death is not viewed as a negative state or as the void within an ecological perspective where all living matter is recycled and reborn. Death is merely one phase and regeneration. All seen as a part of a web of interconnectedness, part of the cycles of seasons, of day and night, of solstices and equinoxes, of the tides, the phases of the moon, and the menses in women. (Orenstein, p. 24)[2]

This is certainly the background the reader discovers implicit in all Hyvrard's books, and rendered explicit in certain texts such as *Mère la mort*, *Les Doigts du figuier*, *La Meurtritude*, *Que se partagent encore les eaux*, and *Canal de la Toussaint*.[3] Here we see why Hyvrard uses the moment of tension between chaos, the ultimate interconnectedness, and (biblical) Creation as a metaphoric node in her writing, and why the Garden of Eden, Adam and Eve would be important too. To Adam was attributed the power to name, separate and control. Eve was sentenced to silence and bodily suffering through childbirth. Birth, its hazards, suffering and bleeding are important and frequent images in Hyvrard's symbolic system. Indeed, as we have already seen, whenever she sets out to write about economics and colonisation, she usually writes about her womb, her sexuality, pregnancy, miscarriage and her pain as a woman – mother and daughter both, alienated from her reproductive labour.

Pregnancy is connected both physiologically and emotionally to cancer for Hyvrard. In pregnancy the proliferating cells create a baby, in cancer the cells also create autonomous life. In *Le Cercan*, Hyvrard and her co-discussants in the chemotherapy group make clear the protective attitude some of them have to their cancers. There is even a section in the book entitled 'It's as if it were a child that's been taken from me'. (This unlikely association is an example of 'contraration' in Hyvrard's thought: growth which produces life from the womb, growth which produces death.)

The conversation between Hyvrard, who had breast cancer, and her mother, who had uterine cancer, shows that for Hyvrard the cancer is a bodily attempt to fill an emotional need – a view she iterates in *Ton nom de végétal*. Where love is lacking so grows the tumour. Breast and womb for daughter and mother. I am reminded of the remark in *La Jeune morte* that the daughter must somehow wean her mother one day in order to establish her own autonomy. So her breast cancer is for her the mark of resistance. The scapegoating of cancer sufferers by society at large is a mark of the link of the dis-ease with the sacred.[4] The scapegoat bears the transgressions of the community and is cast out of society as a symbol both of the cathartic liberation of society from that which the group wants to ignore, and of a sacrificial atonement for that which is cast out. The scapegoat is the shadow side of society, rejected, feared and never eliminated. This is the role of all Hyvrard's narrators. They make visible what has been hidden; they bear witness to the unspeakable; they live the transgression.

Hyvrard situates the sacred at points of tension in the web of inter-connections. Motherhood is certainly one of these points. There is a tremendous tension between the matristic view of women as daughters of Mother Earth and the everyday exchanges between birth mother and daughter. The former is positive and desired, the latter destructive.

Most of Hyvrard's work addresses mother-daughter relationships in some way and we have already seen the oppressive aspects of them in some detail. It is in *Mère la mort* that the questions of female genealogy and of a female divinity are addressed most fully.

The context is one of women's need to recover cultural and linguistic memory specific to their sex and gender. The knowledge and traditions that were blocked by the silencing of Eve must be re-membered, put back together from the distorted fragments that remain in patriarchal society, and its mythology. As Orenstein remarks:

> Today's feminist matristic literature has the awesome task of dis-mantling those patriarchal cultural constructs which have masked the historical verities of female empowerment over eons of time, and which also have denied and degraded the human connection to the spiritual and natural world. (Orenstein, p. 130)

Hyvrard's narrator, Jeanne, is trying to find her way back through the cultural silences to the 'missing piece' that she knows must be there somewhere, to the language that will express her way of being and to the stories that will situate her in her world. Orenstein categorises such a narrator as a 'nonamnesiac living in a world of culturally induced amne-sia' (p. 37). She develops her point in directions directly applicable to Jeanne in all of Hyvrard's early work:

> We may, thus, legitimately inquire whether a nonamnesiac, living in a world of culturally induced amnesia, is actually 'mad,' or whether

she is 'illuminated,' and stepping to the beat of a different drummer. At what point does the culture drive the woman of eco-matristic-shamanistic-memory mad, and send her over the brink from being the woman of awakened memory in a world of amnesiacs to being a woman driven mad by the persecution she undergoes for her memory in a culture that judges her to be insane rather than awakened? (Orenstein, p. 37)

Hyvrard would use similar terminology. (In fact she and Gloria Orenstein have met to discuss *Mother Death*.) These are the circumstances we have already looked at from the perspective of the modes of persecution invoked to bring about madness in the narrator. Now let us look at what her awakening memory reveals.

Just as the Jeanne of *Les Prunes* remembered the colonising of Martinique by the French and the cultural destruction that ensued, so the Jeanne of *Mère la mort* remembers the invaders who desecrated the shrines of the Goddess:

> . . . But the invaders came. They said stones weren't living. They tore out trees without seeing the blood flow . . . They said a man had landed and had killed the python protecting your cave . . . They said the king of Hades had carried away earth's daughter one day while she was gathering poppies . . . They said reason was born from the creator's thigh wearing a helmet . . . They thought they appropriated me. But I became the world. (*Mother Death*, pp. 38–9)

The Goddess is not named and, indeed, she first appears in a passage where fragmentary references to pagan and Christian stories and symbols are juxtaposed, and where the ambiguous nature of the 'she' who is waiting becomes apparent.

> She's at the edge of the rye field. She holds a flower. She waits very calmly to devour me. The river's almost dry. I've no more water. She's going to smother me. Her womb contracts. She's at the edge of the rye field. Crows fly around her. She digests me in her belly.
> Stone slab for what feast? Stone slab for what liberation? Bread and wine on tombs. Masses celebrated on altars. On an island, a python protecting your cave. A dragon devouring a princess. A fruit eaten in a garden, a fruit that makes us mortal. A man in a fish's

belly. A man thrown up on the sand. For what exit? For what rebirth? Shared bread. Crabs eaten in cemeteries. Painted eggs placed on graves. In what language the same word to say to be beaten and to die? In what language the same language to say feast and funeral?

Mother death. I cry out to you . . .

Mother death. In what deck are you the only card without a name? (*Mother Death*, pp. 24–5)

The 'she' in the rye field diversifies into Demeter, Mother Goddess, who nurtures the earth and is at one with her daughter Persephone, and the 'woman in mauve', who oppresses Jeanne. The story of the original separation of mother and daughter is retold and the connection made to the situation of women in the present and to Jeanne's madness.

They tore you away from yourself to make you many. With as many cults as they've given you names. With as many attributes as they've devoted cults to you. With as many attributes as they've erected temples for you. I run toward you, seeking the name they tore from you. I run toward you. (*Mother Death*, p. 89)

The 'missing piece' that the narrator needs is the name of the divinity and together with that name the language which permits the entry of women into a symbolic universe, cultural creativity, and intra-gender communication. In this way Hyvrard is re-configuring the holistic network, actually thinking it against what she has to think with – namely the logos. Luce Irigaray addresses the same topic in much the same way as does Hyvrard:

We lack, we women with a sex of our own, a God in which to share, a word/language to share and to become. Defined as the often obscure, not to say hidden, mother-substance of the word/language of men, we lack our *subject*, our *noun*, our *verb*, our *predicates*: our elementary sentence, our basic rhythm, our morphological identity, our generic incarnation, our genealogy.[5]

And, close by in the same volume, Irigaray connects lack of a female divinity with women's inability to connect and communicate with each other within their gender:

If women lack a God, there is no possible communication or communion between them. One needs, they need, the infinite in order to share a *little*. Otherwise, the sharing leads to fusion-confusion, division and conflict in (each of) them, between them. If I cannot be in relation to some sort of horizon where my genre is accomplished, I cannot share while protecting my becoming.[6]

Hyvrard's narrator's search is similarly linked to a matristic language which will allow her to be part of a fusional, universal network:

They're the stronger ones. I can't find the forgotten language. The language from before the invaders. The language without pronouns. The language in which words also mean their opposites. The language in which substantives are conjugated. The language that liberates. The language that leads me back to the living beyond the mirror. The language even older than the statue with naked breasts. The language of souls of the dead in stones. The language of women walled in the river's alders. The language of your caverns' paintings, your soil's pottery, your ashes' silica. The language of the naked woman, her thighs like mountains. She has a swollen belly and curly hair. They tore her from you and put her behind a window. (*Mother Death*, p. 27)

Jeanne is in despair. She is searching for herself, for a connection with her mother, and her foremothers, for the collected wisdom and stories of female empowerment that have been repressed. Meanwhile the figure who is apparently her mother works with the men to oppress her and keep her locked in 'madness' and separation from her mothers:

No. They've turned us into dribbling mouths with upturned eyes and twisted bodies. They force us to speak a language that isn't our own. To nourish a body that isn't our own. To live a life that isn't our own. I won't find anything. Except her womb that contracts and suffocates me. Except the river's water drying up. Except the red acids she secretes in my brain. Consciousness forming. I am she and I. She suffocates me. I suffocate. I resist. She resists. A fight to the finish. In depths of her body's cavern. In what language do words also mean their opposites? I am both I and she. In what language is there not yet a pronoun? Power. Identity. Two sides of the same coin. Of the same error. We're not two. We're one, in the feminine singular. To have and to be, two auxiliary verbs of a cosmic gestation. We're one. She suffocates me if I'm someone other. If I stick to her, I survive. The missing piece. Consciousness forming. If I resist, she kills me. If I disappear into her, I survive. (*Mother Death*, p. 28)

The image of struggle of the baby to survive birth is one that was already present in *Les Prunes*. In Hyvrard's logarchical/patriarchical world, a daughter's first enemy is her mother − because of the loss of connection between women through time, the mother has been co-opted as the agent of logarchical behaviour modification. Abject herself, the mother is incapable of giving life to her daughter. The daughter must re-birth herself through female memory. Survival will come with full remembrance:

Mother death, I run toward you for survival. I run toward you seeking your name. I read it once in a book. But they'd mixed it up so much I didn't recognize it. And yet I know it. I heard it beating in my bloody vulva. I hear it beating without conjugating in my belly. I hear it beating in my digesting body. (*Mother Death*, p. 109)

Language is the means of transmission of the sacred which finds its existence in the female body, either in the physical and generational link between mother and daughter, when it is good, or in the connection between men and women which is created by physical love as a re-embodiment of fusion and chaos.

Just as there is tension between the Great Mother and the narrator's mother in Hyvrard's work, so there is tension between 'You' (*tu*) the male lover and 'they' (*ils*) the mass of persecutors. In *Mère la mort* 'they' are the people who keep Jeanne in a psychiatric hospital whereas 'You' toils patiently to render habitable a house to which he can take her. In the hospital she is interrogated, threatened and tortured. (Comparisons with concentration camps bring political concerns into the strata of self-similarity in ways that I discussed earlier.) In the house she is protected, loved and nurtured. The threat of return to hospital is ever present, however, so that the couple's emotional structure is vulnerable. Similarly, the house is seen to be fragile, built directly against the rocks that fall frequently from the overhanging cliff. 'You' spends much of his time excavating and rebuilding the damaged building. It is evident that the ruined state of the house is a metaphor for the effects of long-term pressure on the individual relationship and on the male-female relationship in patriarchal society. As Jeanne struggles to reconstruct her history and identity from the fragments she can recall, so her husband reconstructs their family home out of the debris. Both activities take place under dangerous circumstances; each careful construct could be destroyed again at any time.

'You' hears, accepts, believes and encourages Jeanne; 'they' work against her all the time. At one point in the novel, she bursts out into an all-encompassing indictment of the attitudes and behaviours of men to women:

> What have they done, those oh-so-normal men, in response to the open arms of their mothers, sisters, wives, daughters, lovers? Who are those men who say we're sick? What do they know about women's bodies, those men who speak in our place? What do they know of our love? What have they done with their lives, those men who say we're mad? What have they done with their memories from when they were ten years old? What have they done with their oaths of love? What have they done with their desire for truth? Who are those men who say we're mad so they can be rid of us? Who are those men who fix on words when we speak and hear only what they can tolerate? Who are those oh-so-normal men who have sold their souls to raise their stature? Who are those frauds who don't know how to distinguish between true and false anymore? Who are those weathercocks who turn with the wind? Who are those mighty men who cover us with incense so they can bury us more easily? Who are those hungry deaf men who are so greedy they need to devour? Who are those deaf men who act as our megaphones so they can distort us more easily? (*Mother Death*, pp. 74–5)

The pain of oppression is very strong in *Mère la mort*, but so is the indefatigable nature of daily love. The novel ends on an optimistic note as the couple ford a river and walk away from the malevolent mother figure sitting on a balcony watching them. They are bonded by their love in its physical expression, and that expression is centred in the woman's body.

The main focus of *Mère la mort* is on the lost sacred mother. The novel outlines the narrator's search for matristic culture, language and self-reflection in a female deity. Sexual love is here less important. The sacred union of the heterosexual couple is presented as a major theme in *Que se partagent encore les eaux*.[7] In this long poem Hyvrard returns to the chaos before (biblical) Creation and develops the twin themes of unity and separation. For her, in the fusional world at the opening of the Book of Genesis everything was part of everything else, man and woman were undifferentiated parts of total matter. Then that matter was divided into ever more precise categories, differentiated, separated and named. For Hyvrard the sacred nature of the union of woman and man lies in its function as physical re-embodiment of what had been and all the tensions in their relationship stem from the differences between them conceptualised in the knowledge of separation.

> He created them so they might keep within themselves the memory
>   of the whole
> In his image he created them
> Male and female
> And already he did not know what to do about language
> Even though he had not yet spoken
> But he did not know how to say to himself
> That he was making them two to be one . . .
> Not knowing how to make himself both singular and plural
> Because he had no word to say it
> Except body*
> (*Que se partagent*, pp. 121–2. *Note: in French *corps* (body) has the
> same form in singular and plural.)

In Hyvrard's re-separating of the waters, survival of the couple, and ultimately of the species, comes through life and through the fusional nature of sexual intercourse. At that moment female and male come together in a recreation of their original wholeness and one-ness. The act is a sacrament of re-membrance of the time before separation. As such it is sacred. And by reverse self-similarity it is an act of bringing the waters together to recreate the Great All, in her original form. Hence heterosexual union is transformed into a revolutionary act, a direct link with the Great Mother, and a repudiation of the logarchy through the female body.

> Adam man and woman one close to the other

Beginning the world again
Because that is how it is in all love
Provided that unrestrained
It tries in turn to fill the gulf
When the male through being in the female makes himself female
    too by being with her a single body in her
When the female through having the male take root in her becomes
    male herself by having the entire male in her sex
(*Que se partagent*, p. 124)

The language of the text is such that the first and second person pronouns sometimes seem to refer to the original waters and the spirit moving over them, sometimes to Eve and Adam, sometimes to a couple in
present time. (This is the technique of superimposition we have seen frequently in Hyvrard's writing – the self-similarity of chaotic systems.)
Together they are the original completeness, remembered, re-enacted
across time.

In the middle of the bed
In the body of memory
She and he
These mountains and these valleys of flesh . . .
Together in eternity

Undefined bodies perfectly entwined . . .
For she never has enough of him in her
Because it is only there
That ends the suffering caused by want
Memory of the whole

Let the waters part again
Remembrance of the sky's and the earth's gesture in their created
    being . . .
(*Que se partagent*, p. 134)

However the legacy of Genesis has not been so beneficient. There are
two creation narratives and in the second Adam dominates:

Created alone he thought himself alone

Created first he made himself leader
Created leader he believed himself unique . . .

But no woman found he among the animals
Or rather he was so enclosed in himself
That he did not recognise her
(*Que se partagent*, pp. 137–8)

The woman has neither place nor identity: 'You do not even see me' she says, 'Preoccupied as you are/Organising the world for your domination' (p. 138). The struggle continues between the two situations. The man, heir to the attitudes of domination and possession, is concerned with his place in the world. The woman yearns for the wholeness through desire and fusion. There is no apparent irony in the line 'They were con-fused in this place' (p. 149). To be acknowledged as different, not separate or dominated. Hyvrard presents woman and man as the possibility of one flesh, one body in love. From this flesh comes life and survival in the future and memory of a lost sacred union with all things. Hyvrard's argument is essentialist in that it is rooted in the body, but it is scripted to show that women and men are separate and cannot understand each other. (See the beginning of *Canal de la Toussaint* in particular.) Sexual intercourse is necessary as a connection to the past and to the future for the woman. Conception of the child is enception of the sacred – and subversion of the logos.

Ultimately, in the whole body of writing, survival is the sacred mission of all the narrators: to survive in the flesh and in the text, to survive in woman-spirit and woman-memory. Whether she be given the role of scapegoat or divinity, lover or mother, the narrator-daughter must survive to bear witness to her experience in the oppressive world of male-logos domination. Sacralisation of her role in the maintenance and transmission of life and love and language is a defence by universalisation which sustains the narrator as she is being oppressed. She must remain female and human, with all that that comports of sexuality, irrationality, eccentricity, individuality and non-conformity, in a context that represses such freedoms ever more ruthlessly. The concept of oppression is shifting towards that of destruction as Hyvrard's work enters its third phase with *Ton nom de végétal*. The focus remains that of survival.

The tension between the universal-ideal and the individual-real permeates the corpus, existing not only within individual books but between books, between the narrator and her situation, the author and her creation. I see four nodes in the network: one around the notion of mother, one around the female body, one around the role of women, and one around reproductive fusion.

Already in *Les Prunes*, 'mother' was one of the words Jeanne saw as multifaceted and problematical. Looking across the work we see the desire for a matristic culture, a Great Mother. Chaos is female for Hyvrard. Therein lies un-reason, non-linearity, connectedness, life and death – a holistic thought process. Non-divine mothers are more difficult to deal with, though no less central and no less paradoxical. The contraration here is not between the sacred and the profane, but rather between the sacred and the abject. Mothers are diminished by the logarchy and so oppressive to their daughters. They are also the potential source or withholder of all that is desirable: love, safety, nurture. And motherhood is desirable, because in the act of attaining motherhood, one touches the divine. However, as men seem to see all women through a projection of the stereotypical portrayal of mother in our society – says Hyvrard in *La Pensée corps* – then women are trapped and objectified, as oppressed mothers internalise the stereotype and continue the oppression. For Hyvrard, the crucial issue that must be debated in the furtherance of equality is that of motherhood. This is not an unusual spectrum of perspective – it reminds me again of the cast of characters in a fairy tale – but it is rare to find all the paradoxes together in one body of work.

What Hyvrard is struggling to do here is to claim what Irigaray also claims in her writing, namely the 'unsymbolized relationship between mother and daughter [which] constitutes a threat to the patriarchal symbolic order as we know it'.[8] Hyvrard's narrators, by their search for language and memory and by the rooting of these in the female body, are taking the first necessary steps to insert the female body into the reconfigured symbolic order. This is a female representation of a woman and her mythology, a woman and her spiritual genealogy, a woman and her social situation. The continuous struggle between the 'mad' narrator and her male oppressors is a metaphor for women's desperate attempts to create and establish their own symbolic order in the teeth of opposition from the patriarchal-logarchical power structure.

Here Hyvrard's thought and Irigaray's are very similar. Hyvrard provides her female narrator with no female contact other than her mother and the mother provides no support for her daughter. Irigaray writes:

If women don't have access to society and to culture:
– they remain in a state of dereliction in which they neither recognise nor love themselves/each other;
– they lack mediation for the operation of sublimation;
– love is impossible for them.[9]

and goes on to argue that women need a language in order to be able to speak to each other, understand and love each other. Included in this predicament of non-communication and non-love are mothers and daughters whose relationship is complicated even further by a problem of non-differentiation. Margaret Whitford identifies this problem as 'a pathological symptom of a cultural discourse in which the relation between mother and daughter cannot be adequately articulated',[10] and goes on to quote Irigaray:

But there is no possibility whatsoever, within the current logic of sociocultural operations, for a daughter to situate herself with respect to her mother: because, strictly speaking, they make neither one nor two, neither has a name, meaning, sex of her own, neither can be 'identified' with respect to the other ... How can the relationship between these two women be articulated? Here 'for example' is one place where the need for another 'syntax,' another 'grammar' of culture is crucial.[11]

This is the struggle Hyvrard identifies and depicts so graphically in *La Jeune morte*; the struggle between the narrator and her mother for the right to autonomy, borders and jouissance.[12]

We see now why and how the tension between divine and daily mothers comes to be so important in Hyvrard's descriptions of women's fight for survival and for representation within an andocentric and logarchical context. It is clear also why the idealised matristic vision must be sacred. The fragments of it that remain are indeed the 'missing pieces' of a suppressed female symbolic. (The existence of which would seem to be affirmed by the presence in the Gnostic Gospels of a female divine power.[13])

Hyvrard's treatment of the female body is similar to that of the 'encept' of the mother. There is again the juxtaposition of viewpoints, focused for the most part on female sexuality. Delight in the physical processes and cycles versus social opprobrium and silence. Love-making and rape. Good birth, bad birth and miscarriage. Cancer as a false birth. Pain: violence against mind and body – the treatment of madness and cancer as metaphors of the female condition. Sensuality: merging with the male body, with the plant world. (Any reader wondering about the title of *Ton nom de végétal* will find innumerable instances of the blending of human body with vegetable nature from the earliest of the novels on.)

The role of women is presented in the same way. At the centre is the struggling survivor rebelling against behaviour approved and imposed by society, stereotypes of various kinds: dress, behaviour, speech. The ideal is a re-valuation of the modes of female occupation prevalent before industrialised consumer society. These are described at length in *Les Doigts du figuier* and again in *Canal de la Toussaint* where the woman at home in her kitchen is the counterbalance to Magellan the soldier-explorer travelling as the circumference to her centre.

Hyvrard's writing makes no place for a woman out in the world, active, political and fighting from a base of health if not strength. Her vision of woman in contemporary society is of a woman so damaged that she must first fight for survival within herself. There is no energy to go further. Survival is in itself an act of resistance, a statement of revolt, a bearing witness in the teeth of overwhelming and continuous hostility. Hyvrard's view of the universe is very sombre and yet the energy that comes through the writing itself is a force for life, and a political statement for which the most frequent metaphor is that of volcanic eruption – disruption of the status quo by Mother Earth.

Heterosexual love is where Hyvrard situates all physical and emotional sustenance for her damaged narrators. And this is where Hyvrard's own experience shaping her work creates its flaws. She acknowledges the fact of rape and violence perpetrated by unknown men on individual women. She writes about the oppression of women by men, individually and as groups. However, in discussion with her, just as in her books, there is not yet any connection, no continuum that moves from the 'they' to the 'you'. In her work there is always an understanding 'you' making love to the damaged and struggling narrator. This fusion of bodies is the one sacred and necessary connection in a dangerous world and she refuses to problematise it consciously and/or publicly. A reading of the 'Paradis-Fiction' section in *Ton nom de végétal* will make her reasons clear. I am not offering the text as a justification. Hyvrard's personal world is a world of post-traumatic stress and serious (possibly somatic) bodily disorders.

Out of this experience comes her writing. In her work the maternal body is not perceived as safe and neither are any male bodies, other than that of the beloved. Around the beloved, Hyvrard creates a sacred space, and until she develops this persona further and integrates a more complex version of the male figure into the schema that I have tried to make clear, that space disrupts the network that connects all the rest of her work. Here there is no ambiguity, no paradox, no confusion, no contrarations as in the presentation of mother or narrator herself. There is no questioning. Clearly, for the author, this love must exist if the narrator is to survive, and to take the risk of analysing it is still too dangerous to contemplate. Designated sacred, it is hinted at, implied by sensuous imagery and recalled in moments of crisis.

The lover is present in all the novels with an adult narrator, but supportive and crucial though his role may be, he never occupies much place in any of the works until *Ton nom de végétal*. In the central section of that book, a section curiously entitled 'Paradise-Fiction', the lover encourages, entices, forces the woman back into sensation, re-enactment of old feelings and finally emotional response after she has been to all intents and purposes mummified by chemotherapy. His role is similar to that of 'you' in *Mère la mort*, except that instead of rebuilding a material and physical home for the couple, this time he builds an emotional and physical home which is her reawakened body: sacred space and sacred survival brought together by means of the sacralised union of man and woman in love. 'Paradise-Fiction' is a tale of 'tough love'.

In Hyvrard's universe, when a woman is fighting desperately for survival, it is absolutely necessary that she have a lover – or she will not survive. However, it appears extremely difficult for a man to love a woman in such circumstances, because she is not existing on the same plane as he is – mad or mummified are the alternatives Hyvrard offers – so that the love must find material or physical expression. Their union is always depicted as a union within the woman's body, a fusion of male and female, life and death, bringing together the moment of origin and the present.

The tension lies between that moment of origin and the present or, as in *Que se partagent encore les eaux*, between the two descriptions of the human creation: simultaneous and successive. The simultaneous creation would give equality and unity between woman and man; the successive creation, the one privileged by Western society, has given a male-dominant relationship, represented here by the struggle between the narrator and 'they'.

The relationship between narrator and lover cannot be filled out further if the relationship is to remain unproblematic. The gap Hyvrard maintains rigorously between the loving and supportive 'you' and the persecuting 'they' can only exist as long as 'you' does not enter the log-archical world. He is always juxtaposed to the oppressors, always separate from them, living in an extra-institutional space where he can protect the narrator.

He can protect and give life to her mind and body. He can merge with her body but his mind cannot merge with hers. The realm of under-standing is another place of tension. Women and men do not inhabit the world in the same way. The philosophy of this fundamental difference is explored in *Canal de la Toussaint*. Much of the first, and more abstract, part of the book, the 'Traité du désordre' (Treatise of disorder) is spent comparing how and why women and men are different when they are born of the same (biblical) creation and in the same biological fashion.

The book opens:

Man cannot think fusion, born of woman, he is from the beginning in contraration.

Woman cannot tell fusion, for born of woman, she is never quite born.

Drama. (*Canal*, p. 11)

It continues with numerous variations and developments of this initial premise. They run together and apart in wonderfully chaotic evocation of natural disorder. This one extended quotation will suffice because it contains all the elements discussed earlier in this chapter:

Darkness cannot be conceived of. It takes in conception. It is enception itself.

Song is its doorway. Collective memory, deformed, deforming, reforming, reformed. Man cannot live darkness. He has closed the door to it. Fixed speech. Solidified. Writing. Earth. Fall.

Woman cannot speak darkness. She is the female body. Con-ceived and conceiving. Enceiving. Permanence. Continuity. Entity. Infinite from the beginning of time. Outside time. Inside time. In time. The abolition of time. Time itself. Eternity.

Man, born of woman, cannot encept eternity. He can only concept it. In so doing, he excludes himself from it. He dreams it.

Man, born of woman, can only concept. He has always a remain-
der. Fortune.

Woman born of woman can only encept. Woman born of woman
is never closed. Nightmare. Her body swells to infinity in the stars
without end. They are of the body. They are the body. She is the
body. No distinction. Darkness. Fall.

Man cannot think fusion. Part of the body, he remembers it. He
dreams.

Woman cannot speak fusion. Part of the body, she knows it.
Lamentation.

Man and woman dream and lament. The lament of the woman
does not fill man's dream. Man's dream does not cover woman's
lament. And yet they love each other.

Dream. Lamentation. Man cannot live his dream. Woman cannot cease her lamentation. Misfortunes. Misfortune. (*Canal*, pp.
14–16)

The difference for Hyvrard lies here, in the nature of the female body
which conceives of eternity and through eternity. Survival, life through
time, belong in woman's experience. Man, having no conception, has no
concept of how woman is in the world, and so, not understanding her
way, sets up his own in opposition. From here a more paradoxical figure
of the beloved could (and perhaps will) be constructed. Hyvrard does not
see this as biological essentialism but as matristic power, an expression of
the sacred nature of survival. It is this need to survive that defines her
perspective and gives her world its particular characteristics. Survival is
personal and global. For a woman to survive she needs a mother (though
she might survive in spite of her), and a loving (male) partner. Thus she
has a past, a present and a potential future (as mother). But in Western
patriarchal society the mother has become the enemy from whom the
daughter cannot free herself. Thus, when the daughter is of an age to
become a mother in her turn, the danger she is in becomes acute, unless
she has a partner who can help her protect herself both from the 'they'
of society and from her mother:

Rather than an identification with mothers, we experience an alienation and sense of betrayal when this powerful and original symbol
is unable to protect us from male violence, and we don't recognize
how the potential mother has been threatened in every woman.

The value of procreativity, and the neolithic symbols of a cosmos that was centred on the process of life, have been stolen; the origins of creation, the matrices of value, have been masculinized. Blaise elaborates:

> Men's theft of the sacred, accomplished through a historical and politico-symbolic matricide, and repeated daily for centuries, reveals itself as a theft of Origins. Origin of the creation of the world which a male god appropriates – the first feminine sacredness ousted – Origin of humanity – the woman, mother denied and supplanted by the Father – Origin of culture, the feminine rejected and relegated to nature.

> According to a Hebrew saying, hell is the place where there are no mothers. This desacralization, devaluation, and desecration of the female sex as life-giver is the basis for patriarchal power and knowledge. Male dominance is achieved through the eternal murder of the mother.[14]

Hyvrard achieves this by creating two loci of sacredness: the lover who will protect the woman against a mother-murdering society and the Mother who will protect her against a daughter-murdering mother.

It is interesting to realise that within this world of violence against the narrator, this world of self-defence and survival, that Hyvrard sees the writing of *La Jeune morte* as a mother-murder.[15] She speaks of the book as a transgressive act, a female tragedy parallel to that of Oedipus and equally necessary in order for the daughter to write the representation of her relationship into the realm of a female symbolic. So, in order to get back to the Great and Sacred Mother, the patriarchally-allied devouring mother must be eliminated.

Chapter 8

RESISTANT VOICES

For most of this book I have been writing about Hyvrard's fusional thought. The way in which she 'encepts' a dynamic network, which she sees as infinite, everlasting and all-encompassing, and in which paradoxes, complexities and 'contrarations' abound. Within this 'cosmic dance', according to Hyvrard's philosophy, the binary oppositions on which French culture is structured would be thought together, losing, in the process, the competitive and hierarchical elements of their opposition. However in my last chapter, the dynamics of survival reveal at the individual level a clearly oppositional set of 'characters' in Hyvrard's work. On the one side are 'they/*ils*' the (implied) male enemy oppressors and 'you/*tu*' the identity-denying biological mother, on the other 'you/*tu*' the desired and present (male) lover and 'she/*elle*' the desired and re-membered spiritual Mother. The narrator is located between them in a state of shifting equipoise which she characterises as survival. There is a tension here that I intend to explore further, because it throws light on the different levels and directions of resistance within the texts. For it has become clear that the major energy in the texts is that of resistance.

The resistances are all inter-connected, but seem to fall into three general categories: resistance to exclusion and dispossession; to being invaded, dominated and oppressed; to the negation of one's world view and the elimination of one's identity. All of them can operate at all levels – global, group and personal – so that cross-metaphoric reference or self-similarity is maintained throughout the work. But also, in practice, each category is more closely linked with one level of operation than the others. Thus the exclusion and dispossession struggle is played out in the Western tradition between the logarchy and Mother Nature: Christ and the goddess in the wine-press, Adam and his two wives; that is, between naming, separation and logic on the one side, interconnection and chaos (Lilith's unruliness and Eve's sexuality) on the other. Invasion, domination and oppression surface most clearly in the political sphere: the exploration of the state of Martinique in *Les Prunes*, of the state of colonial Africa and post-colonial Paris in *Le Corps défunt de la comédie*, and Solidarity and the Polish state in *Le Silence et l'obscurité*. Psychological oppression, resistance to denial of world view and impediment to the on-going process of identity are developed in the early texts narrated by Jeanne and in *La Jeune morte*. But, without exception, all levels are present in all the texts, as are all forms of resistance from physical and political rebellion through political non-compliance and personal refusal, which situate themselves in the body as madness, illness and playing dead in order to survive later (like She who was entombed in the wine-press and Annie in *La Jeune morte*).

The voices of resistance are, of course, expressed in language and in a language forged by struggle, stubbornness and sensitivity out of the official and approved language of the oppressors. Not for Hyvrard the position expressed by Adrienne Rich: 'This is the oppressor's language, yet I need it to talk to you'.[1] Even in her theoretical writings and the papers she writes as a social scientist, Hyvrard creates neologisms and twists grammar in order to prevent the structures of the French language from disguising or destroying the world view she is putting forward. Her resistance to the biases within her language are at the core of her entire work. (Her ways of manifesting that resistance are similar to those of Wittig and Daly – reclaiming, redefining, recreating. In particular all three have written dictionaries laying out systems of female meaning.) Hyvrard has three clear aims. She wants to express in all its specificity the pain of the female body that is being oppressed. She wants to expose the restrictions, constrictions and ideologies imposed by the gaps, imprecisions and compulsory forms of French. And she wants to expand the possibilities of the language to the point where it will permit her to think and express a fusional, inter-connected network of 'encepts', as well as it expresses a clearly differentiated series of concepts.

bell hooks sees language as a site of struggle in much the same way. She writes:

> I have been working to change the way I speak and write, to incorporate in the manner of telling a sense of place, of not just who I am in the present but where I am coming from, the multiple voices, inarticulateness. When I say, then, that these words emerge from suffering, I refer to that personal struggle to name that location

from which I come to voice – that space of my theorizing. Often
when the radical voice speaks about domination we are speaking to
those who dominate, their presence changes the nature and direction of our words. Language is also a place of struggle [. . .] We are
wedded in language, have our being in words. Language is also a
place of struggle. Dare I speak to oppressed and oppressor in the
same voice? Dare I speak to you in a language that will move beyond
the boundaries of domination – a language that will not blind you,
fence you in, or hold you? Language is also a place of struggle. The
oppressed struggle in language to recover ourselves, to reconcile, to
reunite, to renew. Our words are not without meaning. They are an
action, a resistance. Language is also a place of struggle.[2]

This could well be the voice of Hyvrard both in what is being said and
in the manner of writing.

This struggle is expressed in two complementary ways in Hyvrard's
work – in language and in the female body. Etymology and genealogy
are parallel processes (except that genealogy traces back in a way that
taxonomy cannot); both writing and reproduction are gestures of recon-
figuration. The toxicities of language and the metaphor of miscarriage
are connected to bad birth, abject mothers and ecological devastation.
Good birth produces text and baby, so that the child offers/is the new
linguistic possibility in fleshly form. The word is made flesh but in a way
that challenges, in-corp-orates and expands the possibilities of the logos.
Hence we find ourselves back in biblical metaphors which have been
re-configured. Hyvrard, working in resistance to logarchical expression
and yet with it because rational language is the only one available, is
managing to pull Adam (naming) and Eve (reproduction) back into one
flesh/word and re-produce the wholeness she idealises through the nos-
talgia for male-female unity that she writes into her works. The fusion
of orgasm then comes into her system as the re-membered interconnectedness of primeval chaos and the beginning of both genealogy and
etymology – not as an affirmation of the heterosexual bond *per se*.

But to return to the resistant voice in Hyvrard's work, the question
arises as to whose voice this is – a question immediately followed by
others: whom is she speaking to? Whom is she speaking about? And
these issues bring us back round to the binary and oppositional grouping
of the 'characters' in the fictional writing.

The narrator of Hyvrard's texts, when identified, is always female and is named Jeanne. She writes out of her own bodily experience: birth, miscarriage, madness, cancer and chemotherapy. All of these experiences are also Hyvrard's. We should not, however, jump to the assumption that narrator-Jeanne and author-Jeanne are one and the same voice.

The resistant voice is not that of the radical and marginalised victim resistant to the dominating centre; it is rather a stream-of-consciousness narratorial voice posing problems for the reader. In the first novel the voice is explicitly multi-layered and identified by gender, race, geographical and historical location, even though the boundaries between voices are deliberately blurred wherever the overlap of situation permits inter-referentiality of metaphoric superimposition. After *Les Prunes*, the narrational voice becomes as nearly as possible that of a generic female speaking out of her female condition. Birth, miscarriage, breast and uterine cancer are all biologically designated female, and madness has been thus attributed socially by the direct linguistic link between hysteria and the womb created by the first categorising psychologists.

But is there such a person, even in fiction, as a generic woman?

The one who is all and only woman, who by some miracle of abstraction has no particular identity in terms of race, class, ethnicity, sexual orientation, language, religion, nationality.[3]

The answer is, of course, no. Hyvrard's first narrator is a French girl living in a colonised Martinique. Jeanne is then moved to a psychiatric hospital and village in the high plateau country of south central France and on to Paris. She speaks French, is heterosexual, has a knowledge of Roman Catholic liturgical practice and is a goddess seeker; she is versed in the Bible in various translations, in Greek mythology, European archaeology and exploration literature, watches French films on television and is familiar with the topology and transport systems of Paris. Also, as her race is never identified, whereas that of the Arab and African immigrant men is, we can probably assume that, marginalised though the voice is in other ways, it is always a white voice, speaking from that assumption of centrality that removes all need for specific identification.

It is an inner voice. Conversations are reported and other voices are incorporated into the main flow of thought, but this voice speaks directly to no-one. There is no exchange between the narrator and the other persons in her life, and her relationship to those persons is as close to the biological and the generic as possible also: daughter to mother, female beloved to male lover, victimised female to dominant male(s) (rapist, psychiatric nurse, torturer, prison guard ...). The voice is thinking aloud: observing, commenting, sorting and connecting. It is bearing witness to what it perceives, clarifying patterns and systems of power and oppression, searching for a way of making connections across time and through language.

The movement that is repeated across the whole body of work, and more and more clearly within each work as the body develops, is a movement from raw pain and brute oppression to the gradual reappropriation of self, followed by the externalisation of understanding into political awareness. The three stages are most obvious in *La Jeune morte*, where Annie discovers and analyses them before our eyes, and in *Ton nom de végétal*, where they are written successively in the major sections of the book.

Until this point I have been talking about the narrational voice of the poetic (apparently) fictional texts, but what of *La Pensée corps* or the treatise that opens *Canal* or documents such as those quoted in the appendices of this text? The authorial voice is that of Hyvrard herself. How different is this voice from that of the fictions/realities? – Let me call them the literary texts in order to avoid the debate between reality and fiction here, given that the texts are all more or less overt examinations of female oppression in the Western world and the economic effects of post-colonisation – It seems to me that the literary texts are concerned with personal suffering expanded in scale until it becomes self-similar with the global situation. They are emotional, poetic and highly metaphorical. The understanding is physical and intuitive. The challenge for the reader is to allow herself or himself to enter imaginatively into the mental space and perceptions offered by the text. And the challenge is quite different for a female reader and a male one. A woman, whatever her background and experience, will have female body-knowledge as a starting point from which she can, literally, feel her way into the proffered world if she so chooses. A man will have to make a much greater leap of imagination, first to enter to physical realities of the other sexual body. Then both, according to their particular marginalities and privileges, will accept or resist the patterns of power, victimisation and support. It is probably useful to remember here that Hyvrard is better known and much more appreciated amongst the Francophone writers, critics and teachers of Quebec and the French-speaking university populations of Canada, the United States and England than she is in France amongst her literary peers. I suspect that the immigrant populations of France would understand her point of view quite easily. Everything she is concerned about is an explicit or implicit calling into question of the core of French culture: language and a complicit, exclusive centrality. The more closely identified the reader feels him or herself to be to 'traditional' (literary) forms and values, the less s/he is likely to be a non-resistant reader of Hyvrard's texts.

It should be harder for even the traditional reader to discount the more theoretical writings, for these are political critiques developed consciously and rooted in philosophical and economic expertise. (Unless, of course, this reader maintains an inflexible requirement of classically correct, rational and separational prose . . .) In a sense the theoretical works are intellectual justifications of the global awareness manifest in the literary texts. Hyvrard's control over these writings has grown and been refined over the years to achieve intellectual and linguistic elegance, but the fact remains that each of the literary texts is a chaotic system. It is the product of an overwhelming amount of information that Hyvrard has received, like the rest of us, from a multitude of sources. At a given point for her it makes pre-rational sense; she intuits the economic and political consequences. There is far too much information for her to process through to a state of conscious understanding at this time and what is more (as in all chaotic systems) the material is too complex, too inter-related, too paradoxical to be reduced to a linear and rational ('classic') form. So it pours out in juxtaposition, metaphor, pattern and self-similarity in scale. Those of us who read it easily read it as poetry. Because we think it is poetry, we accept its peculiarities and juxtapositions and we find we understand it. It is when we call it politics and economics that we can get confused or resistant because the shift of categories is too great and too unexpected. At this point the fact that the narrator is labelled mad actually gives us permission to tell ourselves that we have not understood what we have read for however long we need to come to terms with the reality of our situation, which is that we have understood but we have not got an adequate language to express our understanding. And we find ourselves in the same quandary as the narrator.

The question that I ask myself at this point is, is Jeanne (I include both mad-Jeanne and Jeanne Hyvrard here) part of what is described by chaos theory? Is she a system who is exquisitely sensitive to local conditions and who can translate the consequences of those conditions for the rest of us, albeit indirectly? And is that a definition of a prophet? Or, more curiously, has each of us the capacity to express our world view in the physical conditions of our body? And conversely, does our physical state shape our perception and interpretation of the world?

The logical extension of a fusional universe (if I dare write such a thought!) would indeed be that each body, being part of a universally interconnected and dynamic system, would be integrated into that system, and connected in some real sensory ways to the rest of it. This is certainly the way Hyvrard writes. Her political and economic vision, which has so far proven accurate in her reading of the increasing trans-nationalisation of peoples and globalisation of economies, is rooted directly in her body as barometer and living metaphor of world conditions.

Out of this understanding comes a philosophical and political resistance that is clear and purposeful, a bearing witness to the state of the world, not a proposing of solutions. All of this would fit with a fusional view point. And a fusional view point would seem congruent with marginalisation and oppression. It is in the interest of the oppressed to see as wide a picture as possible. It is not particularly in the interest of the privileged, dominant group to see any way but theirs – justified by power and leading to their goal.

Curiously, however, Hyvrard shows an interconnected network of dominant (logarchical) males, all working to the same end, yet her fusional thought does not bring her to envisage any kind of female network, either political or supportive. It is as though there are only three women in existence: goddess, mother and daughter. This is, I think, because Hyvrard's writing is fully ego-focused – which is what gives it such intensity. Her words are projected in both directions, outwards and inwards through her body like light rays through a prism.

I have said that Hyvrard writes out of her physical experience, using her body as trope for the world's ills. It is also true to say that she writes in from her physical body to her deep emotional self of which the body is also a reflection. Political and philosophical resistance to oppressive systems are almost inevitably an externalisation of an inner sense of injustice and oppression or trauma against which, as a child, one was powerless. Of such childhood feelings is the oppositional imagination born. And Hyvrard makes it clear that she has seen this connection both by the working of *La Jeune morte* and by her interpretation of it as an example of a cannibalising system representing many others on the political scale.

As we have seen, she studies in great detail the experience of internal oppression and of the way from non-self through resistance to individu-ation. The gendered and oppositional characters in her early books come from this place. They are expressions of the world as she saw it, struc-tured in ways taught regularly to Western children.[4] On the bad side are the narrator's mother/wicked step-mother and the father's household/ (masculine) system supporting her. Both persecute the girl/heroine. On the good side is the fairy godmother, translated back here into the matristic vision of a Mother Goddess, and, of course, the loving prince. Throughout the early books, this is the core structure around which swirl the overwhelming amounts of chaotic information.

Later the structure will be modified as Hyvrard manages to analyse her innermost need for resistance. Her understanding and analysis emerge as *La Jeune morte*, in which the mother figure is portrayed as both destructive and loving-in-her-way, both hated and loved. As I have said previously, Hyvrard sees this book as the female vision of the Oedipus myth.[5] So for the woman, also, total individuation can only be achieved by the ultimate transgression – total destruction of, or rupture with the same-sex parent and the total transfer of love (emotion and sex-uality) to the opposite sex. But this is a move out of the fusional world which for Hyvrard is rooted in the act of birth. Or is this rupture only necessary in the case of 'bad birth'? If so, then the contrarations of the chaotic system can incorporate it without any problem.

The total transfer of love (in her own experience) would explain to some extent the absoluteness of the sexual bond in Hyvrard's work and her utter refusal to examine it in any way. The loving male figure who always saves the narrator thus becomes both the lover/husband and also the (absent) father figure whom she called on for help against the oppressor both in *Les Prunes* and in *La Jeune morte*. The transfer here is so complete that the author seems to offer no way of thinking-together the enemy 'they/*ils*' and the saviour 'you/*tu* [he]' to form some equivalent to the complex female figure represented by the many forms of the god-dess: Mother Nature, Mother Africa, Mother Anguish, Mother Death, *La Grande Toute* (The Great All) and the nurturing and destructive living mother who has finally emerged through the work. If, however, the male lover is the vestige of the male part of the lost wholeness of pre-Adamic chaos, as I postulated earlier, then the male 'they' become the abject father-equivalent, obstructing 'good birth' through genealogical time by constantly re-creating abjection in women by their oppressive practices. Perhaps the named symbolic male figures who wander through the third major section of *Ton nom de végétal* are the beginning of a search for the synthesis of a complex male figure who will emerge in the next cycle of Hyvrard's thought.

What has happened also, however, is that while the role of the male sexual partner remains absolute, that of the woman in relation to the man is beginning to shift. The little girl in *La Jeune morte* is attributed, and takes for herself, the (intellectual) male role in the family. Her father entrusts the mother to her, not to her brother or elder sister. And while this may be a verbal conceit of a fond parent to the precocious littlest child, it is also true that she claims the newspaper immediately after her father as a sign of her role and family status. In *Ton nom* the presence of a previously existing female divinity is acknowledged by the male creator for the first time. So the putative beginning of different kinds of inter-connection is now visible.

The struggle, between remaining fully female, thus risking engulf-ment by the mother, and achieving some presence within a male system, requires two orders of resistance and two non-compatible ways of being in the world. Hyvrard shows the problem clearly in *Canal*, the book which she has long considered the major statement of her world view. The first part of the book is a treatise on disorder (or chaos). In the sec-ond part, one of the main themes, and the nearest thing to a story in the work, is a fragmentary re-telling of Magellan's voyage from Spain to the Magellan Straits. Through the 'characters' in this story, we can see the divergent ways of being that Hyvrard is describing together. Contrararations. The woman stays at home in Spain, dreaming and carry-ing out the age-old female tasks. Magellan goes exploring, following his vision of a spherical, and therefore interconnected, world. The fact that he does not walk in a straight line, the circularity of his thought and his capacity to navigate across the curved surface of the globe using flat maps make him in some respects a metaphor of Hyvrard's own enterprise.

At the same time he is a trope of the resister. First he is a warrior and a survivor – hence his wound. He resists the prevalent world view and scientific expertise of his time and persuades kings to finance his expe-dition. He resists the officers of his fleet who do not trust his leadership and try to take control. Meanwhile, by his very being, he breaks down the previous trope of the linear, upright, rational man, he who goes straight to his goal (all the while believing the earth is flat – oh irony!). But he is cut off from the embodied, supportive woman also. Magellan is gendered male but he is completely out of phase with his supposed peers. Hyvrard presents him as the first example of an emerging species. A faulty example, however, in that he cannot break completely with separationary, logarchical ways, and yet he is disconnected from the interconnections of femaleness. He remains in (dire) straits, neither returning to the known context nor yet able to advance into a new one.

By using Pigafetta's account of the journey in the way she does, Hyvrard takes the traditional literary concept that an account of a real or fictional journey (which is usually shown as a more or less linear passage through time and space) serves as the metaphor for an equivalent mental and emotional journey (with the implicit suggestion of cause-and-effect rational development here also), and inserts it into a contemporary world of incessant dynamic exchanges. Thus she again subverts literary logic and linearity, showing them to be sub-forms within a larger, ever-shifting network of information communication.

Hyvrard presents man and woman as different in their way of being in the world because of the differing nature of the birth bond, and of their orgasmic pattern, she suggests in her early writing (see Appendix III). In *Canal* she sets up that difference showing that man moves away from woman. Man is outward by nature. Woman is inward. Man is separational. Woman is fusional. Yet by the way Magellan is constructed he is shown as a possible joining point for the two. He is depicted as different from his linear-thinking peers but is not capable of moving out of the cultural space in which he was raised. Hyvrard leaves him between the Atlantic and the Pacific, like a baby in a birth canal, not ready to be born into a new world. Annie claims her own re-birth in *La Jeune morte* and the figure in *Ton nom* has also just emerged – but the pull is still in both directions.

Likewise the narrative voice speaks both outward and inward passing through the body of knowledge to attain the global and the personal. Thus the child's resistance to the invasiveness of the mother and her desire to make direct contact with the world for herself finds its parallel in the cancer patients' response to the doctor's attitudes and their decision, because of their bodily experiences, to work together to explore the social aspects of their condition. On another level Hyvrard, though still publishing under a pseudonym, claims her own birth name publicly at the end of *La Jeune morte*. In her next work, *Ton nom de végétal*, the physical, emotional and global elements of the text are divided into three sections as though the distinctions between inner voice/spirit, body and

context/world are now clearly visible and must be made so in the text –
though they are not separate, having continuous cross-reference of
themes and leitmotifs. The major themes continue to be resistance and
survival, but here the struggle is not against human opposition in any
direct form but against all that is toxic to earth and human. The paradoxes arise in the ambiguous and shifting nature of toxicity. Once again
we find ourselves in a chaotic system in all its complex potential for
destruction as well as for healing.

Hyvrard works within the process of resistance which she sees as constant. As all the various economic, political and physical systems of the
world continue in their evolution so the points of danger – oppression,
destruction – shift. At these points resistance is necessary for survival, be
this the survival of woman, of identity, of group culture, of political
rights or of the planet in a form that will permit human life. Hyvrard
offers no solutions. She sees the writer as ever vigilant, survivor and
scapegoat, bearing witness early enough to permit others to respond to
what she describes. Her situation in France reminds me of Cassandra,
condemned by Apollo to be right and to be disregarded by her people.
Certainly her fusional thought and chaos writing has a Sibylline quality
to all readers imbued with Apollonian logic. Framed in this way, the
struggle between two thought processes becomes very familiar and is not
unexpected at the end of the millennium.

There is another question that arises here in the context of language
and literature, rather than in the philosophical struggle between interconnectedness and taxonomy, and that is the issue of whether it is
possible to move out of a chaotic system. Is the only possible state one
of perpetual adjustment to circumstance in order to achieve equipoise
and hence survival? There is no place outside from which to observe, and
there is no linear path, both of which seem necessary to the concept of
solution.

APPENDIX I

At the Edge of the Unnameable (1988)[1]

[. . .] Codification was really the pain of the beginning of the world.

I questioned resolutely the separation and the break and finally the order itself set up by a Genesis locking in binarity a substance that did not want any. 'Let the Waters Part Again' (1982/85), this poetic spoken word on the creation of the living, was taking its place in the oldest genre of the world, the commentary on the sacred text. I could not stop myself from questioning the anomaly of the second day. It seemed to me that Elohim had not succeeded in parting the waters as well as he would have wanted to, and that our whole thought was resting on this badly shaped rib. I could not bring myself to expand the break, panicking like all inventors at the moment of infringing a taboo, that is breaking with their time. Pain! Anguish! Misunderstanding! Day none the less! Night always! . . . [. . .]

In questioning the unnameable so much, I contracted long and painful stigmata. The unnamed (fem.) cancer. The chemical treatment that was inflicted upon me without asking my permission nor informing me of the possible consequences finished the dissolving away of alienation, schooling and cultural codes, whatever psychoanalysis had left in existence. In the alchemist's crucible of an era in total transmutation, I was myself the metal in fusion.

As the months passed, I walked down the Champs-Elysées, and knew nothing of my own disappearing. It was only after the fact that I understood that in *the place of that*, soul and culture had disappeared. They had taken away from me that which the living believe cannot be taken away from them. This *white garden* modified the world map. Yet, I did not die. Something essential was resisting: animal nature, breath. I had no other

[1] Text presented to the Writer's Workshop (Atelier des écrivains) Montreal, April 1988.

163

life but that of the group. Deprived of my humanity, I could only take back human shape by mimicking the thousands of others swarming in the *human-nest*.

In order to go back among the living, I copied daily the gestures of my family, my friends, my neighbours, my colleagues and my fellow citizens. That is how I learned that those who abandon themselves to the species are spared what one may consider as the greatest of all solitudes, the exclusion from one's own species.

In leaving me half-dead, the chemical poisoning gave me back at the same time the savage distress of the beginning, its innocence, absence of prejudices and of conditioning. I discovered that culture was only the codified shape of the jungle and that predatoriness was the world's faith. This devouring of all flesh, this frantic cannibalism where each one tries to make the other into a shape in which he will be able to use him, I knew to be the foundation of the world: the effort of all living beings to remain alive. Dare I tell you of the solitude of the prey in the mouth of the predator? In the cavern of night, mouth full of fangs and slobber tasting of my own corpse, working at not letting go of the stick which I had managed to grasp, I survived. Is what sets me aside from the others, having seen behind the curtain? There are no words to express that horror. There is no after-it, the world then remains eternally unveiled.

Yet, there was always an anonymous beast against which to lean the misshapen flesh that my swollen legs could not hold up anymore. [. . .] body pinned to the species, I have known fusion with the species. As I did not despair of it, it did not despair of me. Convinced of the necessity of going to sound the alarm, I stubbornly persisted in rediscovering all my faculties one by one by one. I had to regain shape to warn of the ravages caused by the new treatments. They were ruining my body and destroying my brain. Their physiological barbarity was, finally, less worrying to me than the ontological questionings that they were raising. [. . .]

Disorder appeared to me then as an effort of organisation which the concepts in force could not account for. I was forging other tools with their innocence, faith and urgency that are found only in the suburbs of death. In the glacial enthusiasm of the boarding of the eternal boat, I invented the new concepts of *chaic* and *encept* to think what the conceptual logic of the excluded third had constantly left aside. 'Treatise of Disorder' is a philosophical meditation on the (re)creation of the world.

APPENDIX II

These entries are taken from *La Pensée corps* (Body Thought), which is Hyvrard's non-static dictionary. All definitions are interconnected. Each word in italics has its own entry so that a reader referring to any word has a series of possible paths available. To give readers the experience, I have chosen to start from *chaos* as a basic concept and to provide the entries for the first seven words italicised in that section. Many of them refer to each other also, so that it is possible to get a sense of the movement within the book and the interconnections of Hyvrard's thought.

Chaos

The open form, *logos'* black shadow.

The *logarch* names chaos what he can not seize because he believes it to be without form. It is thinkable in terms of magma, darkness and fusion. The logarch represses it to make clear the place of his own existence as an individual on a *territory*. The logos governs the enclosed fields of the *nomes*. Chaos allows them to communicate.

The form of chaos is a *form* the logarch does not know. He calls it *disorder*. It is not within the domaine of *order* but of open organisation in perpetual formation. It integrates it itself. Not capable of mastering it, he declares it *formless*.

Chaos is not *fusion*. It is the first form, intelligible to the logarch, that escapes him. The projection of darkness on the *grid of the noun/name*.

Between order and fusion, chaos is the *womb* of logos, as the totality gestates the part.

Like everything that allows *communication*, chaos relates to magma. The *individuation* of the logarch relies on its repression. How could he think it?

Magma is not the order of chaos. It avoids the rupture between logos and chaos. It prevents the projection of *darkness*. It is its margin, its memory, its threshold.

Chaos and magma are not of the same order. Chaos is, in the *universe* of the *noun/name*, that which has no name. It is, in the order of logos, that which can not shrink into it. Chaos is, in the universe of the noun/name, the name of that which has no name. The wide opened *mouth* of the opened concepts, of the abyss and the chasm.

Striving to name rather than encircling, the logarch deprives himself of the resources of curved *thought*. In these terms, *the* [feminine] darkness can only evade him. The unknown does not reach him. His mind is closed. He can only exclude that which is not integrated, reject it in the *unnameable* and use it as a scapegoat.

Chaos is the shadow carried from the fusion on to the grid of speech that encloses it.

Speech can exist out of what he calls *reason*. He calls it *madness*, like speech without cause, whereas she is defending an other.

Speech is not a *power* as such, what makes it a power, is to name it, mistakenly, sole reason.

The budding of the being cannot exist in *logical speech*. Another one exists. The reason of chaos. The chaic. Life itself. Organisation. The living *body*. Thought organising itself. Thought in motion.

The noun/name can not reflect that since it is fixed. The chaical thought is not the image, but the image is the meditation of it, the *projection*, the place between the world and the *being*. Before the time of the image, it was *poetry*. With the time of the image, it becomes the new verb. Juxtaposition.

He can not conceive of the existence of an organisation of images for he knows only of the administrative arrangement of order. The organisation of images is *chaical organisation*. It differs from logical order. It is its contrary and not its negation. The complement of *totality*.

Read also: Cosmo.

Logos

The thought-which-separates is not the reality of the organisation of the world. It needs to stay attuned to the fusional universe. Hence the reasonary through the mad, the man and the woman, the assistant and the assisted, the dominant and the dominated, the logarch and the fusionary. The relationship that links them, the relation, the staging, the play of two articulated pieces, the taking and the continuing hold, that is the logos.

Read also: Log—.

Logarch

Emptiness, the beginning of time. Time begins before the time when he makes time begin. *We* know that. He confuses emptiness and chaos.

For he cut her off. For he cut himself off from her. To create *the (masculine) world*, he forgot *the (feminine)*[1] *world*. She, not.

The history of man and of woman does not begin at the same time.

Night. Night, the day without morning, the day he believes day, the day he names day. Night, the thought of the logarch who cannot forget. Haunting dreams in the gaps of the I do not know.

We inhabit that very place, the place of the beginning, the place of the reduction. The logarch authorises the beginning only from the beginning.

Womb, the name of what is lacking. Womb, the piece that is lacking. Womb, the place that is lacking. Womb, the tense of the grammar he failed to construct. Womb, the cover of what he constructed. Womb, the extension of sense. The inception, the concept which remembers the archaic.

The logarch confuses what the world is and what he would like the world to be. He cannot bear the distance separating him from the stars.

He believes that naming can bring him closer. He is right. He orders it in order to abolish it. So he believes. He does not succeed. He succeeds anyway. The body-thought has no administrative *arrangement*. It has an organisation.

The world in the process of making itself exudes body-thought to talk to itself of what is happening, the integration.

The one making himself. Herself one. For the (masculine) one can not understand the whole. And, without the whole, the (masculine) one is incomplete. Totality.

Read also: Log—.

Territory

The territory is the space on which a living being imposes his/her *order* by force. All who find themselves there may be predatored. Without this order imposed by a master, it becomes *earth* again. Masked by apparatus, it is a *nome*.

---

[1] 'The' is the translation of both 'le' and 'la'; here, Hyvrard plays with the standard form which is 'le monde'. In order to conserve her intention as much as possible, and to distinguish between the two, we will indicate in parentheses whether she refers to the feminine or the masculine form.

In the notion of *environment*, from the beginning, man rules himself out.

The attempts he makes thereafter to re-establish the balance by the means of ecology are doomed to fail since he has decided not to take himself into account, considering the rest of the *world* as exterior. He places himself, mastering what he looks at. He creates the notion of space which is exterior to him whereas he is an active part of the *place*.

Space is an abstraction whose function will be excluded because the subject believes himself and thinks himself out. He establishes *rights* that no longer correspond to functions. That is possible because they are pure orders. The function re-emerges in a conflictual way as, for each one, space must submit to the order he advocates because he perceives it as his territory. Other masters ruling other orders can only be perceived as rivals.

These orders can only be conflictual as they are rigid. As for every order of which it is the reason for being, the administrative arrangement and the formatting. They rule out *organisation* which refers to a creating organism. So that the mastery of space ceases to be conflictual, it is necessary to integrate these different orders in order to replace them by functional connections between the organs of the collectivity. This passes through a reconsideration of the notion of surroundings to which man is no longer exterior. That can not happen in a framework of thought from which man has excluded himself from the start.

The cybernetic revolution creates new territories overlapping the old ones. New uses of space appear that can no longer be analysed in terms of *property*. Hang-gliders and images create territories that cannot even be expressed in relation to the ground. If, until then, the problem of fundamental mastery were expressed in terms of confrontation between the public and the private, this question has no object for the mediatising fields even though the notion of space remains operational within them.

The new space contains territories, spaces newly ordered that no longer refer to property and less and less to the ground. The mediatising field is common whether it be public or private. The new space structures the ground otherwise. A new territory settles in the very inside of the preceding one. The master of the territory is no longer as much the master as he believes himself to be. His private space becomes a common place. One may then think in terms of *in*, of in-thinking, what is thought in terms of *out*, and substitute for the notion of space and environment the one of place and surroundings which include the subject in the heart of the thinking act. This terminology is not as archaic as it seems. If the original communities have been historically dissolved in individuation and private appropriation, the mediatising fields, computer sciences and bionomics, in short corallisation, give a glimpse of the creation of new communities requiring management of the planet in global terms: geonomics.

Read also: circumscription, courtyard, jungle, jurisdiction, littoral, ontology, place, round, rural economy, society, *surroundings*.

Nome

The logarch reigns over the nome that he ordinates according to the *logarchy*. He needs it as support to reinforce his fiction of *individuation*. When the nome is based on a landed place, it is a *territory*. All its inhabitants then are at the logarch's disposal.

The ancient nome is the portion of space within which a *rule* applies. The question is to know whether it is a matter of *order* or of organisation. Organisation is the true functioning of things and order the form the master of the territory attempts to impose on it. Order can partially intersect organisation, but it can also have no relation with it, as it is the case between man and woman. He attempts to give her a form, to impose on her an order that does not correspond to organisation.

The formless is that which cannot be put into form, into order, by the logarch in the actual state of his territory. The formless is without contour, that which is unappropriated and unordered.

The nome is not necessarily a territory. It can be just an ordered space. Administration. The sciences. The disciplines. What one properly calls a domaine.

Read also: being-place, circumscription, computer science, domestication, earth, economy, geo, grid, jurisdiction, law, log—, mediatic fields, noun-name, *order*, *organisation*, out, production, property, quoted, reason, role, round, rules, scapegoat, separation, society, speech, surroundings, taking, universe.

Forms

Insuring the *connections* between the two universes, they relate to *order* and to *organisation*. They use all kinds of connections to link things, people, and *heterologous* ideas. The logarch only knows some of them. Those he can master because they are homogeneous, parts of the whole, protecting him from the one. He believes the others to be *formless*, but they connect the parts and the whole. They are heterogeneous. They re-emerge differently. They are *incepted*, preventing the rupture between the mother-concepts and the daughter-concepts.

Disorder

The logarch calls disorder the *order* it can not conceive of, that of the *other*. In logonomics there is only room for one order. The beings who inhabit its territory can not be beings-in-themselves, not that the logarch does not regard them as peers, but, in his frame of mind, he cannot conceive of them. Hence the permanent gamble called power. It does not come from an intrinsic taste for power, but of a necessity to make function an order of which the essence is control of the environment. Technical thought.

Read also: chaos, environment, log—, obstacle, *power*.

Order

Order is the shape a dominant person imposes on his territory. He constructs it with closed concepts, sealed words and a dry grammar. The nome is territory ordered in this way. Everything that does not submit to this order can not be taken into account. It is the case for heterogeneity and movement.

Order cannot integrate what contradicts it, nor anything new, without changing itself. It cannot take itself to pieces without dying and giving its place to an other dominant imposing an other order.

Orders are multiple, contradictory and sometimes incompatible. Trying to impose themselves one on another, they never stop making war, making and unmaking themselves. The system is inconceivable without order.

Logarchy is one order amongst others. The one that represses the so-called chaos. When it [chaos] re-emerges, it [logarchy] does not recognise it. It has nevertheless never stopped. The logarch calls the passage of one order to another crisis. Thus cybernetic globalisation. It is the articulation of the various orders and of organisation.

The ordinancer establishes order. In logarchy, it is the system, the code, the grid, the writing, the grammar. To order is to put in order, arrange, line up, command. In fact, it is one and the same thing, two variations of the forming information. The ordinancer easily becomes the computer.[2]

---

[2] In French, Hyvrard plays on the fact that from 'ordonnateur' (ordinancer) to

The confusion between the forming-knowledge and the forming-commanding is the very essence of logarchy, its computerised version. Cybernetics is together government and communication. It is not a coincidence, it is the very conception of relationships.

For homo faber, the use of information is not knowledge but control. Some simply call the calculator computer. Is it by this sign that one recognises the logarch's favourite language? Nevertheless the administrative arrangement can only be the establishment of the nome, the putting of it into order without the hierarchy, the formatting of logonomics while it is not yet logarchy.

Ordinary means conform to the normal order of things, but is also said about food, especially in the military. What must be deduced from that? Is this normal order of things only devouring and conquering?

Ordinal: 'Marking the position in order and in rank'. How then to state the place in the organisation, the concentric and fragmentary integration in a totality which is infinite, indefinite, open, expanding, chaorganising?

Read also: *articulation*, chaos, *code*, communication, *computer science*, contradictory, *cybernetic*, *grammar*, *grid*, log—, noun/name, *organisation*, other, *sign*, territory, *writing*, word.

Formless

The logarch believes formless whatever he does not yet have a form for in order to think it. Is it not rather that to which he has not been able to give a form, that which he has not been able to assign residency in a form, that which he has not been able to format in his nome? The formless escapes him because he it resists the forming.

Concentric and fragmentary, the form of the living body in the process of organisation. He does not know it. Not this one or the others, nor any of the thousand forms of chaos. Foreign to his thought, he does not know how to *incept* them. However they are not as obscure as he thinks. They have the clarity of the maternal belly, of earth and roots.

Read also: big, chaos, computer science, confusion, disgust, disidentity, I-one, in, interface, feminine, *fragmentary* fusion, gestation, heterologous, hunger, one, ontology, *organisation*, religion, round, soul, thought, unnameable.

'ordinateur' (computer) there is basically only a difference of a vowel. This is unfortunately impossible to keep in the translation.

APPENDIX III

On the Edge of the Marshland (1982)

[...]
I. Phenomena of which the present intellectual economy cannot give an account.

A. The Feminine Universe

My starting point is the acknowledgement of the impotence of the French feminist stream to create with men new relationships leaving French women the choice between the traditional situation and the construction of a segregated society (men/women) when it isn't a position of withdrawal. I don't underestimate the difficulty for men of giving up their privileges (and in the name of what would they do it, has History ever seen the rich abandon theirs other than under the extreme pressure of the poor?) but I think that this isn't sufficient to explain the phenomenon.

I have been struck by the fact that progressive men, in their trade-union and political fight, turned out to be incapable of perceiving feminine oppression in terms other than economical and social. Not satisfied to consider them as simple 'jerkocrats',[1] I asked myself if the difficulty didn't reside in the co-existence of two mental universes until then without communication. That is to say, that men would not understand what women mean, not because of ill-will of the privileged but mostly because women would not yet have succeeded in telling their universe in a manner comprehensible to them, nor in constructing a mental mode of expression that could account for their living experience.

Thus it seemed to me, the suffering being great on both parts, that the urgent task was to succeed in thinking The otherwise [*sic*] (that is without neglecting of course the other aspects of feminism).

In order to deal with the issue of relationships between men and women I will not use the concept of inequality. While it unquestionably allows one to account for the economic aspects of women's oppression (double work for half pay), it does not allow one to account for the phenomena that concern me. The concept of inequality of men and women is not operational, because there will always be people to say that the biological superiority of females (longer life-expectancy, etc. . . .) compensates for their social inferiority, or others who will find arguments to claim a social superiority in the name of physical superiority. We are in the absurd or in the unacceptable. The notion of inequality applied to men/women relations is not very adequate either in the sense that there ensues from it a warlike and/or revolutionary problematic that does not favour love relationships in all senses of the word. Thus it can't be the way for those to whom feminism is the movement whose goal is the improvement of women's lives. Let us note, concerning love (sexuality and affection), that the total control of reproduction by the scientocrats (in vitro fertilisation and cloning) can change many things in this area. But it is difficult to know if that can be considered progress.

Women and the feminine should not be confused. If women have a place, 'baking in the morning, washing dishes in the evening, and bathing at night',[2] the feminine, or rather the [feminine] feminine* does not. Its place is exactly nil. (And how could it be otherwise since women have not yet been able to name it, having only just started to say it.) The (feminine) feminine has no place, the reified woman lives in a permanent state of annihilation. She is but a series of organs that function for man's benefit, these organs having no links between them. She is disorganised in the biological sense of the word. Virtually outside life, as one would say of an excluded person that he is an outlaw. This is paradoxical given that she gives birth. I will not go over analyses that have become commonplace. I will only make a few remarks on points that seem underestimated to me or with which I do not agree.

About the clitoris, I will evoke the African practice of excision,

* Translator's note: 'the feminine' in French is actually a masculine word – 'le féminin'. Hyvrard claims it as 'la féminin'.

extreme pole of a behaviour that each one of us women has known. However, it would seem that a preliminary clitoridian orgasm allows for better conditions for penetration physiologically speaking. As though it is a metabiological function that makes the pleasure that the woman feels gives her the desire to have a child by this man? I am really conscious of the 'reactionary' nature of this sentence, and that it might shock many feminists and give arguments to sexists trying to remind women of their maternal 'duties'. That's not it at all. To evoke the link between love, sexuality and procreation does not mean that we must only mate when we love and we desire a child, it only means that this is the deep meaning of any mating, even though the imperfections of life result in the fact that it cannot be lived fully by the two partners in these three aspects. I do believe (but it's an axiom) that there is a link between biology and metaphysics. I believe that metaphysics is nothing other than the extreme pole of our understanding of biology. This is what I call metabiology or more simply knowledge.[3] The woman-organ is supposed to have no clitoris. Whereas it is the place of the infinite-indefinite orgasm. Must one go so far as to consider that it is in their different sexual climaxes that men and women base their different mental universes? For man, a discontinuous universe in which separation has an important place, for woman an infinite universe without break, orgasm not necessarily putting an end to desire. In order to analyse these phenomena we need more freedom of expression and more thoughts than people have, moulded as they are by stereotypes of all kinds and from all milieus.

As for the 'vagina-woman', her usefulness is clear. What is worrying in this area is not only the contempt in which man holds woman (that was denounced long ago by feminists) but above all the contempt in which man holds his own sexuality. The expression 'it's only for sex' signifies the degree zero of the relationship and is considered by legitimate spouses as mitigating circumstances in adultery. If we think about it carefully, this magic sentence should not console women for the polygamous situation in which they live (having fewer differences from the Third World than some occidental women imagine), but on the contrary should make them become conscious of what women (all women) are for men. That is, apparently nothing.[4] Indeed what idea of sexuality can a man have who hires a prostitute? It seems, however, that this relationship is the prototype of other relationships. It seems that women do not provide an appropriate analysis of this question. It is astonishing to see certain feminists militate for freedom of prostitution when it seems that everyone should demand abolition according to the same logic as the abolition of slavery and the death penalty. Real improvement in women's personal lot will only come in direct proportion to the priority given by the feminist struggle to abolition. Indeed how can a man ever respect a woman as long as he is at liberty to buy or rent one like a simple piece of furniture? It seems that this problem has been on the whole avoided by women who, wrongly, see in these practices a relief for their condition (I prefer this to a mistress, they say) when it is in fact the bolt on the door of their oppression.

Many things have also been said about the 'womb-woman'; one notes, however, that in her mother role, sexually, she is hardly of interest to man. Is it due to a metasexuality[5] that pushes him to impregnate first females who are not yet mothers, for the benefit of the species (how is one to know?), or else the projection he makes of the image of his own mother which hence forth forbids sexual relations in the name of the prohibition of incest? Or else is it a silent but tenacious grudge toward the female who bears children, or finally a jealousy precisely toward this little one who captures part of the mother's attention? Let us indicate that it is in her maternal function that the contradiction within the female condition appears most clear, or rather her nothingnessisation.[6] Indeed on the one hand the maternal function is supposed to be everything for her. (To show the slightest doubt about this social arrangement in France is still considered bad taste. Books dealing with the problem of the non-love of certain mothers for their children are still considered courageous books.) But at the same time this (re)productive function, considered as the sole element of woman's life, does not give her any social power, the production of human flesh not being taken into account in classical Political Economy. It is by this logic that work accidents, pollution, coups, torture, the wounded and the war dead are not taken into account . . . The degradation of human flesh is not considered unacceptable because its fabrication and maintenance are the free production of quasi-slaves, themselves considered nothing. If woman were not herself considered nothingness, just like her production, the priority of all priorities would be the abolition of torture and the death penalty, as well as the taking into account of disasters jeopardising health. Until now appeals have been made for struggles against the death penalty and torture in the name of human [men's] rights. Never because of the economic mess that it represents. Certain feminists start from this analysis to ask that this production of human flesh be paid for. That seems to me a serious error. If this demand were to be met, it would have the effect of monetarising an additional sector of life and allowing capitalism to penetrate further, introducing everywhere the mercantile society separating labour from capital in order to accumulate the latter in the hands of a few. I think on the contrary that the demand should go in the other direction, that is that life, suffering and death should at last be taken into account by Political Economy and the consequences felt in social and economic organisation.[7]

The 'arm-woman' has been analysed sufficiently so that I need not go into it again.

This woman-organ broken up disorganised thus lives in a permanent state of annihilation. This inferiority complex which we all have and which puts us in the position of the psychologically mutilated is neither a neurosis nor the result of a lack of courage. *It is the product of a political system which rests on the annihilation of woman, her production and her universe.* This nothingnessisation system is inaugurated by fathers [*sic*] during the girl's education (it's only a matter of destroying any possibility of autonomous life in her) and then is simply maintained by all men without exception, the difference being only that this maintenance occurs as a joke for the most progressive men, which allows them to get offended in good faith by the harshness of those whose practice is more sadistic.[8] Examples abound. It is no longer of great interest to collate or denounce them. It's now necessary to show that they form a socio-political organisation (it matters little whether or not it is conscious). It's a question of seeing that we are in the presence of a constituted system of which economic analysis alone cannot give a full account, even though we still have to refer to it. Does one dare to go so far as to form new concepts, attempting to measure in 'ergy' the efforts of vitality that women produce and in 'feet' the existential satisfactions that they get from them and to discover that there is a plus-value somewhere (it isn't lost for everyone . . .). Everything remains to be done in this area. Even if Marxism is not the universal panacea, it would be absurd not to use its methods of analysis when they work. Perhaps we must go beyond the domain of economics and forge concepts to analyse this system which cannot be summed up, either as capitalism, or as patriarchy, or as phallocentry, because it's about life itself. This can only be thought with the help of new concepts created by women to theorise their living experience. The world crisis is now making breaches through which these spoken words could pass. The universe which is collapsing is not one belonging to women kept away from its construction, they are in the background, this is the reason for its destruction.

Things start to evolve in so far as women, working, begin to have a place in social life. We know that in fact they have always worked as farmers or factory workers, but this work has a tendency to become widespread. I will not repeat the commonplaces about lower and more badly paid positions. In this area, the inequality concept is perfectly adequate.

They're also starting to carve out a place for themselves in the arts and in literature, but this literature still remains marginal (some bookstores even create special sections between sewing and cooking). This creates phenomena of ghettoisation or anthropology!

This start of women's penetration into social life can be expressed in terms of a female exodus. It can be explained by a technical mutation concerning the domains of sociobiology and organisation of domestic life. The progress (?) of genetic engineering in addition to existent birth control, the decrease in the birth rate (I'm referring to developed countries), the lowering of the age of majority and the socialisation of education, reduce the maternal responsibilities of women. If we add the increase in life expectancy, we understand that little by little a space emerges in women's lives, allowing them at last to hope for a personal life. This space is increased even more by the fact that different organisations of domestic life, school meals, day-care centres, and domestic appliances (while they do not really free women as Moulinex claims), at least allow us to view this liberation as possible, whereas before it had been unthinkable for material reasons. These socio-biological and domestic factors work simultaneously to leave women without occupation or power.[9] A space of freedom appears while places disappear. Collective places, wash-houses and markets, have already disappeared with the disappearance of rural society. But this movement is now reaching that very locus of the domestic emptied of its function. The work that remains to be done[9] [sic] is organised around a power that must be shared with man, leaving woman without either function or place. Woman, who is already nothing, now has nothing. When it comes down to it, our generation of women is even more powerless than the preceding one since the domain that was traditionally reserved for her has been taken away for technical and economic reasons, without there being a place made for her in society. In the present situation, they are in some way thrown OUT. They were already out of life, these givers of life, now they are out of place, these makers of places.

Thrown out and broken up, women are fragments. First because this feminine exodus in process is made up of thousands of activities which any man would declare incompatible. How could they not be fragments since their lives are made of fragments? It must be said that the ongoing socialisation increases this fragmentation, since working outside their homes doesn't mean that they are exempt from their domestic duties. The artists and writers like the others, since we know that the female lot is the same for all of us whatever our social status may be. (Which doesn't mean that a factory worker doesn't work more than a middle-class woman.) It seems that this de-structured and fragmentary writing bears witness to the situation imposed upon her. Fragmentation increased even more by the split she is forced to make between her domestic life and her social life, if she doesn't want to leave her family. Very often, not only does she not get any help but her activities are the sources of additional conflict. One is astonished by the gap that exists between the social and domestic impact, in fact it is the sign of persistent oppression. This de-structured female writing conveys by its form the *present* female lived experience more than does the unspoken female universe. As for the content of this female writing (body writing) as the commentators love to say, it isn't that her universe is limited to that, but rather that this other part reputed to be unnameable has never been named. As for the rest of the female universe (other than the broken up-organ-woman), it is still completely suppressed (as much in woman as in what corresponds to her in man). I don't know if there is a specificity of women's writing. I only know that there now exist men who write 'like women'.[10] In any case, I believe that this writing is transitory, a ford, a threshold, a passage where everything is crushed, a return to chaos in order to be reborn differently. Right now, the female nation finds itself in great misfortune. Having left a land, without yet having found another.

Let us note that this exodus is all the more tragic since the universe to which women strive for access is slipping away more and more. It is no longer credible. The Occident sees the material prosperity for which it has sacrificed everything being questioned. In this exodus, women have no other baggage than the fragments (which, if they are not women, are at least what has been made of them, their pieces of body named by man, dried up wreckage). They no longer have a place and in addition they have to break, in some way, with their past, their traditions, their education, their loves wronged by feminist interrogation, when it isn't a re-questioning that is even more vast. These shattered and broken fragments are gathered together as they can. Setting them side by side they make stained-glass windows from their pieces of being. One can see the design only when one looks through it; making opaque the openings, they transform prisons into cathedrals. When it comes down to it, about the female writings, I would say that they speak of many other things than what they say.

B. *The Universe of Madness*

The present intellectual economy doesn't even attempt to give an account of the universe of madness. It excludes it a priori as irrational by nature, outside the spoken word and thought. [. . .]

(ms pp. 2–10)

II. The insufficiencies of mental economy.

[A. The insufficiencies of intellectual economy.]

B. The Language of the Marsh

It is the symbolic and poetic language restored in its plenitude and not in its mutilation.[11] That is to say not the use of images (restrictive in relation to the concept) but on the contrary manipulating open-infinite-indefinite concepts wider than the concepts we are used to in the present intellectual language. Indeed it is by an impoverishment and a repression of half of the world that the symbol has become an image, that is to say a particular representation in which we believe wrongly when originally the symbol is in fact an element of reunification since the symbol is the sign of recognition.[12]

The language of the marsh reunites in the same word perceptions of the earth, the body, the intellectual and the spiritual. It is the foundation of knowledge in fact repressed.

My language of the marsh allows for a reading of the text at different levels according to need (this refers to the tradition of hermetism denigrated in the name of the philosophy of Enlightenment-brightness), one forgets that if one can force learning, one cannot force understanding because one must love it to be born with it.

Open-infinite-indefinite concepts are in correspondence with one another and establish connections in a faster way than in the intellectual language. They mobilise intuitive knowledge conveyed by the unconscious memory of the species (tales, proverbs, legends, myths, arts). For example if I say fish and marsh, the link refers to infinitely more things than life and non-separity [sic].

The language of the marsh is not specifically female, it belongs to a long human tradition which is being rediscovered today. This language is not exclusively female, but it is certainly the language of relationship with the maternal universe (the one of non-separity). The maternal is an element of the feminine, if it isn't its essence.

This language of the marsh, language of non-separity can allow everybody from this universe to express themselves, cultural objectors until now reduced to silence. But it doesn't confine itself to that, because all women, mad or supposedly normal, have relations with the universe of non-separity since we were all born, and since little by little we have had to serve our painful apprenticeship in mourning for this universe. The language of the marsh can be a unique language, for a unique human condition.

This language is destined for renewal because it is the language of globalisation. This is what I call the phenomenon of mass taking-over of the earth, brutally shortened by telecommunications and transportation, and already largely unified by multi-national firms who have for a long time stepped over frontiers and situated themselves above states.

The language of the marsh can give an account of the phenomenon of totalisation since it is the language of totality. This totalisation will perhaps at last take into account cultural minorities. Moreover (not being the least of its interests) the language of the marsh is also the language of the junction between the Occidental world and the Third World, a junction already well advanced by the creation of a third culture.[13] The cultures of the so-called under-developed countries are at once in the universe of non-separity (which does not mean that they do not resort to differentiation, they are even extremely precise about rituals, roles, rules, the one no doubt compensating for the other).

The present crisis is economic, social, political, but mostly cultural. One world is dying, another is being born. How can one give an account of this transformation other than by the language of the marsh which can say one thing and its opposite at the same time? That's why the language of the marsh is that of the future. The open concepts, the correspondences, allow the integration of what is going on as soon as it happens, even if one doesn't yet understand fully. One cannot integrate the phenomena that are occurring in a language in which concepts are closed. To talk about today, it is necessary to elaborate a language which allows one to give an account of the mental phenomena that are taking place. That is, to be able to say already that which one is not really equipped to think about yet.

(ms pp. 18–20)

APPENDIX IV

The opening of *La Meurtritude*.

I

1 In the beginning the spirit conceived negations and affirmation.
2 Affirmation was chaotic, bottomless fusion, the breath of the spirit brooding over opposites.

3 The spirit says: 'Light will be'. And light is.
4 The spirit sees the light, that is good. And the spirit separates the light from fusion.
5 The spirit calls the light 'Differentiation'. The fusion, he calls 'Confusion'.

It is both union and separation: unique differentiation.

6 The spirit says: 'A dividing line will be at the heart of opposites. It will be separant between opposites and opposites.'
7 The spirit creates the dividing line. He separates the opposites below the dividing line from the opposites above the dividing line. And so it is.
8 The spirit calls the dividing line: 'Negations'.

It is both union and separation: second differentiation.

9 The spirit says: 'Opposites will come together under negations toward a unique place and the thinkable will appear'. And so it is.
10 The spirit calls the thinkable: 'Affirmation'. The coming together of

opposites, he calls: 'Contrarations'. The spirit sees that this is good.

11 The spirit says: 'Affirmation impels impulsion, instinct fertilising fertility; cognition bearing its fruits on its behalf, being fertile in affirmation'. And so it is.

12 Affirmation urges impulsion, instinct fertilising fertility on its behalf and knowledge bearing its fruits, being fertile on its behalf. The spirit sees that this is good.

13 And this is both union and separation: third differentiation.

14 The spirit says: 'There will be rules at the dividing line of negations to separate differentiation and confusion. They will be for the conjunctions and the reflections and the differentiations and the diversifications.

15 'They will be the rules for the dividing line of negations to illuminate affirmation.' And so it is.

16 The spirit makes two great rules: the great rule to dominate differentiation, the lesser rule to dominate confusion and memories.

17 The spirit gives them to the dividing line of negations to illuminate affirmation, to dominate differentiation and confusion, to separate the brightness from fusion. The spirit sees that this is good.

  *

19 And this is both union and separation: fourth differentiation.

20 The spirit says: 'Opposites will abound, swarming with fruitful, confirming ideas, contradiction will hover over affirmation at the dividing line of negations.'

21 The spirit creates phantasms, fruitful confirming ideas that abound in opposites on their behalf and every contradiction contradicting on its behalf. The spirit sees that this is good.

22 The spirit praised them saying: 'Bear your fruits, abound, fill up opposites with contrarations and contradiction that they may abound over affirmation.

23 And this is both union and separation: fifth differentiation.

24 The spirit says: 'Affirmation will pursue the fruitful idea on its

* Translator's note: Hyvrard omits 18. Her numbering follows that of the Book of Genesis.

behalf, intuition, confirmation, the fruitfulness of the affirmation on its behalf.' And so it is.

25 The spirit makes the fruitfulness of the affirmation on its behalf, intuition on its behalf and every confirmation of the declaration on its behalf. The spirit sees that it is good.

26 The spirit says: 'We will make reasoning according to our shape, to our likeness. It will dominate the interrogation of opposites, the contradiction of negations, intuition, every affirmation, every confirmation which confirms the affirmation.'

27 The spirit conceives reasoning according to his shape, in the shape of spirit he conceives it. Analytical and synthetical he conceives them.

28 The spirit praises them. The spirit tells them: 'Bear your fruit, abound, fill up affirmation, conquer it, to dominate the interrogation of contraration, the contradiction of negations, all fruitfulness which confirms affirmation.'

29 The spirit says: 'Here now, I give you every instinct fertilising fertility over the full extent of all affirmation, and all knowledge which bears in itself the knowledge fertilising fertility: for you, this is your nourishment.

30 For all fruitfulness of affirmation, for every contradiction of negations, for every confirmation of affirmation containing in itself the fruitful idea, every instinctive impulse is nourishment.' And so it is.

31 The spirit sees all that he has done.
And here it is, very well done.

And this is both union and separation: the sixth differentiation.

II

1 Negations, affirmation and their entire arsenal are perfected.

2 The spirit perfects, to the seventh differentiation, the work that he has done. He goes away from the seventh differentiation of all the work he has done.

3 The spirit praises the seventh differentiation, he consecrates it, for in it, he leaves the whole of his work that the spirit has conceived in order to act.

NOTES

Preface: The Missing Voice

1 Irigaray and Wittig were both close to the group Psych et Po in its early years, and Cixous is still connected to Antoinette Fouque and to her Paris publishing house, Editions des femmes.

2 Rosi Braidotti, *Patterns of Dissonance*, trans. Elizabeth Guild (Cambridge: Polity Press, 1991), p. 238.

3 Conference on Hélène Cixous and other writers of the feminine, organised by Mireille Calle-Grüber and held at Queens University, Ontario, in October 1991, on which occasion Cixous received an honorary degree.

4 Conversation between Hyvrard and this author, 5 June 1992:

J.H.: Cixous is different. Her books may not be forms in the sense we have been debating for ten years (I am not a literary critic so I don't have the necessary terminology to talk about it) but I think that her being, I would say 'femining', – that is neither feminine nor feminist but 'femining', that there is, in the writing, this overwhelming way of spreading such misfortune (that I understand) that I find in this sort of permanent web of her books that do not take form, that continue to flow, a way of saying the impossibility of being woman, of being, that is why I would say femining. [. . .] Let me continue to explain what I think of the people of whom you are talking; I don't feel I have anything in common with Mme Kristeva. I understand, in what she says, that how impossible living is for us is a crazy misfortune, and that affects me on an emotional plane. She is able to lay out in public this sort of perdition in which one is sometimes, and to say it. So I am ready to defend her books, (not as a literary critic) but I would say that we are fighting the same battle. [. . .] Let me continue with Luce Irigaray also. I would say that she and I are absolutely fighting the same battle, which is, precisely, to try to create a women-thought that doesn't owe anything to the masculine, but that establishes itself beside it. So I have great empathy for a new way of thinking and I consider she is fighting the same battle as I am because we're both situated completely outside masculine domination. That is to say that for Mme Irigaray and myself, it seems to me that the masculine political order dominating us has no power over us. It's because there's a kind of invulnerability to theoretical power (if you can accept this concept). [. . .] I feel something analogous in the kind of tranquility, the kind of historical and political importance of creating a new way of thinking, period. So I tend to be in agreement with her and often agree with what she says. [. . .]

5 All translations will be identified when first quoted. All unattributed translations were made by Annye Castonguay or Marianne Legault together with me.

1: On Writing/Reading Hyvrard

1 Jeanne Hyvrard and I have debated this question of the superiority of the social sciences over literature for many years. While she agreed that she could not have survived her childhood without the support and comfort of literature, she continued to be somewhat irritated that her ideas came out as 'fiction' first, and that she was not able to express them in social science articles until much later. I argued the capacity of literature to deal with the ambiguity, complexity and the lack of separation essential to her way of thinking. She acknowledged the flexibility, sophistication and density possible in literary texts, but still regrets, with her expert economist's rational mind, her inability to speak directly into the political-power discourse of 'accepted' economics.

2 *Les Prunes de Cythère*, 1975; *Mère la mort*, 1976, translated as *Mother Death* by Laurie Edson (1988) – all quotations will be from this translation; *Les Doigts du figuier*, 1977, translated as *Fingers of the Fig-tree* by Helen Frances (1987) – all quotations will be from this translation; *La Meurtritude*, 1977, translated as *Waterweed in the Wash-houses*, by Elsa Copeland (1996) – all quotations will be from this translation.

3 Jennifer Waelti-Walters, *Fairy Tales and the Female Imagination* (Montreal: Eden Press, 1982).

4 Juris Silenieks, '*Mère la mort*', *French Review* LI:2, December 1977, pp. 329–30.

5 Conversation with this author in about 1985.

6 In Hyvrard's terminology, an 'encept' is a concept that is open and inclusive of all neighbouring concepts from which it emerged. 'Chaic' is in the same relation to 'chaos' as 'logic' is to 'logos'. These and other neologisms necessary to Hyvrard's thought are discussed in later chapters. See also Luce Irigaray, *This Sex Which Is Not One*, trans. Catherine Porter (Ithaca: Cornell University Press, 1986): 'To claim that the feminine can be

expressed in the form of a concept is to allow oneself to be caught up in a system of "masculine" representations in which women are trapped in a system of meaning which serves the auto-affection of the (masculine) subject ... In a woman('s) language, the concept as such would have no place' (pp. 122–3).

7 Jardine and Menke, *Shifting Scenes. Interviews on Women, Writing and Politics in Post-1968 France* (New York: Columbia University Press, 1991), p. 94.

8 Fanon, *A Dying Colonialism*, trans. H. Chevalier (New York: Grove Press, 1967), p. 128. (Originally published as *L'An cinq de la révolution algerienne*, in 1959.)

9 Nancy K. Miller, *Getting Personal: Feminist Occasions and Other Autobiographical Acts* (London and New York: Routledge, 1991), pp. 35–6.

10 Trinh T. Minh-ha, *Woman Native Other, Writing, Postcoloniality and Feminism* (Bloomington: Indiana University Press, 1989), p. 141.

11 This is so despite the varieties of avant-garde writing published over the last hundred years or so. The experimentalists, individuals and schools such as Dada or the Pataphysicians, have remained marginal to the French canonic tradition for the most part. Even the Surrealists have not had a significant effect on the writing and reading of prose. The most important shift occurred in the 1950s with the *nouveau roman* (Butor, Duras, Sarraute, Simon, Robbe-Grillet) and has continued through the evolution of Marguerite Duras' writing – she has become something of a cult figure – to Cixous, *l'écriture féminine* and Hyvrard. It is interesting to note that these last writers have a mainly female readership.

12 Trinh T. Minh-ha, op. cit., p. 143.

13 See *Au bord de l'innommable*, Appendix I, and M. Verthuy in *Jeanne Hyvrard* (Amsterdam: Rodopi, 1988), pp. 72–80.

14 But each writer does it for a different reason. Cixous continues to work with the pre-linguistic stage Lacan calls the 'imaginary', while Hyvrard is struggling to emerge from it into a symbolic that will encompass all the qualities of the feminine. Wittig is systematically breaking down all the established forms of the novel. For an over-view of these problems, see Toril Moi (ed.), *French Feminist Thought* (Oxford: Blackwell, 1987).

15 The exception to date is the second part of *Canal de la Toussaint*, where the subject is sometimes Magellan. He is an 'honorary female' because of his logarchical, non-linear 'encept' of the world.

16 For readers versed in the English-speaking tradition, this may be reminiscent of the work of Modernists such as Gertrude Stein and James Joyce (and hence Cixous).

17 R. Braidotti's article 'Embodiment, Sexual Difference and the Nomadic Subject' (*Hypatia* 8:1, 1993) lays out an agenda that could have been drawn from Hyvrard's work.

18 *La Meurtritude*, p. 143; Waterweed in the Wash-houses, p. 130.
19 My colleague Emmanuel Hérique suggested *The Wombd* which, with its echoes of 'womb' and 'wound' approximates the resonances of *baiser* and *blessure* in *La Baisure*. However, Martin Sorrell, the translator of published extracts of *La Baisure*, has made a different choice, 'The Kissing Crust'.
20 A selection of these, translated by Dominic Di Bernardi, was published in *New French Fiction, The Review of Contemporary Fiction*, Spring 1989.
21 Conversation with this author, 5 June 1992: 'I could almost say that I had a first life that was completed in my mother's womb and that in being born I died [. . .] and having overcome this first death, by being born, I have lived and have survived . . .'
22 The poems in *Parole de suicidaires* (Suicidal Speech), a volume by 'Patrick, Annie et quelques autres' (Lyon: Chronique Sociale, Collection 'Nouvelles Pratiques Sociales', 1985), are by Hyvrard, and it is possible that she is the 'Annie' named in the collective (cf. *La Jeune morte*).
23 The relationship which forms the basis of *La Jeune morte en robe de dentelle* (1990).
24 Donna J. Haraway, *Simians, Cyborgs and Women* (London: Free Association Books, 1991).
25 Jardine and Menke, op. cit., pp. 95–6.

2: On the Changing Paradigm

1 'Ce que la littérature des femmes peut apporter aux sciences', Congress of Latin-American Women, Santiago, Chile, 1987. My translation.
2 Fritjof Capra, *The Tao of Physics* (London: Fontana, 1976):

> The paradigm that is now receding has dominated our culture for several hundred years. . . . The paradigm consists of a number of ideas and values, among them the view of the universe as a mechanical system composed of elementary building blocks, the view of the human body as a machine, the view of life as a competitive struggle for existence, the belief in the unlimited material progress to be achieved through economic and technological growth, and – last, but not least – the belief that a society in which the female is everywhere subsumed under the male is one that is 'natural.' . . .
>
> The new paradigm that is now emerging can be describe in various ways. It can be called a holistic world view. . . . It can also be called an ecological world view. . . . Ecological awareness in that deep sense recognizes the fundamental interdependence of all phenomena and the embeddedness of individuals and societies in the cyclical processes of nature. . . .

The ecological paradigm is supported by modern science, but is is rooted in a perception of reality that goes beyond the scientific framework to an awareness of the oneness of all life, the interdependence of its multiple manifestations, and its cycles of change and tranformation. Ultimately, such deep ecological awareness is spiritual awareness. (pp. 357–8)

3 The French 'new novel' was an attempt to situate the reader within a world in motion, within a change as it happened. There is no place from which all action can be observed, no possibility of objectivity.

4 Herbert Read, 'Surrealism and the Romantic Principle' in *The Philosophy of Modern Art* (London: Faber and Faber, 1964), pp. 105–44.

5 N. Katherine Hayles, *The Cosmic Web: Scientific Strategies in the 20th Century* (Ithaca: Cornell University Press, 1984), p. 20.

6 Michel Butor, *L'Emploi du temps* (1956) and *La Modification* (1957), published together as *Passing Time* and *Change of Heart*, trans. Jean Stewart (New York: Simon and Schuster, 1969). Alain Robbe-Grillet, *La Jalousie* (1957), trans. Richard Howard (London: John Calder, 1959).

7 Hayles, op. cit., p. 21.

8 Hayles, op. cit., p. 19.

9 In English, *Degrees*, trans. Richard Howard (London: Methuen, 1962).

10 Hayles, op. cit., p. 19.

11 The narrator's name is Jeanne. Throughout this book I refer to her as Jeanne and to the author as Hyvrard.

12 They were published simultaneously.

13 Hyvrard uses 'logarchy' in preference to 'patriarchy', as the system of thought is not used exclusively by patriarchs.

14 If a concept is an abstract, defined, closed and watertight generalisation, this does not imply that an 'encept' has a concrete, specific object (*La Pensée corps*, p. 68). 'Chaorganisation' is the unceasing process of the *organisation* of the world that began at the beginning. Except in the fantasms of the logarch, there is not order on one side and *chaos* on the other. The logarch uses this separation as the ground of his domination, but it does not reflect the reality of the world (Ibid., p. 31). See also Appendix II.

15 Monique Wittig (with Sande Zeig), *Lesbian Peoples: Material for a Dictionary* (New York: Avon Books, 1976); Mary Daly, *Webster's First New Intergalactic Wickedary of the English Language* (Boston: Beacon Press, 1987).

16 The Royal Game of Goose, which Hyvrard uses as one of the structuring devices in *Le Corps défunt de la comédie* would provide a good example.

3: On Chaorganisation

1 *Le Canard enchaîné* is a weekly satirical journal published in France.
2 J. Gleick, *Chaos* (New York: Penguin Books, 1987), p. 24.
3 A snowflake would be an example of such a system: basically a 'simple' six-branched crystal, each one is formed into its pattern by its passage through very slightly varying temperature, humidity, etc.
4 Water coming to a boil is a good example.
5 John Briggs, *Fractals. The Patterns of Chaos* (New York: Simon and Schuster, 1992).
6 Gleick, op. cit., p. 56.
7 Alchemy assumes a series of seven possible stages by which lead is transmuted into gold. Hyvrard uses these stages to structure *La Meurtritude*. She calls them deaths. 'The first: resignation. The second: submission. The third: oppression. The fourth: possession. The fifth: acceptance. The sixth: fusion. The seventh: confusion' (pp. 134–5).
8 *Le Corps défunt de la comédie*: 'Choose a programme. A game. Only a game. The keyboard. The screen. The list of programmes. Marie. Marianne. Marienbad. Read the rule of the game. The cathode tube. The green light. The screen. The same language. Nothing is lost . . . When the deconstructed language began to fuse together. When the images and words disconnected. Another speech. Another world. The death of writing . . . ' (p. 89). For a synopsis of *Last Year at Marienbad* and *The Rule of the Game* see Chapter 6, notes 9 and 10.
9 The districts of Paris are numbered 1 to 20 in a spiral shape out from the Ile de la cité in the centre to the north-east of the city on the second circuit. In the book they are traced backwards from the Porte d'Italie to the Marais.
10 'Cancer' is masculine in French: *le cancer*. Hyvrard makes it feminine: *la cancer*.
11 Briggs, op. cit., p. 21.
12 *New French Fictions, The Review of Contemporary Fiction* IX:1, Spring 1989, p. 213.

4: Interface: Voices from the Margins

1 Briggs, *Fractals*, p. 21.
2 Gail Stenstad, 'Anarchic Thinking', *Hypatia* 3:2, Summer 1988, pp. 87–100.
3 Carole Anne Taylor, 'Positioning Subects and Objects: Agency Narration, Relationality', *Hypatia* 8:1, Winter 1993, pp. 55–80.

4 Ismay Barwell, 'Feminine Perspective and Narrative Points of View', *Hypatia* 5:2, Summer 1990, pp. 63–75.

5 Linda Alcoff and Laura Gray, 'Survivors' Discourse: Transgression or Recuperation?', *Signs* 18:2, Winter 1993, pp. 260–90.

6 See Catharine A. Mackinnon, *Feminism Unmodified* (Cambridge, Mass. and London: Harvard University Press, 1987).

7 'De la littérature à la philosophie, y a-t-il une pensée femme?' (From literature to philosophy, is there a women's thought?), lecture given by Hyvrard at the French Institute in Santiago, Chile and in Montevideo, Uruguay, in August 1987.

8 Much of the argument that follows was published previously in 'The Body Politic: *Le Cercan* and *Les Prunes de Cythère*', *Dalhousie French Studies*, special issue *Simone de Beauvoir et les féminismes contemporains*, vol. 13, Fall–Winter 1987, pp. 71–6.

9 'Wardback' (*le verlan* in French) is the French student's equivalent of pig-Latin. Each word is split in the middle and reversed to create a 'secret' code.

10 Michel Foucault, *Discipline and Punish*, trans. A. Sheridan (New York: Vintage, 1977).

11 Susan Sontag, *Illness as Metaphor* (New York: Vintage, 1977).

12 Monique Wittig, *Les Guérillères*, trans. David LeVay (Boston: Beacon Press, 1971). See also J. Waelti-Walters, *Fairy Tales and the Female Imagination*, pp. 104–12.

13 E. Neumann, *The Great Mother*, trans. R. Manheim (Princeton: Princeton University Press, 1955).

14 Jeanne Hyvrard, 'Geonomy', trans. Laurie Edson, *Copyright* no. 1, Fall 1987, pp. 47–63.

15 Jeanne Hyvrard, 'Au bord du Bioflower' (On Board the Bioflower), introduction to a reading of *Que se partagent encore les eaux*, given at the University of Victoria, B.C., Canada, in October 1988.

16 Julia Kristeva, *Powers of Horror*, trans. L. Roudiez (New York: Columbia University Press, 1982).

5: Modes of Psychological Oppression

1 Julia Kristeva, *Powers of Horror*.

2 J. J. Bachofen, *Myth, Religion and Mother Right*, trans. R. Manheim (Princeton: Princeton University Press, 1967).

3 Sandra Lee Bartky, *Femininity and Domination* (New York: Routledge, 1990), p. 34.

4 Cf. Iris Young, *Justice and the Politics of Difference* (Princeton: Princeton University Press, 1990).

5 Bartky's emphasis. Her note reads: 'The use of the masculine possessive pronoun is deliberate.'

6 Bartky again. And behind Bartky lies M. Foucault, *The History of Sexuality*, trans. R. Hurley (New York: Pantheon Books, 1978) and others.

7 Hyvrard, *La Pensée corps*, p. 55.

8 In this, Hyvrard's narrators fit well into the model of 'victim' and 'responsable actor' proposed by Susan Wendel in 'Oppression and Victimization: Choice and Responsibility', *Hypatia* 5:3, Fall 1990, pp. 15–46. Hyvrard would probably classify her author-self as 'observer/philosopher'.

9 'Contrarations' are contrary notions in a non-binary, non-oppositional system, in that they are radically different views of the same thing. Not being set up as opposites, however, they neither contradict nor negate each other but co-exist in a system where paradox, ambiguity and all-sides-of-a-question are considered to be desirable enrichments of complexity (rather than untidiness to be eliminated from a linear, logical development).

10 G. Spivak, *In Other Worlds* (New York and London: Methuen, 1987), p. 83.

11 Maria Mies, *Patriarchy and Accumulation on a World Scale* (London: Zed Books, 1986), p. 230.

12 Judith Lewis Herman, *Trauma and Recovery* (New York: Basic Books, 1992).

13 For a development of this argument see Waelti-Walters, *Fairy Tales and the Female Imagination*.

14 Maggie Humm, *Border Traffic. Strategies of Contemporary Women Writers* (Manchester: Manchester University Press, 1991), p. 128.

15 Claudia von Werlhof's analysis of the situation of women in advanced capitalism parallels Hyvrard's reasoning here. See 'On the Concept of Nature and Society in Capitalism' in M. Mies, V. Bennholdt-Thomsen and C. von Werlhof, *Women: The Last Colony* (London: Zed Books, 1988), pp. 102–4.

16 Bartky, op. cit., p. 30.

17 Françoise Lionnet, 'Métissage, Emancipation and Female Textuality in Two Francophone Writers' in J. DeJean and N. K. Miller (eds), *Displacements* (Baltimore: Johns Hopkins University Press, 1992), p. 255.

18 Conversation with this author in August 1991.

19 Kristeva, op. cit., p. 4.

20 Jessica Benjamin, *The Bonds of Love* (New York: Pantheon Books, 1988), p. 82.

21 Bartky, op. cit., p. 31.

22 Ibid.

23 Conversation with this author, 8 August 1991.

24 Conversation with this author, 4 February 1992. Were she to develop this

further, her writing would connect her to research into fascism, family structures, reproductive technology and the language of rights of the individual – with all their political implications. See K. Theweit, *Male Fantasies* (Minneapolis: University of Minnesota Press, 1987).

6: Modes of Economic Oppression

1 Simone de Beauvoir, *The Second Sex*, trans. H. M. Parshley (New York: Alfred A. Knopf, 1952).

2 M. Mies, V. Bennholdt-Thomsen and C. von Werlhof, *Women: The Last Colony*.

3 Jane Miller, *Seductions* (London: Virago, 1990): 'First, women as half the world have participated in colonised as well as colonising societies, and in both they have experienced diverse and multiple forms of dependency. They have, simultaneously, been excluded from the very modes of critical analysis which have addressed their own and others' oppression' (p. 111).

4 N. Katherine Hayles, *The Cosmic Web*, pp. 136–7.

5 J. Waelti-Walters, *Fairy Tales and the Female Imagination*, pp. 104–12; 'Circle Games in Monique Wittig's *Les Guérillères*', *Perspectives on Contemporary Literature* vol. 6, 1980, pp. 59–64.

6 Gregory Bateson, *Steps to an Ecology of Mind* (San Francisco: Chandler Publishing, 1972), p. 1.

7 Erica Grundman, 'La Sub/version de Jeanne Hyvrard: Le jeu de l'oie dans *Le Corps défunt de la comédie*' in J. Waelti-Walters (ed.), *Jeanne Hyvrard: La Langue de l'avenir*, Les Cahiers de l'APFUCC, 11:3, 1988.

8 'Apprenez le geste qui sauve' was a media slogan in France against drunken driving.

9 *Last Year at Marienbad*, 1961, director Alain Renais, scriptwriter Alain Robbe-Grillet, actors Delphine Seyrig as A, Georgio Albertazzi as X, Sacha Pitoëff as M. The film is set in a baroque chateau which is now a hotel. Rich society people walk around, play card games and above all play the game of Nim. Everyone seems disconnected from the surroundings, from other people and all expression or emotion. The sound track is disconnected from the images. The film shifts without warning into flashback and back to the present. *Last Year at Marienbad* appears to tell the story of a mysterious man, X, who tries to remember (or imagine) a time (perhaps now, perhaps last year) when he was involved with a woman, A, who may have been raped or may have been made love to by X, who may or may not have been shot by another man, M (her husband?), who is persuaded (harassed?) by X into leaving the labyrinthine hotel after the stroke of midnight in order to lose herself for ever alone with X.

10 *Le Règle du jeu*, 1939, by Jean Renoir. The film is a satire of high society
    passing time in a chateau, and the intrigues are so many and various as to
    make an intelligible synopsis virtually impossible. Robert, the Marquis de
    la Chesnaye and owner of the château, has a wife Christine and a mistress
    Geneviève. André, who loves Christine, flies his plane across the Atlantic
    in record time and, after a car accident provoked by his disappointment at
    Christine not being at the airport, is invited to the château. (His friend
    Octave, who is a childhood friend of Christine, orchestrates the invitation.)
    Lisette, the maid, is married to the gamekeeper who catches a poacher and
    hires him as a servant. There is to be a party. Robert flirts with Lisette.
    Christine sees Robert embracing Geneviève; she later talks to Geneviève
    and invites her to the party too. Everybody pursues everyone else; the men
    fight in various ways. Ultimately, the gamekeeper sees Christine with
    Octave (whom she claims to love), thinks she is his wife Lisette (who had
    refused to leave to live elsewhere with him) and swears to kill them both.
    By an accident of costume the gamekeeper mistakes André for Octave and
    shoots him.
11 Antonio Pigafetta, *First Voyage Round the World by Magellan*, trans. Paula
    Spurlin Paige (Englewood Cliffs, New Jersey: Prentice-Hall, 1969).
12 Les Editions des femmes were to publish it in Spring 1993. The book is
    now scheduled to be published by Editions Trois in Montreal in the near
    future.
13 In this regard Hyvrard's thought approaches that of Donna Haraway, 'A
    Cyborg Manifesto' in *Simians, Cyborgs and Women*.
14 See Chapter 5: The Great Mother and women as the world made flesh,
    female genealogy and flesh as discourse.
15 M. Foucault, *Les Mots et les choses* (Paris: Gallimard, 1966).
16 Hyvrard brings the God of Genesis and the Great Mother together here
    in a way that acknowledges both chaos and creation.
17 *Le Cercan*:

    Daughter: I wondered whether your cancer and mine . . . I see a link
    . . . It's the same! It's connected to motherhood and daughterhood, so
    to speak, and perhaps to that sort of despair that I feel from not con-
    forming to what you wanted me to be . . .

    And that on your side, your cancer would then also be from not
    knowing how to love me as I was. Mightn't there be something like
    that in it? . . .

    As if, in fact, your cancer and mine were the means of expressing the
    love we had for one another and the memory of how strong it was. I
    have an image that keeps coming back. You'll think it's silly, it's when

we went to Hurand's in Monk Street with the coupons . . . (pp. 213–14)

7: Nodes of the Sacred

1 Hyvrard, *La Pensée corps*, p. 29.
2 Gloria Feman Orenstein, *The Reflowering of the Goddess* (New York: Pergamon Press, 1990). See pp. 144–5 for a discussion of *Mother Death*.
3 Hyvrard's context is not that of the contemporary North American matristic writers, such as Starhawk. Her work is rooted in the writings of European thinkers and cultural anthropologists such as Bachofen, Bachelard, Caillois, Dumézil, Eliade, Girard and Durand, whose work on myth, genealogy, women and the sacred provide the underpinnings of French thought on these topics. See the bibliography below.
4 R. Girard, *The Scapegoat* (Baltimore: Johns Hopkins University Press, 1986).
5 Luce Irigaray, *Sexes et parentés* (Paris: Editions de Minuit, 1987), p. 83, quoted by Margaret Whitford, *Luce Irigaray. Philosophy in the Feminine* (London and New York: Routledge, 1991), p. 140.
6 Ibid. Irigaray, p. 74; Whitford, p. 143.
7 Hyvrard, *La Baisure* suivi de *Que se partagent encore les eaux* (Paris: Editions des femmes, 1984). *Que se partagent* was translated by Erica Grundman in 1988 when Hyvrard read the original text at the University of Victoria B.C. Quotations are from Grundman's translation.
8 Whitford, op. cit., p. 77.
9 Luce Irigaray, *Ethique de la différence sexuelle* (Paris: Editions de Minuit, 1984), p. 70. Quoted in Whitford's translation.
10 Whitford, op. cit., p. 83.
11 Irigaray, *This Sex Which Is Not One*, p. 143.
12 Kristeva, *The Powers of Horror*, pp. 8–9.
13 Christine Battersby, *Gender and Genius* (London: The Women's Press, 1989), pp. 48–9.
14 Somer Brodribb, 'Disincarnate Desires. Thoughts on Sexuality and Post-Structuralist Discourse', *Women's Studies International Forum* 14:3, 1991, p. 139. Brodribb refers to and translates from Suzanne Blaise, *Le rapt des origines ou la meurtre de la mère. De la communication entre femmes* (self-published, 1988).
15 Conversation with this author, 2 February 1993: 'What I mean when I say it's irreparable, that it is a murder, is that the idea of separation from the species [. . .] what separates from the others [. . .] that's transgression. [. . .] I would say that you have a kind of sacrament of murder, which is the

moment in life when you have to say, "There, I'm killing, this is my life. I am naming the unspeakable; I'm inventing something new; I'm the only one who can do it . . .".'

8: Resistant Voices

1 Quoted by bell hooks, *Yearning. Race, Gender and Cultural Politics* (Toronto: Between the Lines, 1990), p. 146.
2 Ibid., pp. 146–7.
3 Elizabeth V. Spelman, *Inessential Woman. Problems of Exclusion in Feminist Thought* (Boston: Beacon Press, 1988), p. 187.
4 J. Waelti-Walters, *Fairy Tales and the Female Imagination.*
5 It is perhaps here and around the issue of relational thought and use of language that Hyvrard's thought comes closest to that of Irigaray.

Appendix III

1 Term heard at the APFUCC (Association des Professeurs de Français des universités et collèges canadiens).
2 Marie France Dutrop.
3 If to know means to love and be born with, we find again here the notion of culture, a grid for understanding the world – ours, mine – mine being metascientific.
4 To many this affirmation will seem exaggerated. But how else can it be explained that so much preoccupation is given to the rights of man, to prisoners of conscience, censure etc. on the one hand – and so little, on the other, to battered women, individual and collective rape (prostitution), daily acts of violence of all kinds, and to physical and psychic oppression under which women live without their partners seeming to be moved by it, the most frequent reaction to this subject usually being derision?
5 How does one know whether there are sexual laws? How to know what is biological and what is cultural?
6 Neologism: annihilation being the result of nothingnessisation.
7 The theme of my book *Le Corps défunt de la comédie (Traité d'économie politique)* published by Le Seuil in 1982.
8 There is an abundance of literature by women on this topic.
9 This does not mean that they are not always crushed by work.
10 Louis-Combet: *Tsé-Tsé* and Ollier, *Marakech-Médine*, both published by Flammarion.

11 In France, poetry is considered to be a minor genre; indeed it's happy when 'poet' is not an insult.

12 In origin, a symbol was an object divided in two to serve as a sign of recognition on meeting again.

13 Third culture: a culture of the twenty-first century which would transcend Western culture and the culture of the Third World, transforming their rending apart into an alliance, and integrating the economic, technical and social changes that are coming about. This third culture, yet to be invented, is not a 'between-the-two' culture, which would only be a compromise.

BIBLIOGRAPHY

1) Jeanne Hyvrard's major works:

Les Prunes de Cythère, Paris, Les Editions de Minuit, 1975.
Mère la mort, Paris, Les Editions de Minuit, 1976.
La Meurtritude, Paris, Les Editions de Minuit, 1977.
Les Doigts du figuier, Paris, Les Editions de Minuit, 1977.
Le Corps défunt de la comédie, traité d'économie politique, Paris, Les Editions du Seuil, 1982.
Le Silence et l'obscurité, réquiem littoral pour corps polonais, Paris, Les Editions Montalba, 1982.
Auditions musicales certains soirs d'été, Paris, Les Editions des femmes, 1984.
La Baisure, suivie de *Que se partagent encore les eaux*, Paris, Les Editions des femmes, 1985.
Canal de la Toussaint, Paris, Les Editions des femmes, 1986.
Le Cercan, Paris, Les Editions des femmes, 1987.
La Pensée corps, Paris, Les Editions des femmes, 1989.
La Jeune morte en robe de dentelle, Paris, Les Editions des femmes, 1989.
Ton nom de végétal, Montreal, Les Editions Trois (forthcoming).

N.B. This list does not include her numerous articles nor texts published in collective works, nor written versions of her oral presentations, nor unpublished manuscripts.

2) Translations:

The Dead Girl in a Lace Dress, trans. J.-P. Mentha and J. Waelti-Walters, Edinburgh, Edinburgh University Press, 1996.
Waterweed in the Wash-houses, trans. Elsa Copeland, Edinburgh, Edinburgh University Press, 1996.
Mother Death, trans. Laurie Edson, Lincoln, University of Nebraska Press, 1988.

The Fingers of the Fig-tree, trans. Helen Frances, Wellington, New Zealand, MA thesis, Victoria University, 1987.

'The Kissing Crust' [*La Baisure*] in *Elles, A Bilingual Anthology of Modern French Poetry by Women*, ed. and trans. M. Sorrell, Exeter, University of Exeter Press, 1995.

'Musical Auditions on Certain Summer Nights', trans. Dominic Di Bernadi, *New French Fiction, The Review of Contemporary Fiction*, vol. IX, No. 1, Spring 1989, pp. 129–35.

'Physics Chemistry', trans. Dominic Di Bernadi, *New French Fiction, The Review of Contemporary Fiction*, vol. IX, No. 1, Spring 1989, pp. 136–7.

'Geonomy', trans. Laurie Edson, *Copyright*, No. 1, Fall 1987, pp. 45–63.

'Jeanne Hyvrard' (interview), trans. Dominic Di Bernadi, *New French Fiction, The Review of Contemporary Fiction*, vol. IX, No. 1, Spring 1989, pp. 213–14.

Jeanne Hyvrard (interview), trans. Patricia Baudoin, in *Shifting Scenes: Interviews on Women, Writing and Politics in Post-68 France*, Alice Jardine and Anne Menke, New York, Columbia University Press, 1991.

3) Critical studies:

Bersani, J. 'Roman de paroles: Ernaux, Raczymon, Hyvrard', *NRF* 297, vol. 1, no. 10, 1977, pp. 95–101.

Bishop, Michael. 'Contemporary Women Poets', *Studies in Twentieth Century Literature*, vol. 13, no. 3, 1989, pp. 129–50.

Bonnefoy, C. 'Le Mystère de Jeanne Hyvrard', *Les Nouvelles littéraires*, 2611, 17–23 nov., 1977, p. 7.

Cartano, Tony. 'Une théorie général du chagrin', Jeanne Hyvrard: *Le Corps défunt de la comédie*, *Magazine littéraire*, no. 182, mars 1982, pp. 48–9.

Cauville, Joëlle. 'Féminin et fusionnel dans l'oeuvre de Jeanne Hyvrard', *Dalhousie French Studies*, vol. 14, Spring-Summer 1988, pp. 122–3.

——. *Mythographie hyvrardienne*, Québec, Presses de l'Université Laval, 1996.

Corzani, Jack. 'La littérature des Antilles-Guyanne françaises (Exotisme et négritude)', *Information littéraire*, 29, no. 5, nov.-déc. 1977, pp. 211–16.

——. 'La littérature écrite d'expression française à la Guadeloupe et à la Martinique', *Europe*, no. 6, 12 avril 1980, pp. 19–36.

Dümchen, Sybil. 'Un entretien quelques moments avant la guerre', *Lendemains* XVI, 61, 1991, pp. 130–42.

Figueiredo, Euridice. 'Interview avec Jeanne Hyvrard réalisée à Paris le 20 juillet 1985', *Conjonctions*, revue franco-haïtienne publiée par l'Institut français de Haïti, 1986, pp. 118–34.

Frances, Helen. '*Les Doigts du figuier*, traduction et introduction', MA thesis, Victoria University, Wellington, New Zealand, 1987.

Gavard-Perret, J. P. 'Jeanne Hyvrard: *Les Prunes de Cythère, Mère la mort*', *Esprit*, no. 10, octobre 1976, pp. 475–7.

——. '*Les Doigts du figuier, La Meurtritude*', *Esprit*, no. 11, nov. 1977, pp 128–9.

Grundman, Erica. 'La Sub/version de Jeanne Hyvrard: Le jeu de l'oie dans *Le Corps défunt de la comédie*' in *Jeanne Hyvrard: La Langue de l'avenir* ed. Jennifer Waelti-Walters, *Les Cahiers de l'APFUCC*, vol. 2, no. 3, 1988.

Henkels, R. M. 'Jeanne Hyvrard: *Les Prunes de Cythère*', *French Review*, vol. L, no. 2, déc. 1976, pp. 371–2.

L[agardère], A[nne]. 'Jeanne Hyvrard: *Mère la mort*', *NRF*, no. 282, juin 1976, pp. 93–4.

Lamy, Suzanne. *D'elles*, Montréal, Les Editions de l'Hexagone, 1979, pp. 57, 61–99.

——. *Quand je lis je m'invente*, Montréal, Les Editions de l'Hexagone, 1984, p. 13.

Le Clézio, Marguerite. 'Jeanne Hyvrard: The Writing of the Night', *Revue de l'Université d'Ottawa*, vol. 54, no. 1, pp. 117–23.

——. 'Mother and Motherland: The Daughter's Quest for Origins', *Stanford French Review*, Winter 1981, pp. 381–9.

Marini, Marcelle. 'Production et reproduction langagières en lisant Jeanne Hyvrard', *Femmes et institutions littéraires*, 34/44, *Cahiers de recherches* (S.T.D. Paris VII), no. 13, 1984, pp. 19–25.

Miguet, Marie. 'La Bible à rebours de Jeanne Hyvrard', in *Recherches sur l'imaginaire*, Cahier XVII, Université d'Angers, 1987.

——. 'Jeanne Hyvrard. Un poète d'aliénation', in *Recherches sur l'imaginaire*, Cahier XVIII, Université d'Angers, 1988.

Minière, Claude. 'Jeanne Hyvrard comme le récit ancien d'une colonisation', *Art Press International*, no. 5, mars 1977, p. 13.

Moscovici, Marie. 'Un langage décolonisé', *Critique*, no. 347, avril 1976, pp. 375–80.

Orenstein, Gloria Feman. 'Une vision gynocentrique dans la littérature et l'art féministe contemporains', *Le Mythe littéraire et l'histoire, Etudes littéraires*, vol. 17, no. 1, avril 1984, pp. 143–60.

——. 'Creation and Healing: an Empowering Relationship for Women Artists', *Women's Studies International Forum*, vol. 8, no. 5, 1985, pp. 439–58.

Pétillon, Monique. 'La parole convulsée de Jeanne Hyvrard', *Le Monde*, no. 10238, 30 déc. 1977, pp. 13, 15.

Reid, Martine. 'Jeanne Hyvrard' in *After the Age of Suspicion, The French Novel Today*, Special Issue, *Yale French Studies*, 1988, pp. 317–20.

Romet, Gilles. '*Les Prunes de Cythère, Mère la mort* par Jeanne Hyvrard', *Magazine littéraire*, no. 112–13, mai 1976, p. 81.

R[oudaut], J[ean]. 'Jeanne Hyvrard: *La meurtrière* [*sic*], *Les Doigts du figuier, parole*', *Magazine littéraire*, no. 130, nov. 1977, p. 51.

Saigal, Monique. 'L'appropriation du corps dans *Le Cercan* de Jeanne Hyvrard', *Atlantis*, vol. 16, no. 2, Printemps 1991, pp. 21–30.

——. 'Le Cannibalisme maternel: L'abjection chez Jeanne Hyvrard', *The French Review*, vol. 66, no. 3, February 1993, pp. 412–19.

Silenieks, Juris. 'Jeanne Hyvrard: *Mère la mort*', *French Review*, vol. LI, no. 2, déc. 1977, pp. 339–40.

——. 'Beyond Historicity. The Middle Passage in the Writing of Contemporary Francophone Caribbean Authors', in *Travel, Quest and Pilgrimage as a Literary Theme*, Studies in Honour of Reino Virtanen, ed. F. C. Amelinckx and J. N. Megay, Society of Spanish and Spanish-American Studies, 1978. (Prod. University Microfilms International, Ann Arbor, Michigan)

Steinmetz, J.-L. 'Les bubons et la peste sociale', *La Quinzaine littéraire*, no. 367, 16–31, mars 1982, p. 8.

Théoret, France. 'Elle n'est pas noire ni antillaise', *Spirale*, no. 27, sept. 1982, p. 15.

Toumson, Roger. 'Un aspect de la contradiction littéraire afro-antillaise: l'école en procès', *Revue des sciences humaines*, vol. XLVI, no. 174, avril–juin 1979, pp. 105–28.

Verthuy, Maïr. 'Y a t-il une spécificité de l'écriture au féminin?' *Canadian Women's Studies/Les Cahiers de la femme*, vol. 1, no. 1, 1978, pp. 73–7 (reprise).

Verthuy-Williams, Maïr. 'Hyvrard, unnamed among the unnamed' in David Bevan ed. *Literature and Spirituality*, Amsterdam, Rodopi, 1992.

Verthuy-Williams, Maïr and Jennifer Waelti-Walters. *Jeanne Hyvrard*, Amsterdam, Rodopi, 1988.

Waelti-Walters, Jennifer. *Fairytales and the Female Imagination*, Montréal, Eden Press, 1982.

——. 'He Asked for Her Hand in Marriage – or the Fragmentation of Women', *Fragments: Incompletion and Discontinuity*, New York Literary Forum, Nos. 8–9, pp. 211–22.

——. 'Ils ont fait de moi la mort: la mère dans l'oeuvre de Jeanne Hyvrard', *Etudes littéraires*, vol. 17, no. 1, avril 1984, pp. 117–29.

——. 'La pensée fusionnelle et la pensée séparatrice chez Jeanne Hyvrard', *Literature and Altered States of Consciousness*, Mosaic, XIX/4, Fall 1986, pp. 145–58.

——. 'The Body Politic: *Le Cercan* and *Les Prunes de Cythère*', *Dalhousie French Studies*, vol. 13, Fall-Winter 1987, pp. 71–6.

——. 'Comment l'homme pourrait-il naviguer droit sur une terre ronde? Introduction au *Canal de la Toussaint*', *Cahiers de l'APFUCC*, vol. II, no. 3, 1988, pp. 75–87.

——. 'Transnational Thought. Butor and Jeanne Hyvrard', *Dalhousie French Studies*, vol. 17, Fall–Winter 1989, pp. 85–92.

4) Selected background:

Abraham, Ralph, Terence McKenna and Rupert Sheldrake. *Dialogue at the Edge of the West. Chaos, Creativity and the Resacralization of the World*, Santa Fe, Bear and Company, 1992.

Abrioux, Yves, ed. *Littérature et théorie du chaos*, Paris, Presses universitaires de Vincennes, 1994.

Alcoff, Linda and Laura Gray. 'Survivors' Discourse: Transgression or Recuperation?', *Signs*, vol. 18, no. 2, Winter 1993, pp. 55–80.

Bachofen, J. J. *Myth, Religion and Mother Right*, trans. R. Manheim, Princeton, Princeton University Press, 1967.

Bartky, Sandra Lee. *Femininity and Domination, Studies in the Phenomenology of Oppression*, London and New York, Routledge, 1990.

Barwell, Ismay. 'Feminine Perspectives and Narrative Points of View', *Hypatia*, vol. 5, no. 2, Summer 1990, pp. 63–75.

Bateson, Gregory. *Steps to an Ecology of Mind*, San Francisco, Chandler Publishing, 1972.

——. *Mind and Nature. A Necessary Unity*, New York, Dutton, 1979.

Battersby, Christine. *Gender and Genius*, London, The Women's Press, 1989.

Beauvoir, Simone de. *The Second Sex*, trans. H. M. Parshley, New York, Alfred A. Knopf, 1952.

Benjamin, Jessica. *The Bonds of Love. Psychoanalysis, Feminism and the Problem of Domination*, New York, Pantheon Books, 1988.

Bohm, David and F. David Peat. *Science, Order and Creativity*, New York, Bantam Books, 1987.

Braidotti, Rosi. *Patterns of Dissonance. A Study of Women in Contemporary Philosophy*, trans. Elizabeth Guild, Cambridge, Polity Press, 1991.

——. 'Embodiment, Sexual Difference and the Nomadic Subject', *Hypatia*, vol. 8, no. 1, 1993, pp. 1–13.

Briggs, John. *Fractals. The Patterns of Chaos*. New York, Simon and Schuster, 1992.

Brodribb, Somer. *Nothing mat(t)ers: a feminist critique of postmodernism*, North Melbourne, Spinifex Press, 1992.

——. 'Discarnate Desires. Thoughts on Sexuality and Post-Structuralist Discourse', *Women's Studies International Forum*, vol. 14, no. 3, p. 139.

Butler, Judith. *Gender Trouble. Feminism and the Subversion of Identity*, London and New York, Routledge, 1990.

Butor, Michel. *L'Emploi du temps* (1956) and *La Modification* (1957) published together as *Passing Time* and *Change of Heart*, trans. Jean Stewart, New York, Simon and Schuster, 1969.

Caillois, R. *L'Homme et le sacré*, 2nd edn, Paris, Gallimard, 1953.

Capra, Fritjof. *The Tao of Physics*, London, Fontana, 1976.

Chesler, Phyllis. *Women and Madness*, New York, Avon Books, 1972.

Cocks, Joan. *The Oppositional Imagination*, London and New York, Routledge, 1989.

Conley, Verena A. *Hélène Cixous*, Toronto, University of Toronto Press, 1992.

——. *Hélène Cixous: Writing the Feminine*, Lincoln, University of Nebraska Press, 1984.

Daly, Mary and Joan Caputi. *Webster's First New Intergalactic Wickedary of the English Language*, Boston, Beacon Press, 1987.

Dumézil, Georges. *Mythe et épopée*, Paris, Gallimard, 1973.

DuPlessis, Rachel Blau. *The Pink Guitar. Writing as Feminist Practice*, London and New York, Routledge, 1990.

Durand, Gilbert. *Les Structures anthropologiques de l'imaginaire* (1960), 6e édition, Paris, Bordas, 1979.

Eliade, Mircea. *The Sacred and the Profane*, trans. W. R. Trask, New York, Harcourt, Brace and World Inc., 1959.

Fanon, Frantz. *A Dying Colonialism*, trans. H. Chevalier, New York, Grove Press, 1967.

——. *Black Skin, White Masks*, trans. C. L. Markham, New York, Grove Press, 1967.

——. *Toward the African Revolution*, trans. H. Chevalier, New York and London, Monthly Review Press, 1967.

Foucault, Michel. *Les Mots et les choses*, Paris, Gallimard, 1966.

——. *Discipline and Punish*, trans. A. Sheridan, New York, Vintage, 1977.

——. *The History of Sexuality*, trans. R. Hurley, New York, Pantheon Books, 1978.

Fraser, Nancy and Sandra Lee Bartky, eds. *Revaluing French Feminism, Critical Essays on Difference, Agency and Culture*, Bloomington, Indiana University Press, 1992.

Girard, René. *The Scapegoat*, Baltimore, John Hopkins University Press, 1986.

Gleick, James. *Chaos. Making a New Science*, New York, Penguin Books, 1987.

Haraway, Donna J. 'A Manifesto for Cyborgs: Science, Technology and Socialist Feminism in the 1980s', in *Coming to Terms*, ed. Elizabeth Weed, New York and London, Routledge, 1989.

——. *Simians, Cyborgs and Women*, London, Free Association Books, 1991.

Harding, Sandra. *Whose Science? Whose Knowledge?*, Ithaca, Cornell University Press, 1991.

Hayles, N. Katherine. *The Cosmic Web. Scientific Field Models and Literary Strategies in the 20th Century*, Ithaca, Cornell University Press, 1984.

——. *Chaos Bound: Orderly Disorder in Contemporary Literature and Science*, Ithaca, Cornell University Press, 1990.

——, ed. *Chaos and Order: Complex Dynamics in Literature and Science*, Chicago, Chicago University Press, 1994.

Herman, Judith Lewis. *Trauma and Recovery*, New York, Basic Books, 1992.

hooks, bell. *Talking back: thinking feminist, thinking black*, Boston, South End Press, 1989.

———. *Yearning: race, gender and cultural politics*, Toronto, Between the Lines, 1990.

Humm, Maggie. *Border Traffic, Strategies of Contemporary Women Writers*, Manchester, Manchester University Press, 1991.

Irigaray, Luce. *Ethique de la différence sexuelle*, Paris, Les Editions de Minuit, 1984.

———. *This Sex Which Is Not One*, trans. Catherine Porter with Carolyn Burke, Ithaca, Cornell University Press, 1985.

———. *An Ethics of Sexual Difference*, trans. Carolyn Burke and Gillian C. Gill, Ithaca, Cornell University Press, 1993.

Jardine, Alice. *Gynesis*, Ithaca, Cornell University Press, 1985.

———. *Shifting Scenes. Interviews on Women, Writing and Politics in Post-1968 France*, New York, Columbia University Press, 1991.

Jones, Roger. *Physics as Metaphor*, Minneapolis, University of Minnesota Press, 1982.

Jouve, Nicole Ward. *White Woman Speaks With Forked Tongue. Criticism as Autobiography*, London and New York, Routledge, 1991.

Kristeva, Julia. *Powers of Horror. An Essay on Abjection*, trans. Leon Roudiez, New York, Columbia University Press, 1982.

Lionnet, Françoise. 'Métissage, Emancipation and Female Textuality in Two Francophone Writers', in *Displacements* ed. J. DeJean and N. K. Miller, Baltimore, Johns Hopkins University Press, 1991.

Mackinnon, Catharine A. *Feminism Unmodified*, Cambridge, Mass., Harvard University Press and Cambridge, Cambridge University Press, 1987.

Mariani, Philomena, ed. *Critical Fictions. The Politics of Imaginative Writing*, Seattle, Bay Press, 1991.

Mies, Maria. *Patriarchy and Accumulation on a World Scale*, London, Zed Books, 1986.

Mies, Maria, Veronika Bennholdt-Thomsen and Claudia von Werlhof. *Women. The Last Colony*, London, Zed Books, 1988.

Miller, Jane. *Seductions. Studies in Reading and Culture*, London, Virago Press, 1990.

Miller, Nancy K. *Subject to Change. Reading Feminist Writing*, New York, Columbia University Press, 1988.

———. *Getting Personal: Feminist Occasions and Other Autobiographical Acts*, New York and London, Routledge, 1991.

Mills, Sara. 'Discourse Competence: Or How to Theorize Strong Women Speakers', *Hypatia*, vol. 7, no. 2, Spring 1992, pp. 4–17.

Moi, Toril. *French Feminist Thought*, Oxford, Blackwell, 1987.

Mortley, Raoul. *French Philosophers in Conversation*, London and New York, Routledge, 1991.

Neumann, E. *The Great Mother*, trans. R. Manheim, Princeton, Princeton University Press, 1955.

Nice, Vivien E. *Mothers and Daughters. The Distortion of a Relationship*, Houndmills, Macmillan, 1992.

Orenstein, Gloria Feman. *The Reflowering of the Goddess*, New York, Pergamon Press, 1990.

Paglia, Camille. *Sexual Personae: Art and Decadence from Nefertiti to Emily Dickinson*, New Haven, Yale University Press, 1992.

Pigafetta, Antonio. *First Voyage Round the World by Magellan*, trans. Paula Spurlin Page, Englewood Cliffs, N. J., Prentice-Hall, 1969.

Pritchard, Annie. 'Antigone's Mirrors: Reflections on Moral Madness', *Hypatia*, vol. 7, no. 3, Summer 1992, pp. 77–93.

Roach, Catherine. 'Loving Your Mother: On the Woman-Nature Relation', *Hypatia*, vol. 6, no. 1, Spring 1991, pp. 46–59.

Robbe-Grillet. *La Jalousie* (1957), trans. R. Howard, London, Calder, 1959.

Robinson, Jenefer and Stephanie Ross. 'Women, Morality and Fiction', *Hypatia*, vol. 5, no. 2, Summer 1990, pp. 76–90.

Robinson, Lilian S. *Sex, Class and Culture*, New York and London, Methuen, 1978.

Rooney, Phyllis. 'Gendered Reason: Sex Metaphor and Conceptions of Reason', *Hypatia*, vol. 6, no. 2, Summer 1991, pp. 77–103.

Rothenberg, Paula. 'The Construction, Deconstruction and Reconstruction of Difference', *Hypatia*, vol. 5, no. 1, Spring 1990, pp. 42–57.

Schipper, Mineke, ed. *Unheard Words*, trans. B. Potter, London, Fasting, Alison and Bushby, 1985.

Shiach, Morag. *Hélène Cixous: a Politics of Writing*, New York and London, Routledge, 1991.

Sontag, Susan. *Illness as Metaphor*, New York, Vintage Books, 1977.

Spelman, Elizabeth V. *Inessential Woman. Problems of Exclusion in Feminist Thought*, Boston, Beacon Press, 1988.

Spivak, Gayatri Chakravorty. *In Other Worlds*, New York and London, Methuen, 1987.

——. 'The Political Economy of Women as Seen by a Literary Critic', in *Coming to Terms*, ed. Elizabeth Weed, New York and London, Routledge, 1989.

Stenstad, Gail. 'Anarchic Thinking', *Hypatia*, vol. 3, no. 2, Summer 1988, pp. 87–100.

Suleiman, Susan Rubin. *Subversive Intent: Gender Politics and the Avant-Garde*, Cambridge and London, Harvard University Press, 1990.

Taylor, Carol Anne. 'Positioning Subjects and Objects: Agency, Narration, Relationality', *Hypatia*, vol. 8, no. 1, Winter 1993, pp. 55–80.

Theweit, Klaus. *Male Fantasies*, Minneapolis, University of Minnesota Press, 1987.

Trinh T. Minh-ha. *Woman Native Other, Writing Postcoloniality and Feminism*, Bloomington, Indiana University Press, 1989.

Waelti-Walters, Jennifer. 'Circle Games in Monique Wittig's *Les Guérillères*', *Perspectives on Contemporary Literature*, vol. 6, 1980, pp. 59–64.

——. *Fairy Tales and the Female Imagination*, Montreal, Eden Press, 1982.

Wendell, Susan. 'Oppression and Victimization: Choice and Responsibility', *Hypatia*, vol. 5, no. 3, Fall 1990, pp. 15–46.

Whitford, Margaret. *Luce Irigaray. Philosophy in the Feminine*, London and New York, Routledge, 1991.

Wittig, Monique. *Les Guérillères*, trans. David LeVay, Boston, Beacon Press, 1971.

Wittig, Monique (with Sande Zeig). *Lesbian Peoples: Material for a Dictionary*, New York, Avon Books, 1976.

Young, Iris Marion. *Justice and the Politics of Difference*, Princeton, Princeton University Press, 1990.

INDEX

208